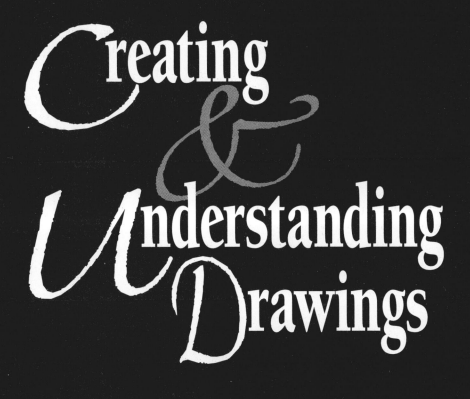

Creating & Understanding Drawings

Creating & Understanding Drawings

Gene A. Mittler, Ph. D.
Professor of Art
Texas Tech University

James D. Howze
Professor of Art
Texas Tech University

Chapter 14 by
Holle Humphries

GLENCOE

Macmillan/McGraw-Hill

New York, New York   Columbus, Ohio   Mission Hills, California   Peoria, Illinois

Send all inquiries to:
Glencoe Division, Macmillan/McGraw-Hill
936 Eastwind Drive
Westerville, Ohio 43081

ISBN 0-02-662228-9 (Student Text)
ISBN 0-02-662229-7 (Instructor's Guide and Teacher's Resource Book)

Printed in the United States of America.

1 2 3 4 5 6 7 8 9   AGK   00 99 98 97 96 95 94

Table of Contents

UNIT  **Realistic Drawings**

UNIT  **Structural Drawing**

UNIT 4

Expressive Drawings

UNIT 5 — Special Topics in Drawing

Features

Sharpening Your Skills

Artists at Work

An Introduction to Drawing

CHAPTER 1

Drawing and the Visual Vocabulary

CHAPTER 2

Aesthetic Qualities and Art Criticism

CHAPTER 3

Drawings and the History of Art

CHAPTER 4

The Media of Drawing

CHAPTER 5

Entering the Studio

▲ Study this composition closely, then explain how the artist has tied the two figures together without having them touch each other. To which figure is your eye attracted?

Antoine Watteau. *Couple Seated on a Bank.* c. 1716. Red, black, and white chalk on buff paper. 24.1 x 35.7 cm (9½ x 14⅛"). National Gallery of Art, Washington, D.C. The Armand Hammer Collection (detail at left).

All artists use the same basic components to communicate visually with viewers. These visual symbols are explained in Chapter 1, "Drawing and the Visual Vocabulary." After you have learned the language necessary to talk about drawings, you need to know what makes them successful. Chapter 2, "Aesthetic Qualities and Art Criticism," introduces and explains three theories of art that will serve as your guides to aesthetic qualities found in visual art.

Chapter 3, "Drawings and the History of Art," provides a chronological outline with information about developments in drawing for each period of history. Chapter 4, "The Media of Drawing," introduces the media and the tools you will need to create works of your own. Chapter 5, "Entering the Studio," provides experiences with the basic drawing materials and techniques.

▲ This artist's work illustrates her skills in making use of the visual vocabulary.
Identify the elements of art used here. Note the lines, shapes, values, and textures.
What principles are employed? (Include emphasis, variety, and movement.)

FIGURE 1.1 Elizabeth Catlett. *Sharecropper.* 1970. Linoleum cut on paper. 45.2 x 43 cm
(17¹³⁄₁₆ x 16¹⁵⁄₁₆"). National Museum of American Art, Washington, D.C.

Drawing and the Visual Vocabulary

Imagine that you are standing in a gallery with a friend, looking at the drawing in Figure 1.1. Several minutes go by before your friend asks, "What do you think of it?"

How would you answer that question? You might begin by saying, "I like it." This is a common answer. Many conversations about art begin with expressions of like or dislike. Unfortunately, many of these same conversations also stop there.

However, suppose your friend, who hasn't had the benefit of an art education, asks another question: "Well, I like it, too, but is it a good drawing? I mean, do you think it is well done?"

Many students have difficulty with questions of this kind. Much of that difficulty occurs because they are not familiar with the language of art. This is especially true in discussions about the way a work is organized or put together. In these discussions, a knowledge of the elements and principles of art—the visual vocabulary—becomes essential.

The Visual Vocabulary

The **elements of art** are *the "building blocks" the artist has to work with to express ideas.* The elements are:

- *line*
- *value*
- *space*
- *shape*
- *texture*
- *color*
- *form*

The **principles of art** represent *the various ways the artist can use each of the elements.* These principles include:

- *balance*
- *variety*
- *rhythm*
- *emphasis*
- *gradation*
- *proportion*
- *harmony*
- *movement*
- *space (can be both an element and a principle)*

The elements and principles of art make up the **visual vocabulary**.

The visual vocabulary is as vital to the artist as the written vocabulary is to the poet. Without words, rhyme, and rhythm, there would be no poetry. Without colors, values, shapes, lines, textures, and spaces, there would be no drawing. Also, without a complete understanding of the various ways these elements and principles can be used in creating art, there would be few good drawings to enrich our lives.

You may be skeptical about the importance attached to this visual vocabulary. As one student put it, "I want to learn how to draw, not learn how to *talk about* drawing." That student failed to understand that learning how to talk about drawing is an aid to learning how to draw. Speech, after all, is our primary means of communication. How can you ask questions—or answer anyone else's questions—about your drawings if you don't know what words to use? Without a vocabulary, the dialogue between you and your teacher, for instance, may be limited to those like-dislike statements mentioned earlier. Statements of that kind have little value in learning or teaching.

Understanding the language of art is also important when you want to learn from the drawings of master artists. A knowledge of the visual vocabulary helps you understand how those artists composed their works. Look at Figure 1.2. What could you tell your friend about the lines, shapes, forms, values, tex-

▲ **If you were trying to describe this drawing to a friend during a telephone conversation, what element of art would you mention first? What would you say about it?**

FIGURE 1.2   Vincent van Gogh. *Café Terrace at Night.* 1888. Reed pen and ink over pencil. 62.5 x 47.6 cm (24⅝ x 18¾"). The Dallas Museum of Art, Dallas, Texas. The Wendy and Emery Reves Collection.

tures, and spaces in this drawing? Would you refer to terms like balance, emphasis, harmony, variety, gradation, movement, rhythm, proportion, and space to explain how those elements have been used? Having a visual vocabulary of art would help you explain this drawing to your friend. However, your friend would also have to know something about this visual vocabulary in order to understand your explanation.

Do you think a knowledge of how the artist used the elements and principles to design this drawing could help you make your own drawings? If your answer is "Yes," then you realize that you can't learn in a vacuum. Your drawings now and in the future will build upon what has already been done by other artists. If you ignore everything that can be learned from past and present art, you will hinder your development as an artist.

Play a Visual Vocabulary Game

Cut a colored illustration of a familiar object from a catalog or Sunday newspaper ad. (Good examples include an automobile tire, a fork, a shoe, or a pair of scissors.) Bring the illustration to class, but do not show it to other students. Prepare as many descriptive statements about the object pictured as you can, making certain that each of these statements includes a reference to an element and/or a principle of art. For example, in describing a book, you might write such statements as:

- It is a symmetrically balanced rectangular form.
- Three sides are white and are made up of repetitious parallel lines.
- The remaining three sides are brown and have a smooth texture.

Make certain that none of your statements name the object you are attempting to identify. Where possible, try to link elements and principles in the same statement.

Read your statements slowly to the class. Are they able to identify the object you are describing? If so, you win. You have demonstrated that you have a good grasp of the elements and principles of art.

Listen closely as other members of the class read their statements. Are you able to name the objects they are describing?

Numerous variations of this "Visual Vocabulary Game" can and should be tried. You will find that they will help make you more conscious of the elements and principles—and contribute to the ease with which you talk about them when discussing your artworks or the artworks created by others.

The rest of this chapter explains the elements and principles of art—the visual vocabulary. This information is essential to students who want to understand artworks created by others and to develop their own drawing skills.

The Elements of Art

In the months prior to his death, Vincent van Gogh painted and drew a variety of scenes observed in and around the city of Arles in southern France. Two of his best-known paintings from this period are café scenes. One of these shows the exterior of the Grand Café at night. Van Gogh wrote that it amused him to be able to paint an outdoor scene after dark. The work you have been looking at (Figure 1.2) is a drawing of that same café. (Figure 1 in Color Section I shows this drawing in color.)

It isn't known whether van Gogh produced this drawing before or after completing his painting of the same subject. A close examination, however, reveals that the drawing isn't a **sketch**, which *is a drawing done quickly in preparation for a painting*. It is instead a carefully designed, finished work of art. You can learn many things from it because of the way the artist used the visual vocabulary.

Did you notice how van Gogh made several kinds of lines in his drawing? He often used several pens with a variety of tips to achieve the results you see here. Working rapidly, as if he somehow knew his time was limited—he was to commit suicide in less than two years—he filled his paper to the edges with an eye appealing pattern of contrasting lines. He created short and long, heavy and thin, straight and curved lines with powerful, confident strokes.

Van Gogh used those lines to define space and the different objects within that space. These lines were also used to create a rich variety of textures that added visual interest to buildings, pavement, and sky. Observe how the placement of those lines adds an exciting sense of rhythm or movement to the drawing. Now, direct your attention to the different light and dark values in this work. Do you see how the light values used to identify the shapes of the café, terrace, and awning contrast with the darker values used to define the pavement, surrounding buildings, and sky? In this way, van Gogh suggests a bright, artificial light that attracts the viewer's eye to the most important parts of his composition.

Clearly he wanted to emphasize the café, illuminated by a huge lantern and surrounded by the shadows of night. The pattern of contrasting lines and carefully balanced light and dark values result in a unified, appealing drawing that expressed what van Gogh saw and felt.

Did You Know?

Few artists accomplished as much work in so little time as Vincent van Gogh. His artistic career spanned just ten years. During this time, he received only one favorable review and sold only one painting. He tried to sell a painting of dazzling yellow sunflowers for 125 dollars but no one was willing to buy it—until long after his death. Yet, in 1987 this same painting of sunflowers was sold at auction for almost forty million dollars!

This brief discussion of van Gogh's drawing shows how much you can learn from an artwork by focusing attention on the elements and principles. To emphasize this point, reread the previous three paragraphs and list the elements and principles discussed. You will find that reference was made to five elements (line, space, texture, value, and shape) and four principles (variety, rhythm, emphasis, and balance). You may have also discovered how the artist used these elements and principles to achieve an overall sense of unity or wholeness in the composition. This drawing demonstrates how the elements and principles of art can work together to produce a satisfying work of art.

Let's examine each of the elements and principles individually. Keep in mind, however, that these elements and principles are not used independently in a drawing. They work together in van Gogh's drawing just as they do in all successful works of art. Considering them separately here, however, will help you learn how each one functions in drawing.

■ LINE

To draw, an artist moves a pointed instrument such as a pen, pencil, crayon, or brush over a smooth surface, leaving marks. The generally accepted name for these marks is line. Line is probably the oldest, and certainly the most direct, means of visual communication. It is also the main element of drawing, although other elements—such as value, shape, and texture—are also important.

Lines can be used in many different ways, depending on the intent and the style of the artist, the instrument used to create them, and the surface on which they are made. Rapidly drawn lines can quickly capture a person's actions and attitude. An artist can use a more unhurried, controlled line to draw an exact likeness of a carefully posed model.

Paul Klee wasn't interested in capturing action or in making an exact likeness in *The Mocker Mocked* (Figure 1.3). He used a single, unbroken line to draw a portrait, although it is not a portrait of a particular person. His line scurries, turns, and twists across the page in a playful way before it finally comes to rest at the point where it started. Klee used what might be labeled a consistent line in his portrait. Notice that the line's thickness and value remain consistent along its entire length, although it twists and curves in many directions.

Lines can change from dark to light or from thick to thin. They can be curving or straight, unbroken or interrupted, long and short. How the artist uses the element of line expresses feelings or ideas about a subject.

■ SHAPE AND FORM

An area that is determined by line, value, texture, space, or any combination of these other elements is a shape. Sometimes a shape may have exact, easily recognized boundaries or edges. At other times its boundaries aren't clear.

When Georgia O'Keeffe was working on the drawing in Figure 1.4, she didn't think only about how to draw the dark positive shapes. She also directed attention to the empty or negative shapes that were created by placing the positive shapes on the paper (Figure 1.5, page 8). *A positive shape* is

▲ Find the beginning or end of the line used to draw this portrait. Do you agree with the statement that this line "actually seems to be moving"? Is this line movement more important than the fact that it is used to depict a head?

FIGURE 1.3 Paul Klee. *The Mocker Mocked.* 1930. Oil on canvas. 43.2 x 52.4 cm (17 x 20⅝"). Collection, The Museum of Modern Art, New York, New York. Gift of J. B. Neumann.

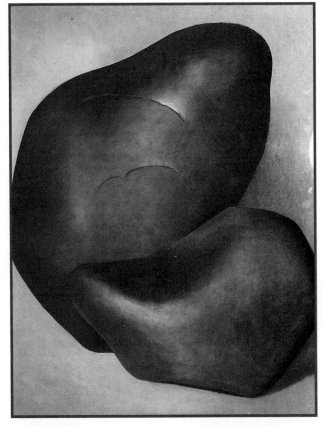

▲ Why would you describe the objects in this drawing as forms rather than shapes? How is a shape drawn to look like a form? Can you find a drawing in this chapter that emphasizes shape rather than form?

FIGURE 1.4 Georgia O'Keeffe. *My Heart.* 1944. Pastel on paper. 69.9 x 54.6 cm (27½ x 21½"). The Museum of Texas Tech University, Lubbock, Texas. Collection of the West Texas Museum Association.

often called a **figure**, and *negative shape or shapes* are referred to as a **ground**. The negative shapes contribute as much to the overall effect of a finished composition as the positive shapes. For example, what if O'Keeffe had decided to place the large positive shapes in the center of the page (Figure 1.6, page 8)? The resulting negative shapes would be quite different. The overall effect of the drawing would be less satisfying. (See Figure 2 in Color Section I.)

SHARPENING YOUR SKILLS

Identify Shape and Form

Examine the drawings illustrated in this book. Can you identify one with precise, easily discernible boundaries and one whose boundaries lack precision and clarity? How do these two different ways of creating shapes affect the overall appearance of the drawings?

Traditional drawings and paintings clearly separate positive and negative shapes. More recent artists, however, for a variety of reasons, seem less concerned about separating the two. As a consequence, it is often difficult for the viewer to determine from the pattern of shapes which ones belong to the figure and which to the ground.

In some drawings, shapes appear solid and three-dimensional even though they are limited to two dimensions, length and width. The flat, two-dimensional appearance of shape sets it apart from form. In drawings and paintings, form has an implied third dimension, depth, in addition to length and width.

Artists usually suggest form on paper or canvas by using *value gradation*. This means that the artist uses a gradual change from dark to light areas to

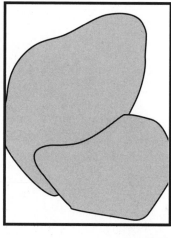

▶ FIGURE 1.5
The shaded areas are referred to as positive shapes or figures. The unshaded areas are known as negative shapes or ground.

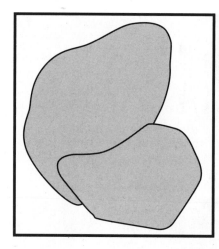

◀ FIGURE 1.6
The placement of positive shapes in a drawing determines the size and configuration of the negative shapes. It also affects the overall design.

create the illusion of roundness and solidity. This technique is clearly illustrated in Figure 1.4, page 7.

Another technique, **cross-hatching**, or *sets of parallel overlapping lines* can also be used to create areas of differing degrees of darkness. When the parallel lines are built on top of each other, a dense pattern of dark area is created. By gradually reducing the density of these areas, an artist can add a sense of roundness to the forms. This is a type of value gradation noted in Gorky's portrait of his wife in Figure 1.7.

■ VALUE

The artist's use of light and dark areas in a drawing or painting is referred to as a *value*. As noted earlier, gradual value changes can suggest the roundness of three-dimensional forms shown on a two-dimensional surface. Abrupt changes of value, on the other hand, result in contrasts that can indicate planes at various angles to each other.

Value is an element that can be used in many different ways. Notice how Rubens used a change of values, from the dark figures in the foreground, or front, to the progressively lighter figures in the background, or back, to create the illusion of space in his drawing of a group of people celebrating a wedding (Figure 1.8). On the other hand, Goya used a sharp contrast of dark and light values to emphasize the figures in his work illustrating one of the disasters of war (Figure 2.4), page 23.

▲ Although later in his career, Gorky became noted for nonobjective art, he also executed literal works such as the one above.

FIGURE 1.7   Arshile Gorky. *Portrait of the Artist's Wife, "Mougouch."* c. 1943. Pen and ink, brush and wash on wove paper. 35.3 x 23.8 cm (13¾ x 9⅜"). Baltimore Museum of Art, Baltimore, Maryland. Thomas E. Benesch Memorial Collection. Gift of Mr. and Mrs. I. W. Burnham II.

▲ This seventeenth-century artist is admired for his large-scale paintings of exciting events. He prepared for these by completing sketches like this one. What has he done to indicate that these people are round and solid and exist in real space?

FIGURE 1.8   Peter Paul Rubens. *The Garden of Love* (right portion). c. Late 1500s to early 1600s. Pen and brown ink, brown and gray-green wash, heightened with light blue paint, over black chalk, on paper. 47.7 x 70.7 cm (18¾ x 27¹³⁄₁₆"). The Metropolitan Museum of Art, New York, New York. Fletcher Fund.

SHARPENING YOUR SKILLS

Find Visual Texture

Vincent van Gogh used a variety of pens to simulate different textures in his drawing of the café (Figure 1.2, on page 4). Can you find other examples of simulated texture among the drawings illustrated in this book? In class discuss the techniques of the artists.

■ TEXTURE

"Be careful, the seat on that old bench is rough!"

"I really like the coarse feeling of this wool sweater."

"I'm going to sand the fender of that old car until it's as smooth as glass."

Whenever people talk about an object as being rough or coarse or smooth, they are referring to its *texture*. This is the element of art that appeals to the sense of touch.

When looking at paintings in a museum, you might have noticed that some are smooth and even. There is little to distract your eye as it glides over their glossy surfaces. In other paintings, however, artists have used heavy applications of paint that produced uneven surfaces of ridges and furrows. This technique adds to their tactile and visual impact. *Tactile* means appealing to the sense of touch.

The desire for a rich, tactile surface has caused artists to go beyond applying thick layers of color.

Some have added sand, plaster, and other materials to paint to change its tactile quality. Others have pasted paper, cloth, and other items to their paintings and drawings to create another kind of *actual* or *real texture*. Actual texture is the kind that the viewer can touch. Some paintings and drawings that are smooth to the touch can still suggest texture. A suggested or implied texture is known as *simulated* or *visual texture*.

■ SPACE

The distance around, between, above, below, and within an object is *space*. In Giovanni Panini's drawing of the Spanish Steps in Rome (Figure 1.9), the artist has focused his attention on creating the illusion of space on a two-dimensional surface.

After examining this drawing, try to list the different techniques the artist has used to do this.

How many were you able to identify? Actually, seven different techniques can be found. They are explained briefly below.

■ **Linear perspective.** Notice how the lines of the buildings slant inward in Panini's drawing, making them appear to extend back in space. This technique, developed by artists in the fourteenth and fifteenth centuries, is called *linear perspective*. It shows the way these buildings would look if you actually viewed this scene. As the lines recede (move away), they seem to meet on an imaginary line known as the horizon line or eye level line. *The point on the eye level line at which all of these lines converge* is referred to as the **vanishing point**.

◄ **The artist used a variety of techniques to create the illusion of space. Find an example of a drawing in this chapter where there is little or no suggestion of depth.**

FIGURE 1.9   Giovanni Paolo Panini. *Spanish Steps.* c. 1730. Pen and black ink, gray wash, watercolor, over graphite. 34.8 x 29.3 cm (13¹¹⁄₁₆ x 11⁹⁄₁₆"). The Metropolitan Museum of Art, New York, New York. Rogers Fund.

- **Size relationship.** As your eye moves back into the picture, the objects become progressively smaller. This technique of making objects in the background smaller than those in the foreground also creates a sense of depth.

- **Placement of objects.** Objects placed higher than others in the drawing appear to be farther back. This technique, especially when combined with a size difference, is an effective method for creating the illusion of space.

- **Overlapping of objects.** Perhaps the most obvious technique for suggesting space is overlapping. This means placing one object in front of another, partially concealing the object behind. Observe how the figures overlap each other in Panini's drawing. This overlapping makes the figures in front appear closer. Some overlapping objects might be miles apart while others appear to touch one another. In either case, the viewer knows that the one in front is closer.

- **Value change.** Did you notice that the figures in the foreground of this drawing appear to be darker in value than those in the background? This is a form of *aerial perspective.* The artist gradually lessens the value and value contrasts for objects that appear farther back in the composition.

- **Detail.** No doubt you noticed that the details of the figures and buildings in the distance are less clear than those of the figures in the foreground. Also, the contours of distant objects seem to blur just as they would if you were actually standing at the foot of the Spanish Steps and looking toward the far off church.

- **Atmospheric perspective.** Another technique for suggesting space should also be mentioned, although it isn't shown in the illustration. Where color is used in a landscape, objects in the distance are painted with hues that appear bluer and less intense or bright. When those distant objects are also made to appear lighter in value, this technique reproduces the effect of layers of atmosphere that exist between the viewer and the distant objects. This technique is sometimes called *atmospheric perspective.*

Of course, artists don't always try to encourage the viewer to look back into their compositions. Many works are produced that provide little or no suggestion of depth. This is certainly the case with Ellsworth Kelly's drawing *Briar* (Figure 1.10). The picture consists of a flat pattern of shapes arranged on the **picture plane**, *the surface of the drawing.* The only suggestion of space is the single overlapping leaf. (This drawing is also an example of the effective use of line. How would you describe the lines Kelly has drawn?)

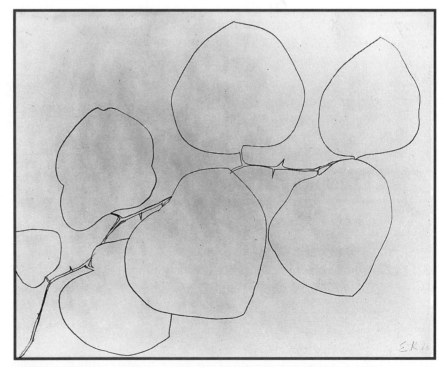

▲ **What adjectives would you use to describe the lines in this drawing? Compare your adjectives with those compiled by other members of the class.**

FIGURE 1.10 Ellsworth Kelly. *Briar.* c. 1963. Pencil on paper. 56.8 x 72.1 cm (22⅜ x 28⅜"). Whitney Museum of American Art, New York, New York. Neysa McMein Purchase Award.

■ COMMENTS ON THE ELEMENT OF COLOR

No doubt you are aware that a composition can be complete and successful without using all of the elements of art discussed. Kelly's drawing, for example, makes no use of value or texture. Like many drawings, it also exhibits no concern for color, demonstrating the artist's decision to work with a black and white medium.

Drawing students are well advised to delay using color in their own work until they have developed their drawing skills with a range of black and white media. Therefore, color will not be considered at great length in this book, although occasional references to color will be made beginning with a brief description of the three properties of color below.

Color is an art element which is made up of three distinct properties: hue, intensity, and value. Hue refers to the name of a color and identifies its location on a color wheel. Intensity pertains to the quality of a color, its brightness or dullness. Value refers to the lightness or darkness of a color.

Colors can be combined in works of art in several ways. One common combination is the use of complementary colors, colors that are opposite each other (blue and orange, for example) on the color wheel. Another combination is analogous colors, colors located next to each other (like yellow-green, green, and blue-green) on the color wheel. Colors are sometimes divided into two groups: cool (green, blue, and violet) and warm (red, orange, and yellow).

The Principles of Art

Each of the following principles describes a different way of using the elements of art discussed earlier. Knowing these principles will be helpful as you continue your education in art. As you know, this education includes studying others' artworks as well as developing your own drawing skills.

■ BALANCE

If you ride a bicycle, you already appreciate the importance of balance. Keeping your balance means that you won't fall off. Leaning too far to one side or the other could produce an imbalance; you and your bicycle could part company.

In art, balance refers to a way of combining elements to add a sense of stability to a work of art. Two kinds of balance are possible. The simpler kind is referred to as *symmetrical* or *formal balance*. In this kind of balance, similar shapes are repeated in the same manner on either side of a vertical, horizontal, or diagonal line dividing the composition in half. One half of the work mirrors the other half. This type of formal balance is illustrated in Mondrian's drawing entitled *Pier and Ocean* (Figure 1.11).

▲ **Describe the lines used in this composition. Notice how this composition is based on a precise balance of horizontal and vertical lines.**

FIGURE 1.11 Piet Mondrian. *Pier and Ocean*. 1914. Charcoal and white watercolor on buff paper. 87.9 x 111.2 cm (34⅝ x 44"); oval composition 83.8 x 101.6 cm (30 x 40"). Collection, The Museum of Modern Art, New York, New York. Mrs. Simon Guggenheim Fund.

A less stationary and usually more visually appealing type of balance is known as *asymmetrical* or *informal balance*. Balance of this kind is based on the apparent weight of the various objects in the work. Weight can be suggested by the careful placement of any of the art elements used in a composition.

For example, in a drawing showing a man jumping on a train (Figure 1.12), Edward Hopper partially balanced the large, leaning railroad car at

▲ **How does the artist's use of asymmetrical balance add to the drama in this picture? Could this same sense of drama have been realized if he had used symmetrical balance? Point out the vertical used to balance the opposing diagonals of train and men.**

FIGURE **1.12** Edward Hopper. *Jumping on a Train.* 1906–14. Ink and wash on illustration board. 47.6 x 38.1 cm (18¾ x 15"). Whitney Museum of American Art, New York, New York. Josephine N. Hopper bequest.

the left with the darker figures of the two men leaning in the opposite direction. The vertical telephone pole helps accent these opposing forces. The shape of the billowing dust cloud at the bottom of the drawing becomes larger and appears heavier at the right. Along with the small house at the extreme right side of the drawing, this dust cloud helps create the feeling of balance in this work.

■ EMPHASIS

Contrast is often used to achieve *emphasis*. It is a way of combining elements to point out their differences. In the process, the artist accents one or more elements to create points of visual interest. The artist can thus direct the viewer's attention to the most important parts of a composition. In

Eugene Amaury-Duval's portrait (Figure 1.13), you can see how a contrast of light and dark values can be used to emphasize the face of a young woman.

■ HARMONY

Mondrian's drawing *Pier and Ocean* (Figure 1.11) demonstrates the principle of *harmony*, as well as formal balance. Mondrian's repetition of horizontal and vertical lines throughout the drawing helps tie the composition together. Harmony can be thought of as a way of combining similar elements in a work to stress their similarities. When the artist decides to use repeated elements or make only subtle changes in elements, the artwork assumes an uncomplicated and harmonious appearance.

■ VARIETY

When artists combine elements to create complex relationships in their works, they are making use of the principle of *variety*. It is this principle that enables them to increase the visual interest in

▲ **What parts of this portrait have been emphasized? How is this emphasis achieved? Find other drawings in this book that use the principle of emphasis.**

FIGURE **1.13** Eugene Amaury-Duval. *Portrait of a Lady (Portrait de Femme).* c. 1850s. Pencil with brush and gold ink on lightweight off-white wove paper. 28.8 x 26.8 cm (11⁵⁄₁₆ x 10⁹⁄₁₆"). Baltimore Museum of Art, Baltimore, Maryland. Purchase, Women's Committee Fund.

◀ **Do you think this drawing would have been as successful if the artist had made use of a consistent line similar to that noted in Figure 1.3? Why or why not?**

FIGURE 1.14 Katsushika Hokusai. *Boy with a Flute.* Date unknown. Ink on paper. 11.4 x 15.9 cm (4½ x 6¼"). Freer Gallery of Art, Smithsonian Institution, Washington, D.C.

their works. They must be aware, however, that too much variety can create visual clutter. The viewer could be confused. Variety must be carefully balanced by harmony.

You can see both harmony and variety in a small drawing of a boy playing a flute, by the Japanese artist Katsushika Hokusai (Figure 1.14). There is variety in the long, flowing lines that are at some places dark and heavy and at others slight and thin. These lines are used to suggest the differences between the boy's delicately pictured head, arms, and legs and the heavy folds of his garment. The long, flowing lines of the boy also contrast with the short, abrupt lines that indicate the pattern and texture of the woven basket and the boy's unruly hair. Value contrasts accent the hair and the decorative pattern of the boy's clothing.

Harmony in the Hokusai drawing was achieved through control. There are obvious differences in line, texture, and value, but these differences are carefully limited. In this case, variety and harmony are effectively combined to create a work of art that is visually stimulating and pleasant to look at.

■ GRADATION

Using a series of gradual changes to combine art elements is called *gradation*. For example, when an artwork makes use of a series of shapes that gradually change from large to small, angular to curvilinear, or rough to smooth, the artist has used the principle of gradation.

Did You Know?

Beginning in the 1920s, Georgia O'Keeffe created more than 200 lush, gigantic flowers during her lifetime. Although later in her artistic career she painted landscapes, bones, skulls, rocks, and cloudscapes of her beloved Southwest, her giant flowers were what brought her early recognition as an artist. At a New York exhibition in 1923, her paintings caused a sensation, eliciting a host of reactions ranging from critical raves to outrage to awe. The size and scale overwhelmed people—her largest work, *Miracle Flower*, was 6 x 7 feet (1.8 x 2.1 m)—yet even her smaller works held the same feeling of monumentality. Using pure color and the principle of gradation, she molded flowing forms that were considered sacred by some and erotic by others. Just as shocking as her subject matter was the fact that these works had been created by a woman at a time when the art world was almost exclusively male.

▲ **What has the artist done to create the sensation of movement in this drawing? Why do you think artists attempt to create this illusion of movement? How does the sense of movement contribute to this work's success or lack of success?**

FIGURE 1.15   Henri Toulouse-Lautrec. *Toulouse-Lautrec Sketchbook: La Comtesse Noir.* 1880. Graphite on ivory wove paper. 16 x 25.6 cm (6¹⁵⁄₁₆ x 10⅛"). The Art Institute of Chicago, Chicago, Illinois. Robert Alexander Waller Collection.

You can see this same principle in drawings exhibiting gradual changes from dark to light values. Changes of this kind are often used to suggest the appearance of rounded, three-dimensional forms. Several drawings you have already seen in this chapter use gradation. Georgia O'Keeffe's drawing (Figure 1.4, on page 7) is one of these. How many others can you find?

■ MOVEMENT AND RHYTHM

In a sketch of a horse-drawn carriage (Figure 1.15), Toulouse-Lautrec used the principle of *movement* to create the look and feeling of action. The drawing conveys this sensation with hastily drawn lines. These lines capture the gait of the horses and the rapidly spinning wheels of the carriage. Placed at an angle, the carriage seems about to burst out of the

picture as it rushes toward the viewer. Movement in this drawing was accented by the way the lines have been made. The hand of the artist must have dashed across the paper as he tried to record as quickly as possible the rapid movement of his subject.

Closely related to movement is the principle of *rhythm*. An artist often creates rhythm by carefully placing the same or contrasting elements throughout a composition. The repetition creates a visual tempo or beat. This tempo invites the eye to leap, skip, or glide from one element to the next as in Max Weber's *Interior in the Fourth Dimension* (Figure 1.16, page 16).

The same shape or line, for example, might be repeated several times in a work guiding the viewer's gaze in a certain direction. Another approach involves using contrasting shapes or colors to lead the eye on a more subtle pathway through the work.

◀ Describe the pathway your eyes follow when you view this nonobjective artwork. Do you like this piece? Why or why not?

FIGURE 1.16 Max Weber. *Interior in the Fourth Dimension.* c. 1913. Brush and watercolor and gouache on heavy watercolor paper. 46.9 x 62.2 cm (18½ x 24½"). Baltimore Museum of Art. Bequest of Sadie A. May.

A series of large and small shapes, for instance, could be placed so the viewer's eye is led forward, backward, then forward again through a work.

PROPORTION

The visual relationship of elements to the whole artwork and to each other is referred to as *proportion.* Often proportion is closely linked to another principle, emphasis. Enlarging objects or figures in a drawing not only shows the importance attached to them by the artist, but also communicates this importance to the viewer.

Artists have used the principle of proportion for centuries. Ancient Egyptian artists enlarged the proportions of pharaohs in tomb paintings as a way of emphasizing their importance as kings and gods. More recently artists have used exaggeration or enlargement of figures or objects in their works to communicate certain ideas or feelings. In Figure 1.17, Charles White exaggerated the sizes of certain parts of the figure to show the strength of a preacher delivering a powerful sermon. In this case, White made the head smaller and the gesturing hands larger than they should be. This exaggeration gives the preacher a more dramatic, powerful appearance.

SPACE

Space, you will recall, is one of the elements of art. You are probably surprised to see that *space* is also listed here as a principle. Sometimes the element of space, like the other elements, is controlled by the principles of art. Since space can be balanced, it can be used to emphasize a certain part of

▲ What parts of this figure are closest to you? How did you determine this? How do you interpret the different actions of his two hands?

FIGURE 1.17 Charles White. *Preacher.* 1952. Ink on cardboard. 54.3 x 74.6 cm (21⅜ x 29⅜"). Whitney Museum of American Art, New York, New York.

Artists at Work

■ MUSEUM ARTIST

Combining Science and Art

"Art is important to me and I'm pretty good at drawing, but science fascinates me too. Which direction should I go when I get to college?"

*A*ctually, many careers require people who are trained in art and knowledgeable about science as well. Preparing exhibits for a natural history museum requires a unique combination of artistic talent and scientific knowledge. As a museum artist, you might draw large background murals one week and prepare models of prehistoric animals the next week. Some jobs could even become a little tedious. For example, models of trees used in exhibits may take more than one thousand leaves that must be made and installed individually to create a realistic effect.

The responsibilities of an exhibition preparator and artist are varied and challenging. The artistic medium changes from project to project and the artist must work closely with a variety of scientists. The museum artist may make architectural or botanical models, draw scientific illustrations, or oversee a complete project from design to construction.

To create an exhibit on dinosaurs, for example, you might study bones and footprints to determine the probable ranges of movements. Scars on bones could help you plot muscle masses. Studying living animals such as crocodiles, birds, and reptiles might aid you in making educated guesses about the behavior and lifestyles of dinosaurs. In addition, reading reports of recent research and consulting with paleontologists (scientists who study fossils) could help you create a realistic exhibit.

Drawing plays an important part in preparing exhibits. For example, as a museum artist you might draw and paint large murals as backgrounds for dioramas (three-dimensional displays). A diorama of a Hindu wedding, for instance, might give the viewers the feeling of standing among the wedding party on a hillside. The background might be a landscape of India with a view of a typical village and distant fields.

This type of exhibit is created in stages. After completing your research, you would create preliminary sketches of the scene that include realistic details. From these sketches, you would plot the drawings onto a grid. Then, the grid would be enlarged and these points are transferred to the larger areas in the diorama. If the backdrop of the exhibit is curved, this step involves careful adjustment to allow for distortion. Next, you would carefully draw the scene with charcoal. Finally, the mural is finished with paints.

Some museums train several interns a year in the exhibitions department. These programs offer talented young people an opportunity to explore the job of creating museum exhibits.

In addition to museums, many businesses require the services of exhibit designers. Galleries, showrooms, trade shows, manufacturer's representatives and department stores utilize the skills of exhibit designers to create effective visual merchandising displays. ■

an artwork, or to suggest a gradual movement into a work. Space can also be used, however, as a principle to control the other elements.

You have learned that shapes can be combined in a composition to create a feeling of symmetrical or asymmetrical balance. You have also learned that several contrasting shapes might be used to emphasize a certain part of a work. Shapes, however, can also be created and arranged so they seem to be placed at different distances in the work. When this happens, the principle of space is used to manipulate the element of shape to create the illusion of depth. Space can be applied to any of the other elements to suggest a three-dimensional appearance in the work. This is clearly evident in Millet's drawing of three women gathering the scattered remains of wheat left by reapers (Figure 1.18). The large, dark, detailed and boldly outlined shapes of the women are clearly closer to the viewer than are the smaller, lighter, less detailed and sketchy figures and objects behind them.

▲ Millet was the son of a peasant. He trained first in Cherbourg and then in Paris under Delaroche. Daumier had a strong influence on Millet's work. How does Millet employ the elements and principles of art for a visually effective work?

FIGURE 1.18 Jean-Francois Millet. *The Gleaners*. 1857. Black conte crayon. 17.5 x 26.4 cm (6⅞ x 10⅜"). The Baltimore Museum of Art, Baltimore, Maryland. The George A. Lucas Collection of The Maryland Institute, College of Art, on indefinite loan to The Baltimore Museum of Art.

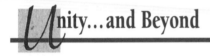nity...and Beyond

When artists design their works, they must organize the elements they have selected by using the principles of art to achieve an overall sense of unity or wholeness. Some artists design their works deliberately and thoughtfully. Others work in a more spontaneous and intuitive manner. Even so, no matter how they choose to work, the result must be inviting and pleasing to the eye. Artists must combine the elements and principles to ensure that all parts of a composition fit together in a visually appealing way. Unity can be thought of as the overall visual effect achieved by carefully blending the elements and principles in a work of art.

It is impossible for anyone to present you with a formula or a list of rules for good design. Instead, you have to develop your own approach to good design. Doing this requires a knowledge and understanding of the elements and principles of art.

There is much more to art than the effective organization of the elements of art. These are merely the building blocks with which artists construct their compositions. A good work of art must go beyond unity. Unless it does, it may be well composed, but it may also be boring, lifeless, and trivial. Consequently, unity must be combined with a sensitive and creative treatment of ideas, moods, and feelings. Only then will the artist create works of art that are complete, unique, and visually exciting.

CHAPTER 1 REVIEW

1. What is the visual vocabulary?
2. Why is the visual vocabulary important?
3. Name the elements of art.
4. Name the principles of art.
5. What is another name for a positive shape? A negative shape?
6. What is the difference between shape and form?
7. What are the two kinds of texture discussed in this chapter?
8. Is there a list of rules for good design?

STUDIO 1

Use the Elements and Principles of Art

SUPPLIES

- ➥ **Reproduction of a drawing or painting**
- ➥ **Pencil, sketchpaper**
- ➥ **Drawing paper or white mat board**
- ➥ **India ink, tempera, watercolor, or acrylic paints**
- ➥ **Brushes, mixing tray**
- ➥ **Paint cloth**

1. You have learned to define the elements and principles of art and observed how artists make use of these elements and principles to fashion their own artworks. Now you will have an opportunity to draw on that knowledge to complete an artwork of your own.

2. To begin this exercise, visit your school or community library and find a drawing or painting that you find especially interesting. Since you will be reproducing and modifying this work, it would be best to choose one that is not overly complicated.

3. After reviewing the information in this chapter, make a list of the elements and principles you would like to make use of when creating your own version of the artwork you selected. To do this, first identify at least three elements of art. Then determine which principles of art you will use to organize each of these elements. You can choose as many principles as you like. Your decisions might well look like the following:

Elements	Principles
Color _____	Harmony
Value _____	Emphasis
Line _____	Variety and Rhythm
Shape _____	Space

4. Complete your own version of the artwork you selected making certain that you use all the elements and principles on your list. Because your choice of elements and principles will differ from those used by the original artist, your composition will take on a different appearance. This difference may be subtle or quite dramatic.

5. The two students who selected Mary Cassatt's painting of *Girl Arranging Her Hair* arrived at two different interpretations of that painting because they chose to use different elements and principles (Figures 1.19 and 1.20). Turn to Color Section I and examine the artworks in color and compare them to Cassatt's original (Figures 3, 4 and 5). When you have completed your composition, place it on display in the classroom and ask other students to determine which elements and principles you chose to emphasize.

▲ **FIGURE 1.20   Student Art.**

▲ **FIGURE 1.19   Student Art.**

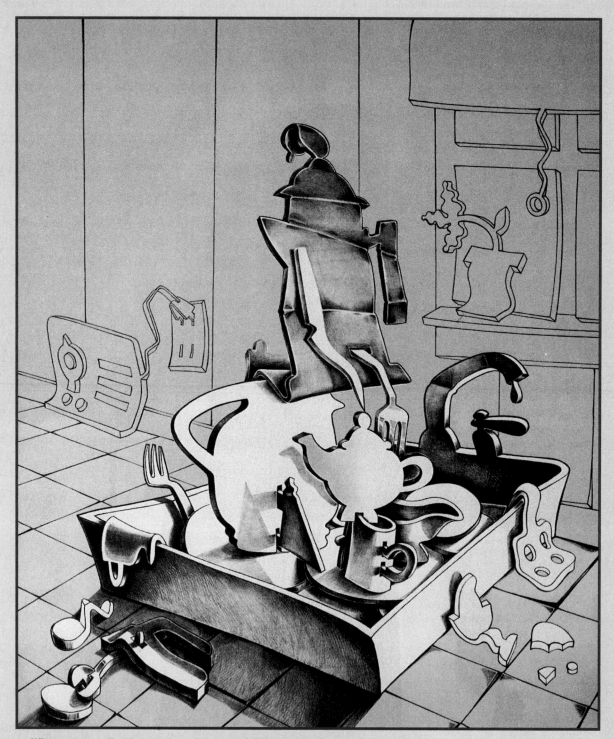

▲ What was your first impression of this work? Since it does not make use of realistic subject matter, must this work be regarded as unsuccessful? What other features or qualities could you take into account when judging this work?

FIGURE 2.1 Lynwood Kreneck. *Hot Day at Cardboard Cottage*. 1985. Serigraph and air stencil. 55.9 x 48.3 cm (22 x 19"). Courtesy of the artist.

Aesthetic Qualities and Art Criticism

Three aestheticians (people concerned with what makes art successful) have gathered at a table in a small café. Jones, Smith, and Veeberholz are involved in an argument that began when they first met many years ago. They are trying to define art!

Pounding his fist on the table, Jones is claiming that a work of art must look lifelike to be successful. "When an artist draws a tree, then it must look like a tree! If it doesn't look like a tree, it isn't art."

Shaking her head violently, Smith outshouts Veeberholz to state her point of view, "That's absurd! There is no reason why a work of art must look lifelike or real. Instead, it must be carefully and effectively composed by the artist."

"What exactly do you mean by that?" Jones asks.

"I mean that it must show a skillful arrangement of the elements of art according to the principles of art. The finished work must be unified and visually exciting. That's what I mean!"

Sensing an opening while Smith catches her breath and Jones covers his eyes in disbelief, Veeberholz leaps to his feet. "Both of you are wrong! A good work of art doesn't have to look real and it doesn't have to be well organized. However, it certainly must communicate an idea, a feeling, or a mood. If it fails to do that, it isn't art. It is as simple as that."

Jones and Smith lose no time standing up to protest. It is clear that the argument will end as it always does, without a winner.

objectives

After reading this chapter and doing the activities, you will be able to:

- List and describe three theories of art.
- List and describe three kinds of aesthetic qualities.
- Explain the difference between *looking* at and *seeing* works of art.
- List the four steps in the art-criticism process.

Terms to Know

analysis	formalism
art criticism	imitationalism
art history	interpretation
description	judgment
design qualities	literal qualities
emotionalism	nonobjective art
expressive qualities	

Theories of Art

Although no conclusions were reached, this discussion is useful to us. Each of these aestheticians values a different theory of art. Theories of this kind have been proposed by aestheticians and philosophers for centuries. Not one theory, however, has emerged that satisfies everyone. Yet they are all alike in one way—each theory tries to define art according to certain necessary and sufficient qualities found in works of art.

For example, Jones feels that a good work of art has to look real or lifelike. Smith thinks that it is more important that a work uses the elements and principles of art skillfully. Veeberholz argues that it is necessary for a work to convey a message of some kind to the viewer. If they didn't enjoy arguing so much, Jones, Smith, and Veeberholz might recognize that there is some truth in all of these theories. Each one alone, however, is too limiting.

A single theory of art, you see, can point to some truths in some works of art. However, it can't point to all truths in all works of art. Therefore, you need to become familiar with several theories of art rather than limiting yourself to accepting a single theory. Together the theories of art can guide you in identifying many different qualities in drawings.

No serious art student approaches a work of art in a neutral way; some preconceived ideas are unavoidable. Your own past experiences with art contribute to your approach. They affect how you look at drawings and determine what you see in them and how you respond to what you see. Knowing about and using different theories of art, however, can broaden your experience of art. The theories can help

▲ Focusing on the details in this picture enables you to discover a great deal about the people in this drawing.

FIGURE 2.2   Norman Rockwell. *Off to College*. Date unknown. Pencil drawing. 106 x 104 cm (41¾ x 41"). Texas Tech University, Lubbock, Texas. Collection of the West Texas Museum Association.

you understand and appreciate not only drawings that are appealing at first glance, but also those to which you might at first respond negatively.

For example, it is unlikely that you would respond positively to each of the drawings in Figures 2.1, 2.2, and 2.3. One of these probably appeals to you more than the others. If this is so, ask yourself why. Do you think that one of these drawings is less successful than the other two? Why do you think it is less successful?

Ask yourself some final questions: Did you judge all three drawings by the same test? If you responded positively to the drawing in Figure 2.2 because it looks so real, did you respond negatively to either or both of the other drawings because they lacked that same lifelike quality? If this is the case, do you think it is right to judge all three drawings by the same standard?

After all, it should be clear that two of these artists didn't care about making their drawings look real. Assume that both were skilled artists who could draw in a realistic way if they wanted to. Since they chose not to do so, they must have been concerned with capturing something other than realistic appearances in their drawings. If you could determine what that is, you might respond differently to their drawings.

Theories of art can direct your attention to different qualities in drawings. Armed with that knowledge, you would be better prepared to understand and enjoy more types of drawings. In this case, you might even find that you could respond positively to all three drawings, but for completely different reasons.

In later chapters, you will study three theories about the nature of art: imitationalism, formalism, and emotionalism. Figure 2.4 might be judged successful in all three theories of art. These theories will help you find different aesthetic qualities in drawings by other artists and make you more aware of those qualities in your own drawings. **Imitationalism** focuses on *literal or realistic qualities*, **formalism** on *design (or visual) qualities*, and **emotionalism** on *expressive qualities*. A brief introduction to these aesthetic qualities follows.

■ IMITATIONALISM: THE LITERAL OR REALISTIC QUALITIES

Literal qualities refer to the *realistic or lifelike representation of subject matter*. Aestheticians who follow an imitationalist point of view (such as Jones) think that the value of any artwork is determined by how closely it imitates the real world. An imitationalist would probably respond favorably to Ingres's *Portrait of Count de Nieuwerkerke* (Figure 2.5, page 24). That same imitationalist, however, would probably react

▲ How is variety demonstrated in the work? How has this variety been tempered with harmony? In discussing the value changes in this work, would you describe these as abrupt or gradual? Do you think this work is unified?

FIGURE 2.3   Paul Cézanne. *Bathers Under a Bridge.* Date unknown. Watercolor over lead pencil on paper. 21 x 27.4 cm (8¼ x 10¾"). The Metropolitan Museum of Art, New York, New York. Lizzie P. Bliss Collection. Maria DeWitt Jesup Fund.

▲ How has the artist emphasized the most important figures in this composition? Does this work represent all three theories of art? How does this drawing make you feel?

FIGURE 2.4   Francisco Goya. *Disasters of War.* c. 1812. Etching and aquatint. The Metropolitan Museum of Art, New York, New York. Mortimer Schiff Foundation.

▲ Many critics credit Ingres for having done some of the greatest portrait drawings of all time. Based upon your examination of this drawing, would you be inclined to agree with them?

FIGURE 2.5 Jean-August Dominique Ingres. *Portrait of Count de Nieuwerkerke*. 1856. Graphite and white chalk on cream wove paper. 33.0 x 24.3 cm (13 x 9⅝"). The Harvard University Art Museums, Cambridge, Massachusetts. Bequest of Grenville L. Winthrop.

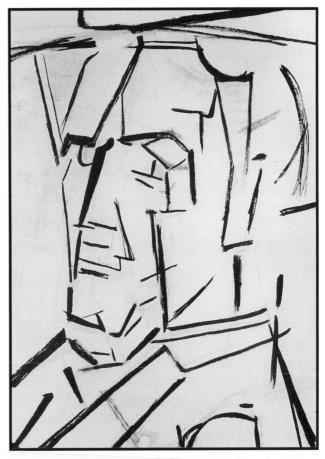

▲ This artist sought to compose his pictures of the simplest elements—in this case, with straight lines.

FIGURE 2.6 Piet Mondrian. *Self-Portrait*. 1942. Ink and charcoal on paper. 63.5 x 48.3 cm (25 x 19"). The Dallas Museum of Art, Dallas, Texas. Foundation for the Arts Collection. Gift of the James H. and Lillian Clark Foundation.

SHARPENING YOUR SKILLS

Examine Visual Clues

Notice also how Ingres provides visual clues about the personality of the count. What do the eyes, the mouth, and the facial expression tell you about the kind of person he was? Observe the pose, the clothes, and the medal the man is wearing. What do these suggest about his wealth, importance, and self-esteem?

unfavorably, or at least indifferently, to Mondrian's *Self-Portrait* (Figure 2.6).

Look carefully at Ingres's drawing (Figure 2.5). Is there any doubt that this is exactly how this French count looked? Sensitive lines indicate the coat and hands. Clearly, however, the focus of attention is on the face, which is drawn as accurately as possible. Gradual changes in value from dark to light give the head a feeling of roundness and volume.

If an imitationalist such as Jones looked at the Mondrian self-portrait (Figure 2.6), he would probably shake his head in dismay. "Surely the artist doesn't ask us to believe that he actually looked like this," he would say. "Why, there is nothing here but a series of hastily drawn lines—straight lines at that. I can see the general shape of a head and facial features, but the portrait isn't realistically drawn. No, in terms of the literal qualities, this drawing is unsatisfactory."

■ FORMALISM: THE DESIGN QUALITIES

Another theorist might regard Mondrian's drawing more warmly. A formalist like Smith, for example, would argue that a work of art should be judged by its design qualities, not its literal qualities. These **design qualities** refer to *the way the elements and principles of art have been used.* Formalists determine if the artist used these elements and principles to create a unified, visually pleasing artwork. They aren't interested in whether or not a drawing looks real. Instead, they are concerned with how effectively the artist has used the visual vocabulary—the elements and principles of art.

As a formalist, Smith might say the Mondrian self-portrait (Figure 2.6) is successful. She would first point out how the repetitious use of straight lines dominate in this drawing and help to give it harmony. The way these lines were applied and arranged creates a sense of rhythm. The lines invite the viewer's eye to move from one to the next.

Small changes in the lines give the drawing variety. There are long, short, horizontal, vertical, diagonal, thick, and thin lines. All of these lines have been carefully organized to create a unified whole. The drawing would make Smith smile in appreciation, even though Jones would turn away with a shrug of indifference.

■ EMOTIONALISM: THE EXPRESSIVE QUALITIES

Both imitationalists and formalists might respond positively to the self-portrait by Käthe Kollwitz in Figure 2.7, but for entirely different reasons. Imitationalists would point out the literal, or realistic qualities, and formalists would emphasize the design qualities.

Another group of theorists, however, would refer to different qualities to justify their positive response to this drawing. Emotionalists such as Veeberholz would say that it is successful because of its expressive qualities. **Expressive qualities**

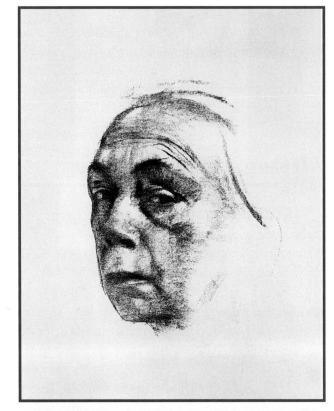

▲ What might this woman be thinking at this moment? What makes you think that she has not enjoyed many joyous experiences in her life? She lost a son in World War I and lived long enough to see her beloved grandson killed in World War II.

Figure 2.7 Käthe Kollwitz. *Self-Portrait.* 1924. Lithograph. 25.0 x 25.5 cm (9¹³⁄₁₆ x 10"). The Harvard University Art Museums, Cambridge, Massachusetts.

mean that *the drawing effectively communicates an idea, feeling or mood to the viewer.*

Veeberholz might begin his study of this drawing by thinking about this woman's frame of mind. Does she appear to be happy and content, or depressed and sad? Notice the furrowed brow, the deeply set, staring eyes, and the straight, expressionless line of the mouth. It is unlikely that anyone, least of all Veeberholz, would suggest that the woman is happy and content. If she spoke, she would probably talk about suffering instead of joy. Will her frown pass and be replaced soon by a good-natured grin? Or is it as much a part of her appearance as her wrinkled brow and sorrowful eyes?

The drawing begs the viewer to ask questions of this kind. The answers help the viewer share the feelings of the woman who drew this self-portrait over fifty years ago. By focusing on expressive qualities, Veeberholz, or any other emotionalist, can discover and respond to the artist's message. When you concentrate on the expressive qualities you can do the same thing.

Looking at and Seeing Drawings

The theories of art point out the different aesthetic qualities in artworks. These theories show you what to look for. You can identify these qualities more easily if you also know how to see art (Figure 2.8).

You may be saying to yourself, "Everyone knows how to see art." However, you may be confusing seeing with looking. People do not need to be taught how to look, but they do need to be taught how to see.

For example, picture yourself walking into a large classroom. It is filled with familiar objects that have four legs, a seat, and a back. Of course you would know at once that these objects are chairs. Up to this point you have been looking. To see, on the other hand, means that you would note the similarities and differences of the chairs.

You would observe that some chairs are made of metal, some of metal and wood, and still others of plastic. Several are painted in bright colors. Other older chairs seem to have faded to a dull, neutral tone. Many chairs appear to be new, but some look as if they have been in use for a long time and badly need repair.

Each chair in the room is in some ways similar to and in other ways different from the others. By examining them carefully, you would see these similarities and differences.

Of course you could hardly be expected to go through this careful observing process every time you encounter a chair or any other object. To do so would be highly impractical, even if it were possible. You reserve the capacity for observing and responding to an object's unique features for special occasions and special objects. If you were buying a chair, that would be a special occasion, and chairs would be special items.

▲ Have you ever observed people in a gallery or art museum? What comments have you overheard? Which artworks seem to command the most attention? To what do you attribute this?

FIGURE 2.8   John Sloan. *Connoisseurs of Prints*. 1905. Etching. 24 x 32 cm (9⁹⁄₁₆ x 12½"). Collection of Whitney Museum of American Art, New York, New York.

■ LEARNING HOW TO SEE

Among the objects that qualify for special observation and response are works of art. Learning from and about works of art leads to the kind of understanding, appreciation, and enjoyment that enriches our lives. To a drawing student, knowing both *what* to look for and *how* to look for it is essential if they are to *see* and respond intelligently and sensitively to drawings. Your art training shouldn't be limited to learning the techniques for making your own drawings. It should also include lessons learned from studying drawings of the past and present and applying those lessons to your own efforts to create drawings.

Art criticism and art history are two different approaches to the study of art. As a drawing student you must have an understanding of the methods used in both of these approaches. When you are mainly concerned with *identifying and responding to the various aesthetic qualities within drawings*, you will use the **art-criticism** approach. When you are mainly concerned with a *search for facts and information about drawings and the artists who did them*, you will use **art history**. In this chapter, you will begin to learn about art criticism. You will be introduced to art history in the next chapter.

Art Criticism

If you have never been involved in art criticism, you should realize from the start that it is not only easy but also enjoyable. Some beginning students mistakenly think that only those with a broad background in aesthetics, art history, or art production can critique art. It is true that such a background contributes to a more knowledgeable and sensitive response to art. Even so, you can practice meaningful criticism while gaining that background. This book is designed to help you learn how to see and respond to drawings through art criticism.

When you critique a drawing, you will use four separate but often overlapping steps or operations. These operations are:

- Description.
- Analysis.
- Interpretation.
- Judgment.

These steps help you identify the different kinds of questions you should be prepared to ask about a drawing. After you answer these questions, you will be able to:

- Identify everything in the drawing.
- Determine how the drawing is organized or composed.
- Explain what the drawing means.
- Make a personal decision about the drawing's degree of success.

Each of the art-criticism operations directs your attention to different aesthetic qualities in works of art. You will recall that these aesthetic qualities are:

- The literal qualities or realistic subject matter.
- The design qualities or the elements and principles of art.
- The expressive qualities or the ideas, feelings or moods communicated.

During description you focus attention on the literal qualities or subject matter and note the elements of art that constitute part of the visual qualities. When analyzing a drawing you observe how the principles of art are used to organize the elements. Finally, during interpretation you concentrate on the expressive qualities as you try to determine the idea, feeling, or moods communicated by the drawing.

Each of these operations for critiquing a drawing is explained more fully below. You will soon find out that using these operations enables you to

SHARPENING YOUR SKILLS

Detect and Discuss Literal Qualities

In small groups, examine a drawing done in an imitational style, such as the drawing in Figure 2.9 on page 28 or another of your choice in this book. Working together, begin by asking questions about the subject matter or literal qualities. If you haven't done this before, you may not know what to ask first. So begin with the most obvious question: "What do I see in this drawing?" To answer this question, carefully study the drawing, and assign one person to list everything your group sees in it.

Next, ask more specific questions, such as:
- How many buildings are included in the drawing?
- What are the buildings made of?
- Are there any windows in the buildings?
- Are there any people in the picture?

Answers to questions like these will help you learn a great deal about the drawing's literal qualities. You will begin to see things that you might have overlooked at first.

Choose a spokesperson from your group to discuss in front of the class the results of your findings.

▲ **Are these buildings drawn in a realistic manner? Do you think it would be comfortable living in them? What do you think may have been a more important consideration than comfort when these structures were erected?**

FIGURE 2.9   Jacob Savery. *The Amsterdam City Gates.* c. 1565–1602. Pen and two colors of brown ink over black chalk. 18.3 x 30.5 cm (7¼ x 12⅛"). Courtesy of the Museum of Fine Arts, Boston, Massachusetts. Louis Curtis Fund.

understand and appreciate others' drawings. It also helps you critique your own drawings—an important step in improving upon your drawing skills.

■ DESCRIPTION

Description, *the first art-criticism operation, involves asking and answering questions designed to help you discover everything in a drawing.* It is the least difficult of the four steps, although this should not be interpreted to mean that it isn't important. You must always try to be as thorough as you can when you describe a drawing. What you learn during description will be of significance later when you interpret and judge the artwork.

Of course there are many more description questions that should be asked in order to find everything in Figure 2.9. Take a few minutes to

study the drawing further, and try asking yourself some questions. As you become more involved in the description process, you will think of questions quite easily—and will soon discover how satisfying this process can be.

This descriptive questioning process might work with an imitational drawing, but what happens when you look at a nonobjective work? **Nonobjective art** *is a style that has unrecognizable shapes and forms. These works contain no apparent reference to reality.* Consequently, how would you describe a work such as the one illustrated in Figure 2.10?

A drawing like this offers few literal qualities to describe. In this case, ask yourself, "What elements of art can I identify in this drawing?"

As you know, elements, along with the principles of art, are the design qualities stressed by formalism. You will consider how the principles are

▲ Were you able to immediately identify the fish in this drawing? Explain how variety of value, line, shape, and texture are shown in this drawing. Judging from the materials from which it is made, is the texture in this work actual?

FIGURE 2.10 André Masson. *Battle of Fishes*. 1926. Sand, gesso, oil, pencil, and charcoal on canvas. 36.2 x 73 cm (14¼ x 28¾"). Collection. The Museum of Modern Art, New York, New York.

used in the next art criticism step. During this descriptive step, your attention is centered on identifying the elements of art in the drawing.

Eventually the descriptive questions you ask about the art elements will become more specific. For example:

- What colors can be identified (in color reproductions)?
- Are light and dark values used?
- What kinds of lines can I find in the work?
- How could I describe the shapes used?
- Are there areas of rough and smooth texture?
- How has the artist suggested depth or space in this drawing?

Actually, you should *always* ask questions about the elements of art when describing a drawing. If you are studying an imitational work, questions about the elements would follow those about the literal qualities. However, if a work is abstract or nonobjective, begin the description process by asking questions about the elements of art.

■ ANALYSIS

The second of the art-criticism operations, analysis, is probably the most difficult. Nevertheless, this step may improve your drawing skills the most. During **analysis** *you use the principles of art to learn how the work is organized or composed.* Your attention centers on the design qualities. Since you identified the elements of art during description, you will focus your attention on the principles of art during this step. The general question you need to ask yourself is "Which principles of art are used to organize the elements in this drawing?"

You will find that a design chart, such as the one in Figure 2.11 on page 30, can be of help when you are analyzing works of art. As you can see, the elements of art are listed vertically on the left side of this chart. The principles are listed horizontally across the top. The blank spaces show possible design relationships realized by combining elements and principles. These relationships determine how a work of art is put together. This chart is useful for analyzing all art, whether it is imitationalist, formalist, or emotionalist.

DESIGN CHART		PRINCIPLES OF ART								
ELEMENTS OF ART		Balance	Emphasis	Harmony	Variety	Gradation	Movement/ Rhythm	Proportion	Space	
Color	Hue									
	Intensity									
	Value									
Value (Non-Color)										
Line										
Texture										
Shape/Form										
Space										

UNITY

▲ **FIGURE 2.11**   The design chart will help you analyze artwork from now on, whether you choose a career in visual art or simply want to appreciate it.

◀ If Rembrandt had used a line of the same thickness throughout this drawing, would he have been as successful in suggesting the illusion of depth and weight? Explain your answer.

FIGURE 2.12   Rembrandt van Rijn. *Jan Cornelius Sylvius, the Preacher.* c. 1644–1645. Pen and bistre drawing. 13.4 x 12.2 cm (5⅛ x 4¹³/₁₆"). National Gallery of Art, Washington, D.C. Lessing J. Rosenwald Collection.

DESIGN CHART		PRINCIPLES OF ART								
ELEMENTS OF ART		Balance	Emphasis	Harmony	Variety	Gradation	Movement/Rhythm	Proportion	Space	
Color	Hue									
	Intensity									
	Value									
Value (Non-Color)										
Line					X			X	X	**UNITY**
Texture										
Shape/Form										
Space										

▲ **FIGURE 2.13   Partially completed design chart for Rembrandt's** *Jan Cornelius Sylvius, the Preacher.*

You can employ this chart in the future, whenever you want to critique a work.

Notice that one or more questions are suggested at each intersection of element and principle on the design chart. For example, at the intersection of line and balance, you might ask, "Are the lines in the work balanced?" Or you might ask a question linking line with emphasis: "Is line used in this composition to emphasize one or more points of interest?"

To practice using the design chart, analyze Rembrandt's portrait of *Jan Cornelius Sylvius, the Preacher* (Figure 2.12). Remember, ask yourself the questions suggested at each intersection of element and principle.

The design chart in Figure 2.13 will help you get started. The Xs indicate three of the more obvious design relationships involving line in Rembrandt's drawing. The X at the intersection of line and variety means that the lines showing the chair and the book edge are wider and heavier than those used for the robe. Thinner lines were used for the face, hair, and beard.

The X at the intersection of line and proportion refers to the relationship of these thick and thin lines. The thick lines of the book and chair make these objects look heavier than the robe, which is drawn with lighter lines.

The third X is placed at the intersection of line and space. The heavier lines in the drawing appear to be closer and the lighter lines farther away. These lines suggest objects at different distances in the work.

Now complete the design chart. How many more design relationships can you identify? The number depends largely on your patience, determination, and powers of observation. Students with experience in analyzing art will probably find more relationships than other students. The more you analyze art, the more easily you can recognize design relationships.

Don't become discouraged if your first efforts seem difficult and unproductive. You certainly don't expect to learn to drive a car the first time you sit behind the wheel. So you shouldn't expect analyzing something as complex as a drawing to be easy the first time you try. You will get better at it with practice—just as your driving skills improve with practice.

■ INTERPRETATION

As the scene below indicates, you may be more familiar with the third art-criticism operation, interpretation, than you realize....

The TV detective pauses dramatically before the roomful of suspects gathered in the library of the old von Scheckel mansion. He was asked to investigate

▲ **What one principle of art would you be certain to mention when discussing this drawing? What is there about this work that suggests the artist's confidence in his drawing ability? Do you think he labored over details or worked over the entire drawing at once? What lesson can you learn from this work that will help you in your own drawing?**

FIGURE 2.14   Honoré Daumier. *Fright.* Nineteenth century. Charcoal over pencil. 20.3 x 23.4 cm (8 x 9¼"). The Art Institute of Chicago, Illinois. Gift of Robert Allerton.

the mysterious disappearance of old Baron von Scheckel. He has just finished presenting his collection of clues. Foul play is obviously involved. As the trench-coat-clad investigator has pointed out, each member of the Baron's family had opportunity and motive. One of them is guilty—but which one?

The camera slowly sweeps across the faces of the unfaithful young wife, the greedy sister, the hateful brother-in-law, stuffy Uncle Fenimore and his quiet but sinister wife, and kind Aunt Frieda. Except for kind Aunt Frieda, they all look guilty. You lean forward, eager to learn if you have identified the culprit. Suddenly, the detective whirls around and points an accusing finger at Aunt Frieda....

In many ways your role as a critic interpreting a work of art is similar to the role of the detective in the scene just described. **Interpretation** *involves using the "clues" gathered during your investigation of a drawing to reach a decision about its meaning (or meanings).* You consider everything you learned from a work during the description and analysis steps before you make this decision.

The expressive qualities are the focal point during this step. You will want to ask yourself, "What ideas, moods, or feelings does this drawing communicate to me?" Answering this question may be the most exciting part of the criticism process. During interpretation you express your own personal decisions about the meaning of artworks. There are no right or wrong answers. Anything as complex as a good drawing is open to many different interpretations. Interpretations often vary because they are colored by each viewer's unique past experiences. For example, a man born and raised in the jungles of Brazil, when seeing an airplane fly overhead for the first time, would interpret the sight much differently than a person born and raised in downtown Chicago.

Different interpretations of a drawing are acceptable, but they must always be based on the clues found in the work. Use logic and common sense to avoid misjudging those clues. For example, to say that a picture of two snarling men wildly beating each other with clubs stands for peace and goodwill would be misreading the work.

Critiquing a drawing by Daumier (Figure 2.14) will give you an opportunity to test your skills in interpretation. Before you try to interpret it, however, be sure to describe and analyze the work as thoroughly as possible. In these steps you will gather the clues—literal and design qualities—to use in making a decision about what the drawing means. (Before you read further, interpret the drawing in Figure 2.14).

Briefly review what you have learned from describing, analyzing, and interpreting the drawing by Daumier. During the description operation, did you identify the figure of a woman? Did you see that she appears to be gesturing wildly while leaning backward? What kind of expression did you observe on her face? During the analysis step, did you notice the variety of thick and thin lines used to suggest form and movement? When making your interpretation, did you use these and other literal and design qualities to identify a woman who is:

- Happy and laughing hysterically?

- Sad and weeping uncontrollably?

- Frightened and reeling back in terror?

- Angry and screaming loudly?

Of course, not all drawings will be as easy to interpret as this one. Some complex works might even be open to several different interpretations. In those cases you might find that your own interpretation (or interpretations) differs from those expressed by others. That is fine—a difference of opinion can lead to a lively exchange of ideas. Such a discussion can be stimulating as well as helpful to anyone interested in learning as much as possible from a drawing.

Remember that complete agreement among viewers is not the goal of interpretation. Rather, each viewer is asked to make a personal, carefully thought-out decision based on information gathered during a complete description and analysis.

The clues in Daumier's drawing are clear. Most viewers will decide that the figure in it is violently jerking backward in terror from some unseen threat. You may have missed one important feature, however, that affects the meaning. Did you notice the way the artist applied the lines in this drawing? Do these lines appear to have been made carefully after a great deal of thought? Or do they seem to have been done impulsively and wildly, like the frightened woman's instinctive and violent reaction to an unknown threat? The way this drawing was done also helps reveal its meaning.

■ JUDGMENT

After you have described, analyzed, and interpreted a drawing, you are ready to make an intelligent judgment about it. This is your chance to express your personal response to a work. It is here that you ask yourself, "Is this a successful drawing?"

Before answering that question, however, you must know the difference between a judgment and a statement of like or dislike. Judging a drawing isn't saying that you like or dislike it. Statements of that kind are emotional reactions to art. They are important, of course, but they don't have to be—and often can't be—backed up with clues from the drawing. Like-dislike statements are based on immediate and instinctive responses. You either like or dislike a work of art—period.

A **judgment**, on the other hand, is *a thoughtful and informed response to a drawing*. This response must be supported by good reasons. It isn't enough to say that a drawing is good or bad; you must go on to explain why you think it is good or bad. When you have expressed a judgment and provided good reasons to support it, you are demonstrating that you understand and appreciate the drawing.

However, you may ask, what are those good reasons and how do I go about finding them? If you have completed the first three art-criticism operations, you already know them. These good reasons are everything you learned about a drawing during the description, analysis, and interpretation steps.

You might decide that a drawing is successful because of its literal qualities. ("It looks so lifelike!") Maybe a drawing is successful because of its design qualities. ("The elements and principles are organized to create a unified whole.") Or you could judge the drawing positively because of its expressive qualities. ("It clearly communicates a certain feeling, mood, or idea.") You could decide that a work is successful for one, two, or all three of these reasons.

Did You Know?

Daumier's drawing of a woman in fright is all the more effective if you know something about the artist's tragic life. After a brief period during which he earned his living as a bookseller, Daumier became a political cartoonist. Eventually this occupation brought him into conflict with the king of France, Louis-Philippe. In 1832 an unflattering cartoon of the king cost Daumier six months in prison. His only complaints while in prison were that he didn't have enough ink with which to draw and that other prisoners were always asking him to draw their portraits.

Daumier's fame as a cartoonist often hid the fact that he was a talented painter, although fellow artists recognized his abilities. Although he barely earned a living as a political cartoonist, he continued in this profession until he was in his seventies, when he lost his sight. The artist Camille Corot, a friend of many years, saved him from being evicted out of his modest cottage by buying it for him. When Daumier died, he was buried in a pauper's grave. The hundreds of drawings and paintings found in the little house were obtained by art dealers for almost nothing. Today, critics realize that Daumier's works foreshadowed modern art.

Artists at Work

■ ART TEACHER

Open the Door to Visual Communication

"I enjoy drawing and painting, but an artist usually works alone. My first love is sharing and working with people. How can I combine these interests?"

Teachers of art are catalysts in the dynamic process of learning about visual communication. They enjoy sharing their knowledge and skills with young people, helping them become visually aware of their environment and the artistic efforts of others. Creative art teachers stimulate their students to understand and respond to new information and situations.

Junior high and high school art teachers present a variety of topics. From aesthetics—to art criticism—to art history—to specific studio techniques, art teachers provide instruction and inspiration to students with wide ranges of artistic ability.

As an art teacher, you would develop courses that satisfy certain requirements determined by school boards, districts, or the state. These courses would be designed to give the aspiring artist a solid foundation for a career in art as well as fostering an appreciation of art in all students.

You would plan and present studio lessons intended to acquaint students with a variety of media and techniques. For instance, as a junior high school art teacher, you might prepare a unit on Native American art to introduce drawing. After examining a variety of art objects created by Native American artists, students could be asked to create bark paintings and ceremonial masks. The students would begin to think about drawing in new ways by making thick and thin lines with sharpened sticks dipped in ink.

Another unit in drawing might teach students how to use grids to transfer and use photographs in their drawings. The grid is placed over the photograph and the students use reference points to draw the picture freehand. This technique assures success for even the most inexperienced young artist.

While all art teachers must be able to explain and demonstrate a variety of techniques in many media, many are also practicing artists. Their artistic efforts are sometimes displayed in banks, restaurants, and other local businesses owned by supportive community members.

Although art teachers enjoy drawing and painting, it is their interaction with students that provides their greatest joy. Sometimes students who haven't succeeded in other subject areas discover that they have artistic talent. Many take pride in their work for the first time and show their artwork to friends and relatives. An art teacher's greatest satisfaction is seeing this pride and self-esteem develop in his or her students.

In addition to elementary and secondary schools, many opportunities for teaching art are found in museums, community workshops, adult art programs, painting workshops, Saturday scholarship courses, summer camps, city arts and crafts programs, church schools and the like. Many art consultants, authors and illustrators of children's books and editors of art magazines and textbooks are former school art teachers. ■

During this discussion of the first three art-criticism operations, you have studied several different drawings (Figures 2.9, 2.10, 2.12, and 2.14). Now make a judgment about each of these drawings. Keep in mind that no one else will make these judgments for you…it is a decision you must make on your own if the work is going to mean anything to you personally.

After making these judgments, study the drawing in Figure 2.15. Complete each step of the art-criticism process—description, analysis, interpretation, and judgment—for this work of art.

If you are tempted look in the back of the book for the "correct answers" to the questions posed by the art-criticism operations, you will be disappointed. There are no correct answers. You must make your own judgments and offer support for them. In that way you become actively involved in art criticism just as you become actively involved in drawing. Actively participating in art criticism will help you develop the aesthetic sensitivity that will enable you to understand the artworks created by others and contribute to the improvement of your own drawing skills.

▲ **Describe the appearance of these two figures. During analysis, is it important to discuss how these figures have been emphasized? What clues helped you arrive at your answer? What aesthetic qualities would you refer to when making and defending your judgment of this drawing?**

FIGURE 2.15   Honoré Daumier. *Two Lawyers*. Nineteenth century. Charcoal and gray wash on laid paper. 24.0 x 19.3 cm (9⁷⁄₁₅ x 7⅝"). National Gallery of Art, Washington, D.C. Chester Dale Collection.

CHAPTER 2 REVIEW

1. Name three theories of art.
2. What are the four operations you do when you critique a drawing?
3. Write a paragraph that explains the kind of responses people who judge a drawing might have and whether they need to support their opinions or not.

▲ Is there anything unusual about the pose the artist selected for her model? What elements of art are used to suggest a solid, three-dimensional form? What aesthetic qualities would you identify when defending your judgment of this drawing?

FIGURE 3.1   Élisabeth Vigée-Lebrun. *Study of a Woman*. Date unknown. Red chalk. 24 x 15 cm (9½ x 6"). Museum of Fine Arts, Boston, Massachusetts. Gift of Nathan Appleton.

Drawings and the History of Art

In Chapter 2 you learned about three theories of art, each proposed by an imaginary art critic. You discovered that a drawing can be successful because of:

- Literal qualities (they represent subject matter in a lifelike way);
- Design qualities (they use the elements and principles of art skillfully to achieve an overall unity); or
- Expressive qualities (they communicate a feeling, mood, or idea to the viewers).

You also learned a process—the art-criticism operations—for identifying these different aesthetic qualities in a drawing. You practiced the description, analysis, interpretation, and judgment steps by critiquing several drawings, which enabled you to gather a great deal of information from each of those drawings.

objectives

After reading this chapter and doing the activities, you will be able to:

- Give reasons for studying art history.

- Explain how the study of art can help you create and improve your own drawings.

- Name, describe, and identify characteristics of several styles and periods of art.

- Discuss the development of artistic styles as they relate to historical events and situations.

Terms to Know

Ashcan School	**Impressionism**
Cubism	**landscapes**
Expressionism	**Mannerism**
Fauvism	**Neoclassicism**
Gothic	**Pop Art**
International style	**Rococo**
	Surrealism

Why You Should Study Art History

Maybe you noticed, however, that you haven't learned anything about the artists who created the drawings, or the drawings' context—how, when, or where they were made. You still have many unanswered questions, such as:

- Who was Ingres, the artist who drew the lifelike portrait of the French count (Figure 2.5, page 24)? When and where did he live?

- What circumstances caused Käthe Kollwitz to create the sad self-portrait in Figure 2.7, page 25?

- What innovation did Vigée-Lebrun (Figure 3.1, page 36) employ in her drawing *Study of a Woman*?

Questions like these are unavoidable after you have critically studied drawings and made judgments about them. Your curiosity is aroused, and you want to learn more about the artists who created these works. Often, too, you want to compare your ideas about their works with the ideas of people who have a greater knowledge and understanding of art than you do. Yet where do you turn to find answers to the questions that remain after the art-criticism process is finished? Where can you find information about how others have responded to the artworks you have examined and judged? The answer is *art history*.

■ ART HISTORY HELPS YOU LEARN TO CREATE ART

Often art criticism and art history are thought of as only vaguely related subjects. To understand one, however, you also need to understand the other. Both of these subjects concentrate on works of art, but they use a different point of view. They often use the same processes, but gather different kinds of information.

Critics describe, analyze, and interpret information from a work of art before they decide if it is successful (Figure 3.2). Historians may also describe, analyze, and interpret, but the information that concerns them is different (Figure 3.3). They try to find

ART-CRITICISM OPERATIONS	
	Internal Clues
Description	What is in the work, discovered through an inventory of the *subject matter* and/or *elements of art* found in the work.
Analysis	How the work of art is *organized* or put together; concern centers on how principles of art have been used to arrange the elements of art.
Interpretation	Possible *feeling, moods,* and *ideas* communicated by the work of art.
Judgment	Facts relevant to making a *decision* about the degree of artistic merit in the work of art.

▲ **FIGURE 3.2   Chart of art-criticism operations.**

out who made the artwork, when and where the artist lived, and how the artist's personal style developed. An *art historian* is a person who judges artists and their works by deciding how much they have influenced art history.

Students who want to expand their awareness, knowledge, and understanding of drawings must recognize the value of both art criticism and art history. They must learn to use both approaches to gain information from and about drawings. To ignore either one is like trying to ride a bicycle with one wheel missing—you aren't likely to go anywhere.

Students are usually eager to try art criticism. Perhaps they feel that it doesn't require the extensive background often associated with art history. Once they know what to look for (literal, design, and expressive qualities) and how to look for it (the art-criticism operations), they can immediately begin critiquing works of art. Art criticism also provides students the chance to become personally involved with a work of art. Students don't need an expert or an authority to help them decide how successful the art is; they can make this decision on their own.

The art-history approach, however, requires that students go beyond the artwork itself. They need to seek out and use the findings of art history scholars. Doing this enables them to acquire information about works of art and the artists who created them.

ART-HISTORY OPERATIONS	
	External Clues
Description	*When, where,* and by *whom* the work was done.
Analysis	Unique features of the work of art, compared to features found in other works, to determine its artistic *style.*
Interpretation	How artists are influenced by the world around them, especially by *time* and *place.*
Judgment	Facts relevant to making a *decision* about the work's importance in the history of art.

▲ **FIGURE 3.3   Chart of art-history operations.**

Some students may try to avoid art history because they think it has little to do with developing their drawing skills. What they fail to realize is that art history can offer valuable lessons to anyone seeking to learn more about the process of drawing.

Learning about art history enables you to take advantage of what other artists have discovered and made use of in their artworks. Maybe you need ideas for subject matter for a drawing or for new ways to illustrate the subject matter you have selected. Perhaps you need help in deciding how to use the elements and principles of art to put an idea into visual form. Or maybe you would like to see what drawing media and techniques other artists have used to convey certain emotions.

Art history can help you identify the artists who have dealt with these same concerns. For example, a knowledge of art history would remind you of the kinds of subject matter Daumier used to draw attention to problems in society. It would help you recall that Ingres was a master of using line to create sensitive portraits, and that Käthe Kollwitz excelled at creating drawings noted for the emotions they expressed. The ideas and techniques of other artists can help you create more successful drawings, and a knowledge of art history is the key to discovering these ideas and techniques.

■ AN OUTLINE OF ART HISTORY

The chronological outline on the following pages will help you study the history of drawing in Western art. Included with the outline are examples of drawings produced during different historical periods. The captions accompanying these drawings contain art-criticism and art-history questions intended to help you understand them. Study the outline and the Did You Know? features about the artworks from each period. Doing this will help you learn how art developed from one year, one decade, and one century to the next.

Prehistoric Art, 30,000 B.C. to 10,000 B.C.

Deep inside the caves of southern France and northern Spain many drawings and paintings of animals have been discovered. They are so well preserved and skillfully done that they have caused endless debate among scholars. Is it possible that prehistoric cave dwellers, working with the crudest instruments, could have produced such works of art (Figure 3.4, page 40)? Maybe they were produced by skilled artists conducting a hoax of some kind. On the other hand, if they are the work of prehistoric artists, why were they made and how did they survive?

Most scholars today agree that the works of art discovered at Lascaux, France, and Altamira, Spain, are the work of prehistoric artists. It is unlikely, however, that they represent humankind's first efforts in art. These works are too sophisticated for that. No doubt they are the result of hundreds, perhaps thousands of years of slow artistic development about which we still know nothing.

These drawings and paintings of bison, deer, boar, and other animals were done deep inside caves, far from living quarters at the mouths of caves. They must have been used in some kind of magic ritual. Since our early ancestors depended on these animals for their survival, they probably held these ceremonies to bring them luck in hunting. Maybe prehistoric people thought that they were capturing the spirit and strength of these animals by making pictures of them. They may have thought that making these pictures would weaken the animals and make it easier to hunt them successfully.

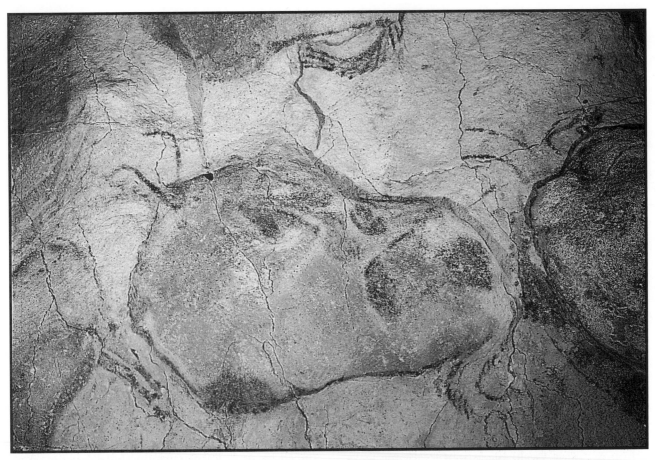

▲ **Can you identify the main features of this animal? What caused the controversy among scholars when works like this were discovered? Why is it thought that these works don't represent humanity's first efforts at art?**

FIGURE 3.4   Prehistoric. *Standing bison. Altamira caves, near Santilla, Spain.* c. 15,000–10,000 B.C.

Since the pictures were done far back in caves, they were well protected from wind and rain. These prehistoric works of art have survived to show us early man's powers of observation, artistic skill, and aesthetic sensitivity.

Ancient Egyptian Art, 2686 B.C. to 332 B.C.

Egyptian culture was based on a complex religion that emphasized a belief in the continuance of the spirit or soul after death. Egyptians thought that the spirit, or *Ka*, needed a body in which to live when it began a new life in the next world. They built elaborate tombs, the great pyramids, for important people in Egyptian society, particularly the *pharaohs*. These tombs were intended to protect the mummified bodies of the pharaohs, who were thought of as both rulers and gods.

Even though the tombs were well protected, they were often robbed and the bodies were damaged or destroyed. To make sure that the spirits would have bodies to live in, artists, were employed to create substitutes—sculptures, drawings, and paintings—for bodies. The Egyptians thought that if a pharaoh's body were destroyed, his spirit could live inside the carved, drawn, or painted substitute.

Since a drawing of a person was to take the place of that person's body, artists had to follow certain rules. Every part of the figure had to be included and shown from the most familiar point of view. If an arm or a leg were hidden behind the rest of the figure, the Ka would have to live in an incomplete body.

For this reason, ancient Egyptian figure drawings combined front and side views. The head was always shown in profile, but the eyes were drawn as if seen from the front. The shoulders were also presented as if seen from the front. The legs and feet were shown from the side (Figure 3.5). Even though Egyptian artists had to follow these strict rules, they still made drawings that are visually appealing.

Did You Know?

It is astonishing to realize that the ancient Egyptian culture lasted longer than the time from the birth of Christ to the present day.

SHARPENING YOUR SKILLS

You, the Art Historian

Choose a work of art illustrated in this chapter and, acting as an art historian, use the art-history operations described in Figure 3.3 on page 39 to learn about the work and the artist who created it. You will have to research art history books in your school or community library. Compile your results to be presented in class. Discuss how the historical information you gathered can be helpful to your efforts to improve your drawings.

▲ Describe this figure. Does he appear to be an important person? Describe the rules that artists were required to follow when creating these works. Does this work follow these rules?

FIGURE 3.5 Egyptian, Old Kingdom, late V to early VI dynasty. *Relief from Ankh-Ni-Neswt's Tomb Chapel.* c. 2600–2500 B.C. Limestone, painted. 160 x 84 cm (63 x 33"). Honolulu Academy of Arts, Honolulu, Hawaii. Gift of Mrs. Charles M. Cooke.

Ancient Greek Art, 1100 B.C. to 146 B.C.

Most of what we know about Greek drawing and painting has been pieced together from ancient writers' descriptions. Many Greek painters, however, were even more famous in their time than the Greek sculptors whose works are better known to us today.

▲ Are lines used to achieve variety or harmony? How is value used to emphasize the figures? Is this an example of symmetrical or asymmetrical balance?

FIGURE 3.6 Exekias. *Achilles and Ajax Playing Morra (dice).* c. 540 B.C. Black-figure amphora. Vatican Museums, Rome.

Ancient writers tell us that a Greek painter's skill was measured by the literal qualities evident in his or her work. The more realistic the work, the more admired the artist was. Sculptors also tried to make their work look as lifelike as possible. An ancient story illustrates how successful they were. According to this story, a Greek citizen was asked why there were so few examples of Greek sculpture. He immediately answered that Greek sculptures were made to look so lifelike that as soon as the artists finished them, they jumped from their pedestals and ran away.

An idea of what Greek painting and drawing may have looked like can be gained by looking at ancient Greek vases. As drawing developed, the figures on these vases became more and more lifelike and often told some kind of story (Figure 3.6). Greek artists were interested in good design, also. They drew their figures to fill the available space in a decorative, visually appealing way. These figures show a concern for accurate proportions, movement, and emotions that are never exhibited in Egyptian art.

Besides being interested in visual accuracy and good design, Greek artists searched for the perfect combination of parts to make an ideal whole. Zeuxis, for example, was a Greek artist who tried to find a woman beautiful enough to be his model for a portrait of Helen of Troy. He finally selected five Athenian maidens with specific ideal features and combined these features in his painting.

Did You Know?

The Greek emphasis on realism in art is revealed in the description of a contest between two Greek painters provided by a writer in ancient times. According to this tale, one of the painters drew back a curtain to reveal a painting of grapes that was so lifelike that birds were tricked into pecking at them. The second artist won the competition, however, when he demanded that his rival, the painter of the grapes, remove the curtain covering his painting. When the first artist attempted to do so, he discovered that there was no curtain—it was a painting of a curtain.

Ancient Roman Art, 509 B.C. to A.D. 476

The Romans greatly admired and imitated Greek art, philosophy, literature, and science, but made few original contributions of their own. They were practical and were more interested in learning about architecture, engineering, law, and government. Roman artists are important to the history of art, however, because they preserved the Greek heritage and spread it throughout their vast empire.

Roman engineers used slave and army labor to construct over fifty thousand miles of roads, a feat that Europeans didn't match until the nineteenth century. This vast network of roads linked distant provinces and made possible the spread of Greek culture from Britain in the west to India in the east.

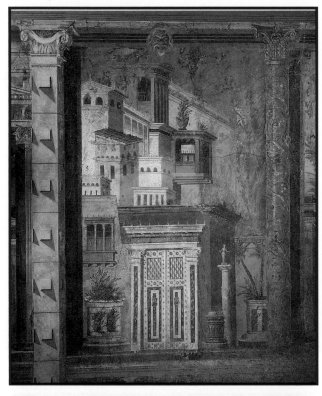

▲ **What do you see in this picture? Are you able to identify any figures? List what you believe are the most important elements of art in this work. How is the illusion of space achieved?**

FIGURE 3.7   Roman. *Wall painting from the villa of P. Fannius Synistor at Boscoreale (east wall, panel with ornate door to fantastic villa from the cubiculum nocturnum).* c. 50 B.C. Fresco on lime plaster. Height 2.44 m (8'). The Metropolitan Museum of Art, New York, New York. Rogers Fund.

The Romans apparently didn't like to hang drawings and paintings on walls. Instead, they created *murals* by painting and drawing pictures directly on their walls. These murals (Figure 3.7) have several features that we find in the works of later Italian Renaissance artists (pages 46–49).

For example, Roman artists used architectural forms to suggest both space and atmosphere. They

Did You Know?

At the peak of its power, Rome had a population of over one million living in an area about three miles square. The city was marked by contrasts. Splendid public buildings, forums, baths, and parks contrasted with narrow, crowded streets and crudely erected wooden tenements where most of the people lived.

had no exact knowledge of linear perspective, which was discovered and perfected by Renaissance artists. Nevertheless, Roman artists' sensitivity to aerial perspective was well developed. They also put figures in dreamy, imaginative landscapes that had either religious or secular themes.

Early Medieval Art, 476 to about 1050

After the fall of the Roman Empire, the only stable organization left in western Europe was the Church. Its influence was felt everywhere, and it gave the medieval period its special character.

The Church saw that art could be used to inspire and teach its followers. Since most people couldn't read, they had to rely on visual images.

A limited number of handwritten books were produced for those few who could read, but the illustrations drawn and painted in these books were intended for the majority of people who couldn't read. The religious carvings on the façade, or front, of medieval churches were meant for these same people.

The task of teaching and spreading the faith belonged to monks. They were dedicated men living together under a strict set of rules in religious communities called monasteries. Besides being teachers and priests, these monks were among the leading artists and craftsmen of the period.

Did You Know?

The façades, or fronts, of Medieval churches were so filled with rich religious carvings that they came to be known as bibles in stone.

Among the tasks undertaken by monks was the production of religious books. There were no printing presses during the medieval period, so all books had to be copied painstakingly by hand. Monks who did this copying were often artists of great skill. They took pride in making beautifully proportioned letters and adding graceful miniature drawings.

The illustrated manuscript, or book, was the most important form of painting in western Europe, from the fall of Rome around 476, until the fourteenth and fifteenth centuries, when easel painting period had been local, rarely reaching beyond the surrounding community. Romanesque art, however, gradually became more international in character. This international character resulted from the exchange of ideas due to the growth in trade and travel during the eleventh and twelfth centuries.

Romanesque paintings and drawings have a flat, two-dimensional look. Their brightly colored and richly patterned figures and objects look like they were cut from cardboard and laid one on top of the other. Romanesque artists made little effort to make their pictures look realistic. Instead, they used colorful shapes and dark lines to illustrate traditional religious stories.

A glance at one of these illustrations quickly brought the story to the viewer's mind. Then the viewer could meditate on the meaning of that story.

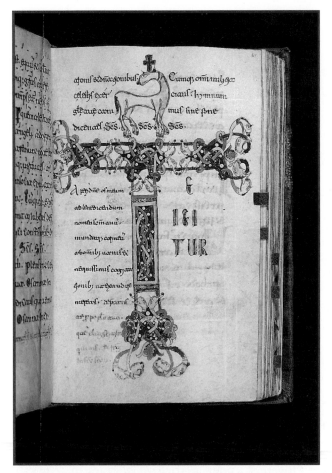

▲ If you were asked to describe this work, which two elements of art would you be certain to mention? What was the most important objective for the artists who created manuscript illustrations?

FIGURE 3.8 Southeastern Italy. *The Lamb of God Atop the Letter "T" of the "Te igitur."* First half of the eleventh century. Walters Art Gallery, Baltimore, Maryland.

and the printing press were developed. The drawings and paintings (Figure 3.8) in these books may seem awkward and even crude to viewers who don't realize the depth and intensity of the artists' religious feelings. The monks sacrificed realism to express as clearly as possible their deepest religious beliefs.

Romanesque Art, 1050 to 1150

Miniature drawings and paintings in religious manuscripts started in early Christian times and became more popular during the early medieval period. It continued to be an important artistic activity throughout western Europe during the Romanesque period. The art of the early medieval

▲ Which of these figures appears to be speaking? Which aesthetic qualities are more important in this work—the literal or the expressive qualities? Why?

FIGURE 3.9 German. Leaf of a breviary or missal. *The Annunciation.* c. twelfth century. Colors and gold leaf on vellum. 15.2 x 12.1 cm (6 x 4¾"). The Metropolitan Museum of Art, New York, New York. Fletcher Fund.

For example, an illustration from a German prayer book (Figure 3.9) tells the New Testament story of the Annunciation. An angel informs Mary that she will be the mother of the Savior. The angel's right hand is raised with two fingers extended to show that he is speaking. Mary turns toward him with open hands. This gesture suggests her willingness to accept the responsibility suddenly thrust on her.

The figures appear still and motionless; neither shows any sign of emotion. The viewer is left to imagine what is going on in Mary's mind at that moment. Clearly this illustration isn't a detailed, realistic drawing. Rather it is an uncluttered arrangement of familiar sacred symbols. Its sole purpose was to illustrate as clearly as possible the story of the Annunciation heard over and over in medieval churches.

Gothic Art, 1150 to Approximately 1500

At no other period in history were the visual arts so closely joined in a common effort than in the Gothic period. Drawing, painting, sculpture, and architecture were combined to create the splendid Gothic cathedral or church, which featured pointed arches, flying buttresses, and weight-bearing pillars. With these innovations in architecture, walls were only required to enclose and define space. Artists and *artisans* took advantage of this by designing walls made of stained glass.

The designs used for stained glass windows greatly influenced the style of drawing and painting used in manuscript illustrations. Gothic manuscript illustrations often showed slender, graceful reli-

▲ Do these figures look realistic to you? How do they differ from the figures in Figure 3.9? Would you describe these figures as round and solid, or flat and thin? Is this a successful work of art? Did you consider the historical importance of this artist?

FIGURE 3.10 Giotto. *Madonna and Child*. c. 1320–30. Tempera on panel. 85.5 x 62.0 cm (33⅝ x 24⅜"). National Gallery of Art, Washington, D.C. Samuel H. Kress Collection.

gious figures in flowing costumes placed inside frames similar to those used for cathedral windows. Solid gold backgrounds were used to emphasize the spiritual importance of the scenes.

Altars inside churches were decorated with tempera paintings created on wooden panels in the same rich designs. This elegant, flowing style of painting became so popular that it became known as the **Gothic International style**, *a kind of art practiced* *throughout western Europe during the late fourteenth and early fifteenth centuries.*

Because the Gothic style of architecture with its walls of stained glass didn't spread to Italy until later, Italian artists could still paint religious pictures on solid interior church walls. First, the artist made a charcoal drawing on the wall. Then a thin coat of plaster was applied, and the charcoal lines seen through the plaster were retraced. Paint, mixed with water and egg whites, was applied to the *fresh* plaster surface. This process gave the painting technique its name, *fresco*. The paint and wet plaster mixed together to form a permanent surface when they dried.

Fresco paintings had to be done quickly while the plaster was still wet. The technique required confidence, boldness, and skill. One artist, Giotto di Bondone, had all of these traits. Giotto's concern for realism shaped the course of art history for centuries. In his *Madonna and Child* (Figure 3.10, page 45),

▲ **Why was Leonardo's artistic output so small? Did he create many drawings? What does this tell you about the importance he placed on drawing?**

FIGURE 3.11 Leonardo da Vinci. *Sheet of Studies (recto).* c. 1470–80. Pen and brown ink over traces of black chalk on laid paper. 16.4 x 14 cm (6⁷⁄₁₆ x 5½"). National Gallery of Art, Washington, D.C. The Armand Hammer Collection.

Giotto used figures modeled in light and dark values to capture the love between mother and son.

The Art of the Renaissance in Italy, 1400 to 1520

During the medieval period, most people were mainly concerned with living in a way that would assure their eternal reward in the next world. Gradually people became more interested in the present world and their place in it. This change of attitude, and the ways in which it was demonstrated in art, literature, and learning characterize a period known as the *Renaissance*.

The Renaissance began in Italy during the fourteenth century and reached its peak in the fifteenth and early sixteenth centuries. One reason it began in Italy was that the tradition of classical art and culture was never entirely lost in this country.

Studying the classics encouraged artists to look for subject matter outside of religion. It also contributed to a growing concern for realism. In drawing and painting, artists developed rules of perspective and refined the practice of using light and dark values to obtain amazingly realistic three-dimensional effects. Artists also studied anatomy in an effort to make their drawings of figures look more lifelike.

Up to the Renaissance, the history of art is mainly the history of styles and ideas to which many unknown artists contributed. After the fifteenth century, however, the history of art deals mainly with the lives and accomplishments of individual artists. Leonardo, Michelangelo, and Raphael were three artists who made up the most astonishing trio of geniuses who ever lived at the same time in the same place. Leonardo da Vinci wanted to learn everything possible about a subject before trying to recreate it in art. This effort, however, took up so much of his time that his artistic output was quite modest.

The human body was just one of Leonardo's many interests. He estimated that he filled 120 notebooks with his figure drawings (Figure 3.11). These drawings were surrounded by explanations and reminders to himself about the many subjects that interested him.

Michelangelo is known for his painting and sculpture, but he depended on drawing skills to design his works. Imagine that you meet him at the

▲ Why have so few drawings by Michelangelo survived to the present time? What do these drawings tell you about the artist? Do you think drawings like this should be regarded as successful works of art? Why or why not?

FIGURE 3.12   Michelangelo. *Studies for the Libyan Sibyl.* c. 1511. Red chalk on paper. 28.9 x 21.3 cm (11⅜ x 8⅜"). The Metropolitan Museum of Art, New York, New York. Joseph Pulitzer Bequest.

foot of a huge scaffold in the Sistine Chapel over five hundred years ago....

The artist peers upward at the dim corner of the ceiling 68 feet (20 m) above where he will paint

a twisting female figure. He reaches for his sketch paper and a piece of red chalk and begins to draw.

Later, in his small studio. Michelangelo takes out a fresh sheet of paper and begins to draw a model, concentrating on the model's feet, hands, and torso. All of these drawings are crowded onto a single sheet (Figure 3.12). All of the available space is used because paper is expensive.

The artist has been drawing a male model, since female models weren't used in the sixteenth century. So Michelangelo makes another drawing at the bottom corner of the paper, changing the face of the figure to look more like a woman's.

Michelangelo is tired. It seems as if the Sistine Chapel ceiling will never be finished. He rarely leaves the scaffold and even has food sent up to him so he doesn't have to stop work. He leaves the scaffold for a few hours of sleep only when he is too weary to continue.

Painting the ceiling seems like a waste of effort. The walls in the chapel are already decorated with great works by well-known artists. Who will bother to stop admiring these paintings and look up at his ceiling?

Unexpectedly the artist reaches for a pen and begins to write, perhaps to express some of his frustration and disappointment.

> "When will the nightmare be over?
> My chin is growing into my stomach,
> My beard has become part of my arm,
> My face is a mosaic of color,
> Now I drink and breathe only paint.
> My body is twisted backward in a circle, and
>   my sanity is completely gone.
> I hate this place.
> Why am I here? I'm not even a painter!"

The next day Michelangelo would begin drawing and painting the new figure on the ceiling. It would be one of 342 figures he would create on a ceiling measuring 40 feet (12 m) wide and 133 feet (40 m) long. The task would demand all of his waking hours for four years. Fortunately, as an eyewitness later reported, when the artist was finally finished and the Sistine Chapel was opened to the public, the whole world rushed to Rome to stare in wonder at the ceiling.

Did You Know?

Great importance was attached to the study of anatomy during the Renaissance. Books were written on the subject to assist artists who wanted to represent more realistically the bend of an arm or the foreshortened appearance of a reclining figure. Like many other artists, Raphael admitted that he made his studies of the figure from live models, but relied upon surviving classical sculptures for proportions.

Apparently, Michelangelo wanted to keep his creative process a secret. He gathered up and burned as many of his sketches as he could before he died. Only a few survived. One of these is shown in Figure 3.12 on page 47.

Twenty-two years after painting its ceiling, Michelangelo Buonarroti returned to the Sistine Chapel to paint his version of *The Last Judgment* on the altar wall. Like the figures he designed earlier for the ceiling, the figures in the painting were carefully planned in detailed drawings that exhibit a concern for form and that were planned on a grand scale. When he was finished with the huge fresco, he signed it simply *Michelangelo, Sculptor*.

Unlike Leonardo and Michelangelo, Raphael Sanzio didn't develop new techniques, but he was able to perfect their techniques to create what is referred to as the High Renaissance style. His figures skillfully blend Michelangelo's sense of movement and full, well-rounded forms, and Leonardo's soft modeling with light and dark values. Yet, even though he borrowed freely from these and other artists, Raphael maintained his own identity by adding his own charm and grace. These qualities are especially apparent in a drawing he made of the *Madonna and Child with the Infant St. John the Baptist* (Figure 3.13).

▲ Describe the figures in this drawing. What is each of these figures doing? Is the artist successful in suggesting three-dimensional form in this drawing? Is this a successful work of art?

FIGURE 3.13 Raphael. *Madonna and Child with the Infant St. John the Baptist.* c. early 1500s. Red chalk on paper. 22.4 x 15.9 cm (8¹³⁄₁₆ x 6¼"). The Metropolitan Museum of Art, New York, New York. Rogers Fund.

Did You Know?

In the spring of 1520 Raphael fell ill with a violent fever. Doctors tended to him and friends told him it was nothing more than a passing ailment—but the artist knew he was dying. He made out his will, made certain his affairs were in order, and died on his birthday, Good Friday. He was buried in the Pantheon in a tomb marked with a simple inscription that reads: "He who is here is Raphael."

The Art of the Renaissance in Northern Europe, 1400 to 1500

The art produced in the countries north of Italy during the fifteenth century followed the traditions of the late medieval period. Unlike artists in Italy, northern European artists showed little interest in the art of ancient Greece and Rome. Instead, they chose to develop further the Gothic International style by making it appear more realistic.

Northern European artists could add more details to their works because of a new oil painting technique developed at this time. The innovative oil paints consisted of dry pigments, oils, and sometimes varnish, making the drying time for oil paintings longer than for fresco paintings. Oil paints gave artists the opportunity to work at a more leisurely pace.

Jan van Eyck is often credited with developing this new oil painting technique. Using the Gothic International style as a starting point, van Eyck created

a new painting tradition, showing scenes as they actually appeared in the real world. He was a master at suggesting atmosphere through subtle gradations of light and the realistic presentation of every detail.

His paintings are characterized by a precision resulting from preliminary drawings completed with a keen eye for accurate detail. In his picture of *The Annunciation* (Figure 3.14), every strand of hair appears to be painted individually.

Rogier van der Weyden (Color Section I, Figure 7), a contemporary of van Eyck, added his own ideas to van Eyck's approach to painting. A popular artist during his lifetime, van der Weyden was especially admired for his strong designs and elegant figures. His works were also noted for their refined, dignified emotionalism.

The new styles of Jan van Eyck and Rogier van der Weyden became less important by the end of the fifteenth century as the impact of Italian Renaissance artists spread northward. Italian influences were introduced into the drawings and paintings of northern Europe. This strange mixture of art styles continued into the sixteenth century, when it finally evolved into a style called *Mannerism*.

The Art of the Sixteenth Century in Italy, Spain, and Germany, 1520 to 1600

The artists of the island city of Venice combined the lights and colors reflected in surrounding waters with a Renaissance concern for reality. The resulting art style was noted for its brilliant use of color, light, and texture; its swirling, full-bodied figures; and its dreamlike atmosphere.

The first of the great Venetian artists was Giorgione. Although only a few of his pictures still exist, he is regarded as one of the greatest painters in history. His paintings changed the way people

◀ **What makes this painting seem so realistic? What new painting technique enabled this artist to include so much detail? What perspective technique suggests space in this composition?**

FIGURE 3.14   Jan van Eyck. *The Annunciation.* c. 1434–36. Oil on wood transferred to canvas, painted surface. 89.9 x 35.2 cm (35⅜ x 13⅞"). National Gallery of Art, Washington D.C. Andrew W. Mellon Collection.

thought about art because they weren't just line drawings filled in with color. He put areas of glowing color next to each other to create pictures noted for their enchanting dreamy moods.

When Giorgione died, Titian became the most important Venetian painter. From Giorgione, Titian gained an appreciation for color, light, and texture learning how to use landscapes to create moods. **Landscapes** are *works of art that use natural scenery as subject matter*. Although he drew and painted all kinds of subjects, Titian was most famous for his portraits of kings, popes, philosophers, and military leaders.

The last great Venetian artist of the sixteenth century was Jacopo Tintoretto. Tintoretto's figure drawings (Figure 3.15) used the same full-bodied form and sense of movement in space as those by Michelangelo.

In his paintings, Tintoretto emphasized emotional aspects of a story rather than illustrating it accurately. His highly unique painting style used contrasting light and dark values to suggest a flickering movement. He stretched out the proportions of figures and often showed them making exaggerated, theatrical gestures.

The church welcomed this dramatic style of painting because it was experiencing a period of disorder and change. Martin Luther had started the Protestant Reformation in 1517 and many people were leaving the church. Its leaders valued the art of Tintoretto and others

48

▲ **How would you describe the line used in this drawing? Point to places where the line seems to be darker or lighter in value. How do these differences in line quality add to the illusion of movement? Name actions this figure might be performing.**

FIGURE 3.15   Jacopo Tintoretto. *Standing Youth with His Arm Raised, Seen from Behind.* Date unknown. Black chalk on laid paper. 36.3 x 21.9 cm (14¼ x 8⅝"). National Gallery of Art, Washington, D.C. Ailsa Mellon Bruce Fund.

▲ How did El Greco differ from other Spanish artists of this period? Why did he use distortion when drawing and painting figures? What name is applied to this style of art?

FIGURE 3.16 El Greco. *Saint Jerome.* c. 1610–14. Oil on canvas. Approx. 1.68 x 1.11 m (5'6" x 3'8"). National Gallery of Art, Washington, D.C. Chester Dale Collection.

because it appealed to the emotions of the people, reminding them that the church was still there to help them find salvation. **Mannerism** is the name of the *dramatic, emotionally-charged style of art* created during this time.

The most striking Mannerist painter lived in Spain. His name was Domenico Theotocopoulos. Since most people had difficulty pronouncing his name, he came to be known simply as *The Greek* or *El Greco.*

El Greco arrived in Spain from the Greek island of Crete after having spent a number of years in Venice and Rome where he was influenced by Titian and Tintoretto. Around 1577, El Greco settled in Toledo, Spain, where he spent the rest of his life.

At this time, artists in Spain were still concerned with representing reality. El Greco, however, was daring enough to express his own inner visions in his work. All of his figures, even in his portraits, were creatures formed by his unique imagination.

El Greco's unfinished painting of *St. Jerome* (Figure 3.16) illustrates his methods. The figure of the saint was drawn with bold, dark contour lines over which layers of brilliant color were added. The figure was deliberately distorted to suggest the elegant, heavenly grace of saints. El Greco didn't intend his St. Jerome to look real; he meant him to look supernatural.

Albrecht Dürer was the only German artist of his time to adopt the ideas of the Italian Renaissance and use them in his work. In 1494 he returned to his native Germany from a trip to Italy determined to draw and paint in the new Renaissance style. He studied perspective and anatomy and then applied what he had learned to his art (Figures 8.6 and 8.7, pages 161–162).

Other German artists, however, weren't as willing as Dürer to accept the new Renaissance ideas

from the south. Matthias Grünewald, for example, chose to use Renaissance techniques only to increase the emotional impact of traditional Gothic subjects such as the Crucifixion.

The Art of the Seventeenth Century, 1600 to 1700

By the beginning of the seventeenth century, the church had regained much of its influence in Italy and was involved in a large-scale program of building and decoration. A new style of church construction known as *Baroque* featured a sculptured, dynamic look realized by using alternating concave and convex surfaces as interior and exterior walls.

These surfaces curved in and out to create a pattern of contrasting light and dark areas that gave the building a look of dynamic, continuous movement.

Many of the features of Italian Baroque architecture are noted in the drawings and paintings created in the seventeenth century. They too exhibited a concern for light and shadow and dramatic movement. Nowhere is this more clearly evidenced than in the work of Michelangelo da Caravaggio, the most influential artist of this period.

Caravaggio was curious about how things actually looked and drew his inspiration from carefully observing the things around him. As he matured as an artist, his style changed to include a greater use of

▲ Why do you think the child has wrapped himself in his mother's apron? What has the artist done to make these figures look round and solid? How is space suggested in this work?

FIGURE 3.17 Annibale Carracci. *A Domestic Scene.* Early 1580s. Pen and black ink, gray wash. 32.7 x 23.5 cm (12¹⁵⁄₁₆ x 9¼"). The Metropolitan Museum of Art, New York, New York. Gift of Mrs. Vincent Astor and Mrs. Charles Payson. Harris Brisbane Dick Fund and Rogers Fund.

a bold, strong light. His figures looked human, not spiritual or supernatural as they did in Mannerist paintings. Caravaggio's style of combining a dramatic use of light and realistic detail had an impact on the entire European art world.

Perhaps the only Italian artist of this period worthy of being ranked alongside Caravaggio is the Bolognese painter Annibale Carracci. He shared Michelangelo's belief that artistic perfection could only be achieved through drawing. His later works used a line quality powerful enough to be compared with Michelangelo's; but Carracci could also use a firm, clear, sensitive line to create a scene of great warmth and charm (Figure 3.17).

Peter Paul Rubens was the greatest Flemish painter of the seventeenth century. While still a young man, Rubens spent eight years in Rome and it was there that his style was formed. The drawings he created at that time show that he studied classical ruins, the works of Renaissance masters, and the paintings of leading contemporary artists, including Caravaggio. The later drawings and paintings of Rubens were noted for their grandeur and flowing rhythm (Figure 1.8, page 9).

Anthony van Dyck, Rubens's greatest follower, gained fame as a portrait painter. His fashionable portraits were noted for their elegance, dignity, and skillful portrayal of rich materials. Besides his famous portraits, van Dyck also made some remarkably fresh landscape studies in watercolor and in ink.

The first great Dutch seventeenth-century artist was Frans Hals. He painted portraits with such dazzling brushwork that he is regarded as one of the most skilled technicians in the history of art.

While other Dutch artists specialized in painting portraits, landscapes, or scenes from everyday life, Rembrandt embraced every subject. He also painted these subjects with such brilliance that he is recognized as one of the supreme artistic geniuses of all time.

Although he didn't follow the lead of many other Dutch artists who visited Italy, Rembrandt went to art auctions and collected engravings that were modeled on the works of earlier masters. His drawing based on Leonardo's *Last Supper* (Figure 3.18) is one of three he did that were inspired by an engraving.

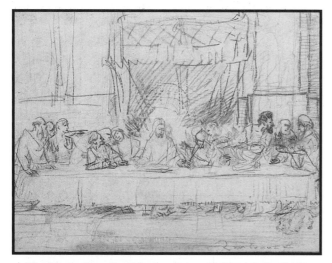

▲ Would you describe this drawing as highly detailed? What has the artist done to emphasize the most important figure in this work? Is balance in this work formal or informal?

FIGURE 3.18 Rembrandt. Sketch after Leonardo's *Last Supper*. c. 1635. Red chalk on paper. 36.5 x 47.5 cm (14⅜ x 18¾"). The Metropolitan Museum of Art, New York, New York. Robert Lehman Collection.

In this drawing, he created an asymmetrical composition by adding a canopy behind and to the left of the seated Christ. The informality of the asymmetrical balance is enhanced by the quickly drawn chalk lines. These lines suggest rather than illustrate in great detail the meaning of the scene in which Christ has just announced that he will be betrayed.

Little is known about the life of Jan Vermeer, also from the Netherlands, and only a few of his paintings survive. Even so, this painter ranks with Rembrandt and Hals as one of the greatest Dutch artists. Vermeer was skilled in handling detail, color, and light to reproduce the exact appearance of his subject.

Diego Velázquez was one of a group of gifted artists who contributed to Spain's golden age of painting in the seventeenth century. As the court painter for King Philip IV, he used sensitive brush strokes to capture the movement of light on figures.

Did You Know?

It is likely that Vermeer completed no more than two or three paintings a year. The total number of paintings known to have been done by him number no more than 40.

The Art of the Eighteenth Century, 1700 to 1800

At the beginning of the eighteenth century a new, lighter style of art, inspired by the work of Rubens and the great Venetian masters of the sixteenth century, appeared in northern Europe. This style used a *free, graceful movement; a playful application of line; and rich colors*. The label attached to this new style is **Rococo**.

Antoine Watteau, a Fleming by birth, developed the Rococo style to its highest level. His drawings and paintings, a haunting combination of grace and sadness, present a make-believe world in which trouble-free young aristocrats pursue pleasure and romance. Watteau valued his drawings more than his paintings because the drawings had qualities that he couldn't render in paint. Often relying on three colors of chalk, he drew figures with a confidence and delicacy often missing from his paintings (Figure 3.19).

The man who continued Watteau's style was Jean-Honoré Fragonard. Fragonard, like Watteau, was a court painter. His gay, romantic subjects were well suited to a painting style that featured delicate color and sound drawing (Figure 6.7, page 117).

Before the middle of the eighteenth century, the Protestant Reformation in England had caused resentment for religious art, and, as a consequence,

▲ What is the name of the art style that Watteau is credited with developing? What are the main features of this style? Which earlier artists inspired the development of this new style?

FIGURE 3.19 Antoine Watteau. *Couple Seated on a Bank*. c. 1716. Red, black, and white chalk on buff paper. 24.1 x 34.9 cm (9½ x 14⅛"). National Gallery of Art, Washington, D.C. The Armand Hammer Collection.

little art of real merit was created. The artist who was largely responsible for adding prestige to English painting was Sir Joshua Reynolds. He was successful in painting the portraits of the aristocracy and became the undisputed leader of his profession.

Although Thomas Gainsborough was Reynolds's equal as a portrait painter, he maintained that his preference was to paint landscapes. The colors in Gainsborough's portraits sparkle when viewed from a distance suggesting flowers, feathers, silken folds, and glittering buckles. Viewers are surprised when they move closer to discover the sketchiness of his painted surfaces. Gainsborough created this effect by sometimes painting with brushes attached to handles measuring as long as six feet. Using these enabled him to place himself at the same distance from his model and his canvas.

Another famous eighteenth-century artist was William Hogarth. Many of his paintings were picture stories told in several scenes like the chapters of a novel. They revealed the immoral conditions and foolish customs of his time.

The most significant artist in Spain during this period in history was Francisco Goya. Goya's early works showing the aristocracy at play are similar to Watteau's and Fragonard's paintings done in the Rococo style. Later, however, his style changed dramatically. In a series of etchings entitled *Disasters of*

War, Goya recorded the horrors associated with the invasion of Spain by French troops in 1808 under Napoleon (Figure 2.4, page 23).

The outstanding Italian artist of the eighteenth century was Giovanni Battista Tiepolo. Constantly commissioned to make paintings, he created ceiling and wall frescoes filled with airborne figures and fleecy clouds. In his preliminary drawings for these frescoes, he used broad sweeps of light values over the barest suggestion of a chalk rendering to suggest three-dimensional forms.

Francesco Guardi, brother-in-law of Tiepolo, is the best-known member in a family of Venetian artists. He is famous for pictures showing various views of Venice. These pictures were bought by tourists in the same way travelers today buy picture postcards to remind them of the places they have visited. Guardi's drawings are free and expressive. They suggest rather than describe, hint rather than declare.

Canaletto, another Venetian artist, used canals, churches, bridges, and palaces as subjects. You can see his detached, detailed style in a drawing of a festival presented as a viewer might have witnessed it from a gondola at the fringe of the festivities. (Figure 3.20). As in many of Canaletto's works, the

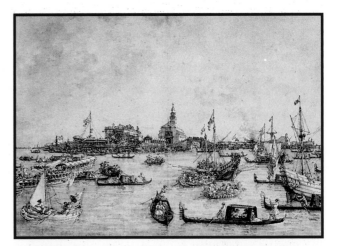

▲ Describe this artist's style. Is it spontaneous, precise, or expressive? What advantages are there in drawing a subject at a distance? Are the expressive qualities important when evaluating this work?

FIGURE 3.20 Canaletto. *Ascension Day Festival at Venice.* 1766. Pen and brown ink with gray wash, heightened with white, over graphite on laid paper. 38.6 x 55.7 cm (15³⁄₁₆ x 21¾"). National Gallery of Art, Washington, D.C. Samuel H. Kress Collection.

subject is seen from a distance in order to include as much of it as possible. The result is admirable in terms of its literal qualities, but disappointing because of its lack of intimacy and warmth.

The Art of the Early Nineteenth Century, 1800 to 1850

The first half of the nineteenth century saw the rise of three successive and important art styles: Neoclassicism, Romanticism, and Realism. **Neoclassicism** was *a reaction to the earlier Baroque and Rococo styles*. Rejecting traditional subject matter, artists turned to the classical art of ancient Greece and Rome and the Renaissance masters for their inspiration. Their works are marked by the importance attached to line and a carefully ordered composition.

Among the foremost artists to work in this new Neoclassic style were Jacques-Louis David and Jean A. D. Ingres. Ingres is considered to be one of the great drafters of history. Forced for a time after the defeat of Napoleon to make a living by drawing pencil portraits of wealthy English tourists, Ingres developed a style marked by a keen eye and a sensitive treatment of line (Figure 2.5, page 24).

Also active at this same time in history was Marie Louise Élisabeth Vigée-Lebrun, one of the most celebrated of all women artists. Extremely talented, Vigée-Lebrun was a successful portrait painter before she was 20 and was painting portraits of Queen Marie Antoinette by the time she was 25. Forced to flee France at the beginning of the revolution she traveled throughout Europe practicing her art. At her death she left behind some 800 paintings, the most notable of which were her portraits. These were executed in a style noted for its rich glowing colors and inventive poses (Figure 3.1, page 36).

Théodore Géricault is usually credited with creating the *Romantic style*, which emphasized the expression of feelings and emotions in drawings and paintings completed in a spontaneous manner. At Géricault's death, Eugène Delacroix assumed the leadership of the Romantic movement. Unlike Neoclassic artists who looked to the calm, ordered compositions of Raphael for inspiration, Delacroix based his art on the glowing color and swirling

▲ **Where did Neoclassic artists such as Ingres and David turn for their inspiration? Can the same be said for this artist? Compare and contrast this work with that of Ingres in Figure 2.5, page 24.**

FIGURE 3.21 Eugène Delacroix. *An Arab on Horseback Attacked by a Lion.* 1849. Graphite on tracing paper, darkened. 46 x 30.5 cm (18 x 12"). The Harvard University Art Museums, Cambridge, Massachusetts. Bequest of Meta and Paul J. Sachs.

action of Rubens. A trip to north Africa in 1832 exposed him to the colorful life of the Arabs. One of his drawings, showing an Arab being attacked by a lion (Figure 3.21), clearly illustrates Delacroix's ability to capture furious action of a rider, horse, and lion locked in battle.

Around the middle of the nineteenth century, a new style known as Realism became prominent. *Realism* rejected both ideal or classical subjects and romantic subject matter in favor of contemporary life rendered in a lifelike way. Artists practicing this new style expressed little interest in exotic, romantic subject matter. Instead, they looked closely at the objects and events around them to find worth-while subjects for their art.

One of the first artists to use the Realistic style was the caricaturist, painter, and sculptor Honoré Daumier (Figures 2.14, page 32 and 2.15, page 35). Although Daumier may have wanted to create more paintings, poverty forced him to spend time making *lithographs* for publication. Lithographs are prints made from inked stones or metal plates. Many of the four thousand Daumier produced criticized the social and moral injustices of his age. His drawings, created with swift, confident strokes of crayon and wash, show us that he was one of the great artists of his era.

Did You Know?

Daumier spent the final years of his life blind and impoverished in a small cottage provided by a good friend and fellow artist, Jean-Bapiste-Camille Corot.

Gustave Courbet was the acknowledged leader of the Realist movement in France. Courbet believed that artists should base their work on direct experience and paint only what they had seen and understood.

Since he exhibited his paintings with Courbet's, Edouard Manet was considered to be a part of the Realist movement. His work, however, is actually a bridge between Realism and the art movement that followed, Impressionism (Color Section I, Figure 8). Much of Manet's work was inspired by his study of the old masters, including Raphael, Giorgione, Titian, Velázquez, and Hals. His approach reveals a concern for technique rather than content. This led him to develop his own unique style, a style marked by flattened forms, sharp contrasts of values, and a loose brushwork that matched that of Velázquez.

Manet's work greatly influenced the next generation of French artists, who came to be known as the Impressionists. Using the contemporary scene, as Courbet and Manet did, and working in the style known as **Impressionism**, they tried to reproduce *what the eye sees at a specific moment in time—not what the mind knows is there.* They were attracted

▲ Do you think this drawing provides a faithful representation of the subject? What has the artist done to give the figure a three-dimensional appearance? How is the principle of variety demonstrated?

FIGURE 3.22 Edgar Degas. *Study for a Portrait of Edouard Manet.* c. 1864. Black chalk and estompe. 33 x 23.2 cm (13 x 9⅛"). The Metropolitan Museum of Art, New York, New York. Rogers Fund.

most often to the landscape, with or without people. This led them to leave their studios to paint streets and fields with dabs and dashes of paint, a technique that enabled them to capture the momentary effects of sunlight reflected from subject matter.

The best known of the Impressionists was Claude Monet. Working outdoors, Monet became fascinated by constantly changing colors. He often painted the same subject over and over again under different light conditions. Thus, color and light were the real subjects for his works.

Auguste Renoir, another Impressionist, carefully arranged his compositions. His subjects were posed to look as if the viewer had encountered them accidentally. His works show a love of warm colors, appealing subjects, and sun-drenched landscapes.

Berthe Morisot's figures live in a world of warm summer afternoons and pleasant, carefree moments (Color Section I, Figures 9 and 10). No less an artist than Claude Monet regarded Morisot's achievements as equal to those of any of the other Impressionists. However, because she was a woman, was wealthy, and held a prominent position in society, her artworks were often overlooked by critics.

Edgar Degas agreed with the Impressionists' views, but he didn't regard himself as an Impressionist. Rather than paint outdoors, he remained in his studio and based his paintings on drawings done from life. He maintained that drawing wasn't recording what the artist sees, but making others see.

Did You Know?

The introduction of the lead paint tube lined with tin in the nineteenth century combined with the development of new pigments perfected by chemists, freed artists from color mixing in the studio and encouraged them to move outside to paint.

Degas also preferred to draw and paint figures rather than landscapes. Degas's affection for drawing, which was inspired by his admiration for Ingres, also separated him from the Impressionists. His study for a portrait of Edouard Manet (Figure 3.22) is an excellent example of his drawing style.

Mary Cassatt, an American, pursued a painting career in Paris and became an Impressionist through her friendship with Degas. Although she never married, Cassatt often created enchanting scenes of motherhood (Figure 10.7, page 203).

Two unique landscape painters, John Constable and J. M. W. Turner, charted the direction that art was to take throughout the nineteenth century in England.

John Constable tried to create a feeling of the momentary, a glimpse of nature at a particular movement. For this reason he focused attention on color, light, and atmosphere. For Constable, the sky

with its moving clouds was the focal point of any landscape. Working outdoors, Constable completed countless sketches of the English countryside which were the basis for his large, six-foot wide paintings.

Did You Know?

Constable believed that clouds could be collected and labeled. He completed scores of cloud studies noting on the back of each the month, time of day, and even the direction of the wind.

Joseph Mallord William Turner is regarded as one of the most original landscape painters. Like Constable, he was fascinated by light and atmosphere, but he combined this fascination with an active imagination. In his paintings, forms seem to dissolve in the golden glow of light. His dazzling color and vaguely defined forms encourage viewers to use their own imaginations to fill in the details to complete the image.

On his many travels, Turner filled sketchbooks with studies of every kind. Space and light dominate in his pencil drawing of the Scottish highlands (Figure 3.23, page 59). In this drawing you can see the barest hint of a landscape beyond the darker figures of herdsmen and their livestock.

The Art of the Late Nineteenth Century, 1850 to 1900

As the nineteenth century entered its final quarter, a number of artists, including Georges Seurat, Paul Cézanne, Vincent van Gogh, Henri de Toulouse-Lautrec, and Paul Gauguin, tried to solve the problems they associated with Impressionism. Their efforts greatly influenced artists in the next century.

Georges Seurat developed a style of art known as *Neo-Impressionism* or *Pointillism*. He deliberately applied tiny, uniform dots of pure color to his canvases instead of using a more uneven color pattern of dabs and dashes. According to the scientific

Artists at Work

■ ART HISTORIAN

The Past Influences the Future

"I enjoy researching the past, but I also enjoy art. I'll never forget the first time I saw an ancient statue in a museum. How can I combine my two interests into a career?"

Art historians are involved in communicating the history of art and relating the impact that art has had on the world's societies. They are involved in a wide range of activities and specialties including teaching, lecturing, film production, writing, research, and library work in books, films and slides. Many specialize in the art of one area, country, or period, while others focus on a field such as architecture or sculpture. Although some art historians may do work for businesses with commercial interests in art, such as insurance companies and auction houses, many are employed by museums, colleges, and universities. Art historians are concerned with the effect of art on society, the influence of one generation of art on another, and the reasons that people create and value art.

The art sections of bookstores and libraries are filled with books written by art historians who seek to illuminate the art and artists of the past. To write such a book authoritatively, you would need to do a tremendous amount of research. While the knowledgeable writings of other experts is an important source

of information, you would also need to travel internationally to view art for firsthand study.

Sharing information about art with the next generation of artists and art historians is an important concern for an art historian. As a college professor, you might teach survey courses to the general student population, or specialize in one area or period. You would also discuss your views and discoveries with your colleagues and with other experts at national and international conferences.

Films about art and famous artists are increasingly popular on art-oriented television stations, public television, and in classrooms across America. As an art historian, you might play a major role in creating accurate and visually exciting documentation for such productions.

Art historians must have an intense feel for the value of uncovering the past as a means of understanding the present.

To become an art historian, you will need to earn an advanced degree from a college or

university. A bachelor's degree is the minimum requirement for a curatorial career.

Begin now to develop broad interests. Many art historians are practicing artists themselves. Take all the drawing, painting, and sculpture classes you can. Of course you will be taking art history classes, especially advanced placement or college classes if they are available to you, but don't neglect regular history classes. They can be an important source of background information and may reveal insightful links to the present. Composition and literature classes will improve your communication skills. Expose yourself to art firsthand by visiting museums and galleries of all types. Part-time or volunteer work in a museum or gallery would provide valuable experience. ■

▲ **Carefully describe the literal qualities in this drawing. If you were evaluating Turner's sketchbook, what grade would you assign to this sketch? What comments would you pass on to your "student"?**

FIGURE 3.23   Joseph Mallord William Turner. *Scottish Highlands.* Date unknown. Pencil drawing. 26.4 x 41.3 cm (10⅜ x 16¼"). Museum of Fine Arts, Boston, Massachusetts. Gift of Dr. William Norton Bullard.

thought of that period, these color dots would then be mixed in the eye of the viewer to create new colors. Seurat was also well known for his splendid drawings. He is noted for works done in black conte crayon in which subjects are defined by light and dark values that blend together in some areas and contrast in others. (Figure 3.24).

While the Impressionists were concerned with the appearance of subjects under different light conditions, Paul Cézanne was interested in the underlying structure of objects. His paintings seem to be made out of cubes of color that turn in a variety of directions to lead the viewer's eye in, out, and around what appear to be solid forms (Figure 2.3, page 23).

In 1886 Vincent van Gogh moved first to Paris and later to Arles in the south of France to develop his artistic skills. His style is characterized by vibrant colors, twisting lines, and heavy applications of paint. He employed this style in an attempt to communicate his feelings rather than his perceptions. (Figures 1.2, page 4; 8.9, page 165; and Color Section I, Figures 1 and 11). An increased emphasis on drawing separated him from the Impressionists. His lack of realistic accuracy and smooth, finished technique aroused critics who scorned his works.

Paul Gauguin began his artistic career in his middle years after leaving his family and a secure position as a stockbroker. In his work he distorted or

exaggerated natural forms and colors for expressive and compositional reasons. Seeking exotic subject matter, Gauguin spent much of his career in the South Seas. An ink drawing with watercolor (Figure 3.25, page 60) shows the way he used flat shapes to make decorative patterns rather than realistic images.

Although he didn't belong to any group of artists or art movement, Henri de Toulouse-Lautrec also contributed significantly to the development of modern art. In his drawings, Lautrec was able to capture a scene, a character, even an emotion with a few quick strokes of pencil, pen, or brush (Figure 1.15, page 15).

Lautrec often visited a cabaret (a night club) owned by a friend, Aristide Bruant. Bruant wrote songs about the painful, often desperate lives of the people who came to his cabaret. In 1887 one of his songs was published, accompanied by an illustration drawn by Lautrec. You will study this drawing later in this book (Figure 9.6, page 170).

By the close of the nineteenth century, the United States had become a world leader. The country's change and growth were reflected in American art. The art of this period is best represented by the works of three artists—Winslow Homer, Albert Pinkham Ryder, and Thomas Eakins.

▲ **How does this seated figure differ from the seated figure by Edgar Degas (Figure 3.22, page 56)? Explain how the principle of gradation is used.**

FIGURE 3.24   Georges Seurat. *Seated Boy with Straw Hat.* 1882. Conte crayon drawing. 24.1 x 31.1 cm (9½ x 12¼"). Yale University Art Gallery, New Haven, Connecticut. Everett V. Meeks Fund.

▲ **This drawing by Gauguin reveals his unique style. Describe the main features of that style. How are line and value used to organize this drawing? How would you describe the shapes used here?**

FIGURE 3.25 Paul Gauguin. *Nave Nave Fenua.* c. 1894–1900. Brush, gouache, and india ink with pen and india ink on dark tan wove paper. 42.2 x 26.2 cm (16⅝ x 10⁵⁄₁₆"). National Gallery of Art, Washington, D.C. Lessing J. Rosenwald Collection.

Homer's work reflects his lifelong affection for saltwater, ships, and sailors. He was largely self-taught and worked for many years as a lithographer before directing his energies to serious painting. Often his pictures show man opposing the powerful forces of nature.

Albert Pinkham Ryder's small paintings show that he ignored technique. He layered on paint to thicknesses of one-quarter inch and often returned to work on a picture while it was still wet. As a result, his paintings have cracked and faded with age. Even so, Ryder

achieved a position as one of the dominant American painters. His imaginary subjects were painted in a simple style using large areas of color and texture. Claiming that the artist should avoid becoming a slave to detail, he included in his works only what was essential to suggest mysterious, dreamlike images.

Thomas Eakins valued precision and accuracy so much that when he was painting a crucifixion he strapped a friend to a cross for a model. When drawing or painting a surgical operation (Figure 6.5, page 113) Eakins didn't try to soften the impact of the scene. Works showing such harsh subjects in such startling detail prevented him from becoming a popular artist.

The Art of the Early Twentieth Century, 1900 to 1925

Artists like Goya, Cézanne, van Gogh, and Gauguin were leaders of a revolution in art that began in the nineteenth century and came to dominate art in the twentieth century. Inspired by the creative efforts of those earlier painters, twentieth-century artists used their own personal visions to produce unique works of art—works that frequently did not mirror nature and did not attempt to meet the requirements imposed by patrons.

During the early years of the century, a group of French artists who became known as the Fauves (French for *wild beasts*) appeared. **Fauvism** ignored realism and used *a heavy, bold application of brightly colored paint to express emotion.* One of these artists was Henri Matisse. Matisse is often referred to as the first modern artist. He saw the world as simple, flat shapes of pure color. He attached more importance to those shapes and colors than he did to the subjects that suggested them in the first place.

Matisse's approach to drawing was similar to his approach to painting. He carefully examined the subject of a drawing to determine the essential shapes and lines to be included in the work (Figure 8.8, page 164) those that were felt to be unnecessary were eliminated. In his compositions, the figures are presented as flat, decorative shapes and are defined and decorated with lines.

An art movement known as **Expressionism** dominated in Germany in the first quarter of the twentieth century. It stressed *the artist's need to communicate to viewers his or her emotional response to a subject.*

Ernst Ludwig Kirchner, a leader in the Expressionist movement, used flat, brightly colored shapes in his early works. Later he used unusual contrasts of colors; large, simple shapes; and distortions to express his feelings and moods. In his final works, Kirchner's shapes took on a more angular look, his colors became even more brilliant, and the distortions more pronounced. In 1937, Kirchner's art was condemned in Germany by the Nazi Party, and 600 of his works were seized. Many of these were destroyed.

Another artist associated with German Expressionism is Käthe Kollwitz. Although human tragedy, suffering, and death are themes of many of her powerful works (Figure 2.7, page 25), Kollwitz is also known for her sensitive portrayals of motherhood.

The Expressionists were influenced not only by the Fauves, but also by Vincent van Gogh and a Norwegian artist named Edvard Munch. On a visit to France while he was still in his twenties, Munch encountered the work of Gauguin and was impressed with Gauguin's simplified shapes of intense color. He recognized that similar shapes and colors could be used effectively in his own expressive approach to art. When his powerful compositions were first displayed in France, they caused so much controversy that the exhibition was closed within a week. The controversy, however, made him famous overnight.

Wassily Kandinsky completed his first works in his native Russia; experimented with Impressionism, Fauvism, and other styles in France; and then joined the Expressionist movement in Germany. His approach to expressing inner feelings eventually led him to abandon all references to subject matter in his work (Color Section I, Figure 12). Generally regarded as the first nonobjective artist, Kandinsky arranged colors, shapes, lines, and textures to create works of art that evoke emotional responses in much the same way that musical sounds are arranged to stimulate certain moods and feelings.

Another important movement, known as **Cubism,** was inspired by Cézanne's paintings. His works were composed of *cubes of color arranged to create the illusion of solid form.* Pablo Picasso took

▲ **What style of art is represented by this drawing? Which earlier artist inspired artists like Picasso to develop this style? How would you describe this style of art to someone who had never heard of it?**

FIGURE 3.26   Pablo Picasso. *Nude.* 1910. Charcoal on paper. 48.4 x 31.3 cm (19¹/₁₆ x 12⁵/₁₆"). The Metropolitan Museum of Art, New York, New York. The Alfred Stieglitz Collection.

this concept further. In a figure drawing (Figure 3.26), he presented the same subject from a variety of viewpoints and made a fragmented form out of interlocking planes or shapes.

Picasso didn't extend Cubism into complete nonobjectivity, but other artists did. One of these artists, Piet Mondrian, studied Cubism and eventually rejected any attempt to represent subject matter in a realistic way. His works were composed of a limited visual vocabulary, consisting of the primary colors along with black and white, square and triangular shapes, and straight lines (Figures 1.11, page 12 and 2.6, page 24).

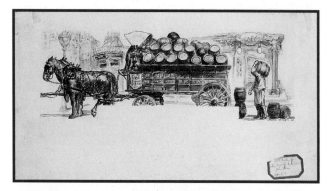

▲ **Would you describe this scene as lifelike? How has the artist used value to create a sense of space in this drawing and three-dimensional form? What has been done to emphasize the important parts of this work?**

FIGURE 3.27 John Sloan. *Medusa Beer Truck.* 1908. Pencil, black crayon, brush and black and gray ink with gray wash on board. 29.4 x 55.3 cm (11⁹⁄₁₆ x 21¹³⁄₁₆"). National Gallery of Art, Washington, D.C. John Davis Hatch Collection; Avalon Fund.

At the beginning of the twentieth century, the most celebrated portrait painter was the American John Singer Sargent. Sargent enjoyed great success as a painter of fashionable portraits. Although these portraits sometimes seem shallow, he always approached each one differently and his compositions were consistently inventive and unique.

One group of early twentieth-century American artists resisted traditional European styles and subjects. Because these artists chose to draw and paint *the American scene—the streets, alleys, cafés, and theaters*—they were laughingly referred to as members of the **Ashcan School** of art. A leading artist in this group was John Sloan. Sloan wanted to portray the colorful views of everyday life in the big city. His drawing of a man loading a truck (Figure 3.27) is characteristic of his vivid style and working-class subject matter.

George Bellows sympathized with the views expressed by Sloan and other members of the Ashcan School. His lifelong love of sports is reflected in paintings that capture the frenzied action of the boxing ring with slashing brushwork. A hearty, friendly individual with a bold approach to life and art, Bellows was also capable of creating sensitive, engaging portraits (Figure 3.28).

On the evening of February 17, 1913, a huge exhibition of European and American art opened in New York City. The International Exhibition of Modern Art, more commonly known as the *Armory Show*, introduced the American public to the most advanced movements in European art. It also motivated many American artists to start the experiments that began the modern era in American art. This exhibition dramatically changed the direction of art in the United States.

Art to the Present, 1925 to the Present

After World War I, Europe experienced a period of pessimism and unrest. Artists associated with a movement known as *Dada* felt that European culture no longer had a purpose or meaning. To them, art objects should no longer be beautiful or meaningful, but ordinary and meaningless.

Although the Dada movement ended in 1922, it had an impact on later artists who were attracted to its imagination and humor. Surrealism, a new art movement, became a significant force in Europe throughout the 1920s and 1930s. During the Second World War, it spread to the United States.

Surrealism was an art style that tried to *express the world of dreams and the workings of the mind* with pencil and brush. One of the best known of these

SHARPENING YOUR SKILLS

Make a Surrealistic Drawing

Surrealists such as Joan Miró relied upon the world of dreams and the inner workings of the mind for artistic inspiration. On a sheet of sketch paper, draw something you could never hope to see in the real world. Use your imagination to come up with the most improbable image possible, such as an animal with wheels instead of feet, an alarm clock struggling to remain awake, a pencil sharpener with a sour disposition. Display your drawing in a "gallery" showing in your classroom.

▶ **What adjective would you use to describe this drawing—precise, objective, or sensitive? What two elements would you be sure to mention when describing this drawing to a friend?**

FIGURE 3.28 George Wesley Bellows. *Studies of Jean.* c. 1920. Black crayon. 26.1 x 23.9 cm (10⁵⁄₁₆ x 9⅜"). National Gallery of Art, Washington, D.C. John Davis Hatch Collection; Avalon Fund.

surrealist artists was the Spaniard Joan Miró. In drawings like *The Kerosene Lamp* (Figure 3.29), Miró tried to record on paper the fantastic sights he encountered in his dream world. It is a work that asks the viewer to abandon any search for logic or meaning in order to enjoy the free and whimsical play of lines and shapes. Laws of proportion and perspective are ignored as the artist breaks away from the confining world of reality to enter the misty world of pure fantasy.

Miró shared a mischievous, childlike humor with the Swiss artist Paul Klee. Klee was a small, gentle man who often worked on as many as six pictures at the same time. Klee thought of painting as a magical journey into the realm of the fantastic (Figures 1.3, page 7 and 9.5, page 169).

Henry Moore's reputation was built mainly on his strength as a sculptor. Even so, some of his most popular works are drawings of people seeking

▲ **Describe this work by listing the recognizable objects. Discuss the elements and principles of art used. What style of art is represented by this drawing?**

FIGURE 3.29 Joan Miró. *The Kerosene Lamp.* 1924. Black and white chalk with touches of pastel and red pencil on canvas. 81 x 100.3 cm (31⁵⁄₁₆ x 39½"). The Art Institute of Chicago, Chicago, Illinois. Joseph and Helen Regenstein Foundation, Helen L. Kellogg Trust, Blum-Kovler Foundation, Major Acquisitions Fund, and Gifts from Mrs. Henry C. Woods, Members of the Committee on Prints & Drawings, and Friends of the Department.

▲ **Franz Kline was one of the leading representatives of the post-World War II American art movement which had a great influence in the 1950s and 1960s. He was an Abstract Expressionist who was deeply influenced by oriental calligraphy.**

FIGURE 3.30   Franz Kline. *Study.* c. 1956. Brush and black ink wash, heightened with white gouache or casein on off-white wove paper. 21.6 x 27.8 cm (8⁷⁄₁₆ x 10¹¹⁄₁₆"). The Baltimore Museum of Art, Baltimore, Maryland. Gift of Dr. and Mrs. Winston H. Price.

protection in underground shelters during the World War II London blitzes, or air raids.

Contemporary art in the United States appears to be developing in every direction at once. In this overview, we can only emphasize the diversity that is largely responsible for the vitality of today's American art.

Edward Hopper's works reflect America during the Great Depression. In some ways, Hopper's drawings and paintings are related to those produced by the Ashcan School artists. He was also concerned with portraying the American scene realistically. His pictures are remembered for showing the emptiness, alienation, and loneliness of contemporary life (Figures 1.12, page 13; 6.3, page 111; and 9.2, page 168). Hopper's works often generate feelings of discomfort—not unlike the feeling one has after smiling and greeting someone only to have that someone quickly look away.

The Great Depression was soon overshadowed by World War II. The destruction and suffering caused in that conflict is recorded in works by many American artists. One of these was the German-born American illustrator, painter, and caricaturist George

Grosz. In drawings and paintings he pictured the horrors of war.

During and after the war years, abstract and nonobjective art became popular in the United States. Artists working in New York in the 1930s and 1940s used media and design qualities more freely to create works with little emphasis on recognizable subject matter. This new art movement was known as *Abstract Expressionism.* Under the leadership of Abstract Expressionists, New York replaced Paris as the art center of the world after the Second World War.

Arshile Gorky, who immigrated to the United States in 1920, was one of the first Abstract Expressionist painters, although he continued to

▲ **What style of art is represented by this drawing? Where do artists who practice this style turn for their inspiration? Why do these artists choose to work on a large scale?**

FIGURE 3.31   Claes Oldenburg. *Drawing for Stake Hitch.* 1983. Pastel and watercolor on paper. 101.6 x 74 cm (40 x 29³⁄₁₆"). The Dallas Museum of Art, Dallas, Texas. General Acquisitions Fund and a gift of The 500, Inc.

draw family and friends in a representational style (Figure 1.7, page 8). In the 1940s, he created works in which brilliant washes of color were contained by or freely flowed out of curving shapes defined by thin, black lines.

Gorky's use of flowing, delicate lines can be contrasted with the wide, slashing lines of Franz Kline, (Figure 3.30). In his huge paintings, ragged black lines overlap and enclose areas of white. They suggest the dramatic outlines of modern bridges or the framework of skyscrapers.

Abstract Expressionism, like all artistic movements, didn't escape the threat of new ideas and approaches. In the 1950s and 1960s many artists again became interested in realism. Responding to the popular culture around them, they based their art on comic strips, magazine advertisements, billboards, and supermarket products. Labeled **Pop Art**, this school of art *focused attention on the unimportant products of contemporary culture.*

Claes Oldenburg's drawing of a stake hitch was done in preparation for a huge, three-dimensional creation installed in the Dallas Museum of Art (Figure 3.31). The figures show the intended scale of the metal stake and rope. Like other Pop Art creations, it is designed to force viewers to see these familiar objects in a new way.

Another kind of realism is practiced by Andrew Wyeth. He may be America's best-known artist. A pencil drawing (Figure 3.32) demonstrates Andrew Wyeth's ability to record detail and express feelings at the same time. The elderly woman in his drawing stares at something beyond the painting and seems to be lost in her thoughts. Alone for the moment, she faces the future with dignity.

This story of art history could continue indefinitely. New artists and new movements are constantly appearing on the scene. We couldn't hope to keep up with the continuously changing events in the art world. It is an exciting time for knowledgeable viewers of art—and a stimulating and challenging environment in which new artists can learn and practice their art.

▲ The artist who drew this portrait is skilled at recording details. What else can be said about his work on this drawing? Defend the argument that literal, design, and expressive qualities should all be considered when judging this work.

FIGURE 3.32 Andrew Wyeth. *Beckie King.* 1946. Pencil on paper. 76.2 x 88.9 cm (30 x 35"). The Dallas Museum of Art, Dallas, Texas. Gift of Everett L. DeGolyer.

CHAPTER 3 REVIEW

1. When art historians describe, analyze, and interpret art, what four things are they trying to find out?

2. Why did the ancient Egyptians always draw figures with combined front and side views?

3. During medieval times, what purpose did religious art fulfill for most of the people?

4. Describe the art that came to be known as Gothic International style.

5. Who is the northern European artist credited with developing oil paints? What did this innovation do for artists?

6. What kind of art would you expect to see at an Abstract Expressionist exhibit?

▲ Did you immediately recognize the medium used to create this drawing? Do you think the artist's choice of medium was a good one in this instance? List other media the artist might have used.

FIGURE 4.1 Edgar Degas. *The Theatre Box.* 1885. Pastel. 56 x 41.9 cm (22 x 16½"). Armand Hammer Collection, The Armand Hammer Museum of Art and Cultural Center, Los Angeles, California.

The Media of Drawing

Whenever you decide to make a drawing, you embark on an adventure of sorts—an adventure marked by a continuous barrage of questions. What will you draw? From what angle will you show your subject? What will you emphasize? What techniques will you use to realize that emphasis? Should you strive for realism, or focus your attention on trying to capture a mood or idea? What art elements will you use and how will you use the art principles to organize those elements?

However, even before these questions can be considered, you must decide what medium or media to use. Should you use pencil, charcoal, or india ink? If you elect to use ink, should you apply it with a pen or a brush? Do you want to create a drawing in color? If so, perhaps you should consider colored pencils, conte crayons, or chalk.

This chapter will provide you with information about the different drawing media that is discussed in this book. This information will be helpful whenever you face the task of selecting the right media with which to express your ideas and feelings through drawing.

objectives

After reading this chapter and doing the activities, you will be able to:

■ Recognize why the choice of media and techniques are important when trying to express a feeling, image, or idea in a drawing.

■ Explain the importance of experimentation with various drawing media and techniques.

■ Explain what is meant by a wash and tell how and why this medium is used in a drawing.

■ Complete a drawing in which you made effective use of mixed media.

Terms to Know

acrylic paint	layout chalks
colored chalks	portfolio
compressed charcoal	powdered charcoal
conte crayon	vine charcoal
dry media	wash
gouache	wet media
india ink	

Making Media Decisions

How important are the questions you ask about art—and the answers they generate? In response, take a few moments to examine the fascinating drawing of *The Theatre Box* by Edgar Degas (Figure 4.1, page 66). To complete it, Degas had to confront and answer these and dozens of other questions pertaining to subject matter, style, media, and technique. Did he come up with the right answers to the questions? The answer to that question is provided by the finished drawing. Let's take a few minutes to examine it.

Did you notice how Degas cleverly uses the dark foreground figures in a theater box to emphasize by contrast the lighter, brighter figures of dancers on a stage? As viewers, we are made to feel as if we too are in the same theater box, peering over our companions for a better view of the performers.

Unlike the attentive, motionless audience members, the ballet dancers are seen spinning, bending, and gliding gracefully across the stage. Perhaps you noted the lack of details in this drawing—shadows conceal them in the foreground and the rapid movement of the dancers blurs them in the background.

In terms of subject matter, and the style of art Degas used to interpret that subject matter, most viewers would probably say that this drawing is successful. Would they respond in this same way if Degas had used pencil, pen and ink, charcoal, or some other black and white medium rather than colored pencils to create this drawing? Certainly the choice of any of those media would have altered this drawing considerably. It would have also altered the drawing's impact upon viewers. Look at this work again without color on page 66, then compare it to Figure 13, Color Section I. Do you think it would be as successful?

The pleasure and satisfaction we derive from his drawing is due in large measure to the materials Degas chose to use in making it—and the methods or processes he employed when using those materials. Did he make the right decisions concerning media and technique? What do you think?

Did You Know?

For the last 20 years of his life, Degas was blind and led a solitary life. He died in 1917 as the First World War was coming to an end. At his simple funeral, a fellow artist, following Degas's instructions, spoke the following words: "He loved drawing very much."

■ KNOW YOUR MEDIA

What is the first thing you do when beginning a drawing? Of course, you reach for something to draw with—and some kind of surface upon which to draw.

▲ More than 200 years ago, the artist employed both wet and dry media in this drawing. The result is very effective. How might the work have changed if Greuze had used other media?

FIGURE 4.2   Jean-Baptiste Greuze. *A Tired Woman with Two Children.* 1750–1761. Pen and brown ink, brown wash over black chalk on laid paper. 22.2 x 27.9 cm (8¾ x 11"). National Gallery of Art, Washington, D.C. The Armand Hammer Collection.

▶ The viewer senses the unseen person who has just left this dinner table. Note the meticulously rendered details and the way the light glistens on the surfaces of silverware and water.

FIGURE 4.3 Antonio Lopez Garcia. *Remainders from a Meal (Restos di comida).* 1971. Pencil and erasure on white mat board mounted on plywood. 42.2 x 54.3 cm (16⅝ x 21⅜"). The Baltimore Museum of Art, Baltimore, Maryland. The Thomas E. Benesch Memorial Collection. Gift of the Apple Hill Foundation.

To make the most of your drawing effort, you should know the advantages and disadvantages of whatever media you decide to use. You should know what you can and cannot do with that pencil, stick of pastel, or felt marker in your hand. You should also know what to expect when you apply that medium to different kinds of drawing surfaces. Keep in mind that the character of your drawings is largely dependent upon the tools you use in creating them and the materials on which you choose to work. In Figure 4.2 Greuze used both wet and dry media to express the subject matter.

To learn as much as possible about media, you must be prepared to experiment with each. Such experimentation is essential if you are to determine what you can and cannot accomplish with each medium. Since we are on the subject of experimentation, it seems appropriate here to remind you of two important factors that you must always keep foremost in mind as you go about developing your drawing skills. These are:

- The need to experiment.

- The need to constantly criticize your own work.

In Chapter 2 you learned how to criticize drawings using the operations of description, analysis, interpretation, and judgment. You can and should use these same four operations to constantly criticize and improve upon your own drawings.

Dry and Wet Media

Media used in drawing are of two types: dry and wet. Dry media include pencil, crayon, chalk, and charcoal. An example of a drawing created with a dry medium is the pencil drawing entitled *Remainders from a Meal* by Antonio Lopez Garcia (Figure 4.3). Wet media include ink, acrylic, watercolor, and tempera paints. Franz Kline's nonobjective study (Figure 3.30, page 64) demonstrates the use of a wet medium. Take a few minutes to examine the drawings by Garcia and Kline.

Do you feel they selected the most appropriate medium for the type of drawing they set out to create? Would Garcia's work have been more effective if he had opted to use ink and brush instead of pencil? Could Kline have achieved the same effects if he had decided to use pencil instead of ink? Would you say that each of these artists selected a medium that best suited their objectives?

It's time to examine more closely each of these wet and dry media. As each is discussed, take a few minutes to experiment with it. In this way you will be able to determine which will serve most effectively in different circumstances to express a particular feeling, image, or idea.

SHARPENING YOUR SKILLS

When to Experiment

When and how should you experiment? Whenever you are using a new medium or a new technique, experiment.

In the case of a new drawing medium, hold it in your hand a few seconds.

- How does it feel? What grip or grips seem most comfortable?
- Apply it to a drawing surface to make a series of different marks and lines. Does it drag or flow on easily?

- What effects are achieved when you apply different pressures?
- How does it compare with other media with which you are already familiar?

Experimentation like this will help familiarize you with the character of the medium and reveal what it can and cannot do. It will also provide you with the information you will need to take into account when you are trying to select the right medium to use to express a particular feeling, image, or idea.

▲ Do you feel this drawing was done slowly or quickly? Why would an artist choose to work this way? Why is pencil a good medium to use for drawings of this kind?

FIGURE 4.4   Paula Modersohn-Becker. *Seated Old Woman.* c. 1906. Charcoal on paper. 25.7 x 17.8 cm (10⅛ x 7"). National Museum of Women in the Arts, Washington, D.C. Gift of Wallace and Wilhelmina Holladay.

■ DRY MEDIA

As the name implies, **dry media** *are those that are free of liquid or moisture and remain that way when they are used.* Dry media include chalks, charcoals, crayons, and pencils. The most common of these is *pencil,* a drawing and writing tool that consists of a slender, cylindrical casing around a marking substance.

Pencils

You are probably most familiar with "lead" pencils which actually consist of a graphite marking substance which is most commonly encased in wood. Artists make use of these graphite pencils in addition to charcoal, pastel, and various other colored pencils.

Pencils such as charcoal and graphite can be purchased in various degrees of hardness. Usually hardness is identified in one of two ways. Some manufacturers use the labels hard, medium, or soft. Others use numbers together with the letters H or B. A pencil identified with an H is hard and will produce light lines. The higher the pencil number, the harder the pencil. A pencil bearing a B is soft and will make dark marks. Pencils range from 9H (extremely hard) to 6B (extremely soft). For most freehand drawing, a collection of 2H to 6B pencils is recommended. Harder pencils (3H to 9H) are used mainly for mechanical drawing or drafting.

Experiment with Pencils

Experiment with a variety of lines and values made with hard and soft pencils. Hold the pencils in different ways—between the thumb and first two fingers and across the palm of your hand. Grip it close to the point, in the middle, and near the end. Vary the pressure on the pencil as you guide it across the surface of the paper. Use several kinds of drawing surfaces and observe the different results. Show your experiments in class and identify the ones that were especially satisfying to you. Explain what you learned from your experiments.

Pencils are convenient for making quick sketches (Figure 4.4, Paula Modersohn-Becker, *Seated Old Woman*), or for creating carefully rendered finished drawings (Figure 3.32, page 65, by Andrew Wyeth). They are also versatile, offering the artist an opportunity of working with a wide range of lines and values. An examination of the pencil drawings by Ellsworth Kelly (Figure 1.10, page 11), Henri Toulouse-Lautrec (Figure 1.15, page 15) will demonstrate how versatile the pencil can be in the hands of sensitive and skilled artists.

Did You Know?

According to his mother, the first word that Pablo Picasso uttered as a child was "lapiz," the Spanish word for pencil. She also claimed that the young Picasso could draw before he could talk.

Colored Pencils offer the artist the opportunity of working with strong, durable colors. They are sharpened easily and resist crumbling. A complete set of colored pencils can consist of as many as sixty assorted colors.

The best-known colored pencils are the Berol Prismacolors. The English Derwent brand is similar and also popular with artists. Conte de Paris pastel pencils are really chalks. They are more suitable for drawings in which colors are blended by rubbing. Colored pencils are waxier, hold a point longer, are more resistant to smearing, and are more durable.

Charcoal

Charcoal is one of the basic and most familiar dry media. It is a black or very dark-colored, brittle substance that consists mainly of carbon. Charcoal is made by heating plant or animal material, such as wood or bones, in ovens containing little or no air. The charcoal used by artists is made from plant materials.

Capture Form with Color

Using colored pencils enables artists such as Terry Morrow to create subtle changes in hue, value, and intensity (Figure 14, Color Section I). Select a round still-life object and draw it, using a colored pencil. Select three other colored pencils and color the object, gradually blending one color into the next. Capture the round form of the still-life object as you apply and blend your colors. Exhibit your drawing in class and discuss the strengths and weaknesses of this medium.

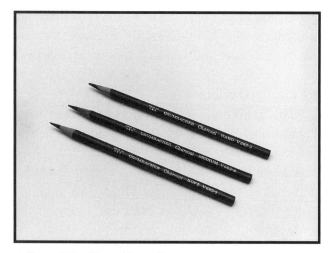

▲ **FIGURE 4.5   Charcoal pencils**

You will find that charcoal is a flexible, easy-to-work-with medium. It can be erased easily and blended or smudged to create different effects. These qualities make charcoal an especially good medium for beginning artists who are often reluctant to make big, bold marks that will be permanent. In the hands of a skilled artist, charcoal can be used to express powerful images and ideas (Figure 10.1, page 194, Harriett Feigenbaum).

Two basic types of charcoal—vine charcoal and compressed charcoal—are used by artists. Vine charcoal is available in sticks only, while compressed charcoal is available in pencil and powdered forms as well as sticks.

Vine charcoal is *charcoal in its most natural state. It is made by heating vines until only the charred, black sticks of carbon remain.* These thin carbon sticks are soft, lightweight, and extremely brittle. You can buy the sticks in thicknesses ranging from that of a rose stem up to nearly one-half inch. The advantage of vine charcoal is that you can erase it and smudge it for effect more easily than compressed charcoal. The disadvantages are that it is less permanent, dirtier, and not as effective in making fine lines.

The medium of **compressed charcoal** is made *by binding together tiny particles of vine charcoal. This process produces a less brittle, finer medium than vine charcoal.* You can buy compressed charcoal in sticks or pencils.

Charcoal pencils (Figure 4.5) have the advantages of being cleaner and will allow the artist to produce fine lines. The disadvantage of the pencils is that the sides cannot be used, thus limiting the types of marks that can be made.

Charcoal pencils are available in both black and white in four degrees of hardness: HB, 2B, 4B, and 6B. Charcoal pencils of a consistent, smooth quality are sometimes difficult to find. Although it is not our purpose to recommend one brand of art media over another, we have found that our best experiences with charcoal pencils have been with those manufactured by Grumbacher. The Ritmo pencil (a Grumbacher Italian import) is also good. If you have difficulty finding either of these products, try those produced by the General Pencil Company.

Powdered charcoal *has the same material makeup as compressed charcoal. It can be used for shading and other special effects* realized by rubbing and erasing the powder sprinkled on the drawing surface.

SHARPENING YOUR SKILLS

Test Charcoal Media

On a large sheet of newsprint, experiment with a variety of charcoal materials. Use the side of charcoal sticks to create a range of broad strokes that exhibit gradation of value. Use the end of charcoal sticks and pencils, pressing firmly or lightly to obtain a variety of delicate and bold lines. Try to create different textural effects by scribbling, smudging, crosshatching, erasing and reworking. Exhibit your sheet of charcoal experiments in class and point out the effects that pleased you the most. Note the different ways other students made use of this medium.

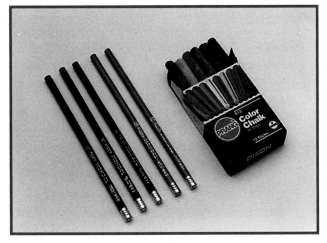

▲ **FIGURE 4.6**   Colored chalks

▲ **FIGURE 4.7**   Pastels

Chalks

Colored chalks *are dry, powdery sticks of pigments* that have been used to create drawings and paintings for centuries (Figure 3.19, page 53 by Antoine Watteau). Chalks range from those that are soft and fine and produce brilliant, lasting color to those that are hard and produce more subdued, less durable color.

Layout chalks *are small, hard, square sticks.* They are also produced in pencil form and are sometimes used by graphic designers, art directors, or illustrators when making rough sketches (Figure 4.6).

The most widely used chalks, however, are *pastels.* Depending on the kind and amount of binder, they can be powdery, waxy, or oily. They can be applied to high-quality surfaces, usually special pastel papers, by hand or with rubbing techniques. Both round and square sticks are available in sets that can include up to almost fifty hues (Figure 4.7).

There are many different papers designed just for use with pastels. Among these are papers with a very fine "sandpaper" surface, velour papers in various colors with a surface like velvet cloth, and charcoal paper in white and other colors.

Many students find that white bristol board or heavy layout paper is the best choice for their needs. Layout paper is a high-quality translucent paper used chiefly by graphic designers and artists. It can be purchased in 13-, 16-, and 20-pound weights. The surface of layout paper is rough enough to make it well-suited for work with pas-

tels. However, because it is translucent, it must be mounted on a white backing in order to show off the drawing.

Crayons

Crayons, along with chalks, are among the oldest of all art media. They are available in both pencils and square sticks. Various degrees of hardness are also available. Crayons provide a wide range of colors, and they can be applied to many different

SHARPENING YOUR SKILLS

Compare and Contrast Pastel Effects

Experiment with chalks and pastels on large sheets of newsprint in the same manner in which you experimented with charcoal. Compare and contrast the different results obtained with these drawing materials. Which do you favor?

surfaces. Because of the adhesive strength of the binder, crayon marks are almost permanent and difficult to erase.

Conte crayon is *the brand name for the best-known brand of drawing crayons.* They are available in various assortments of colors and hardnesses, such as HB, B, and 2B.

Charles Sheeler's drawing, *Of Domestic Utility* (Figure 6.1, page 108) illustrates how conte crayons can be used to obtain a variety of different textures and the subtle gradations of value that suggest the three-dimensional forms in a realistic drawing.

■ WET, OR LIQUID MEDIA

Wet media are *those that come in a liquid state and are applied with brushes, pens of various types, and other drawing tools.* All wet media are permanent and erasing is nearly impossible.

When considering the wet media used in drawing, ink almost certainly comes to mind first. It is a versatile medium used for many purposes by artists since ancient times. You can purchase both translucent and opaque inks in a variety of colors. Special inks are available for use on water-repellent surfaces such as acetate and Mylar film.

Ink

India ink is *black drawing ink.* It is available in two types: waterproof and soluble. The waterproof variety will withstand washes after the ink has dried. The soluble is usually better for making fine lines. Both types can be diluted or thinned with water.

Henri Matisse's pen-and-ink drawing of a girl in a Rumanian blouse is one of several large works based on this subject—Figure 8.1, page 156. Notice how the fine pen lines are used here to create an elaborate design of lively patterns. The line quality, which seems so "right" in this case, could hardly have been realized with any other medium.

However, Thomas Eakins also used ink when he created his drawing of the *Gross Clinic* (Figure 6.5, page 113). Here fine lines are ignored in favor of contrasting areas of light and dark values. While Matisse chose to use a pen to apply ink to his drawing, Eakins opted to use a brush to apply ink to his.

Indeed, any number of different tools can be used to apply ink to a drawing surface. In addition to various kinds of pens and brushes, artists have used sticks, sponges, feathers, cardboard, rolled paper, and even soda straws. Each of these produces a different kind of line or textural quality.

Washes

Wash is *a term used to describe the medium made by thinning ink or paint with water.* It is applied with a brush in a range of light and dark values determined by the amount of water added to the ink or paint. Many artists use a wash to help define or accent the forms created with ink lines in their drawings. The ease with which areas of light and dark values can be realized contributes to the popularity of this medium.

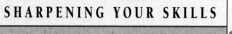

SHARPENING YOUR SKILLS

Use Different Tools with Ink

Apply ink with a variety of different tools to a large sheet of white drawing paper. Try to use as many different tools as possible, noting the different effects realized with each. Exhibit your work in class. What were the most unusual tools used to apply ink to paper? Which effects were regarded as especially unusual and successful?

Annibale Carracci's charming pen-and-ink drawing of *A Domestic Scene* (Figure 3.17, page 52) demonstrates how an accomplished artist can make effective use of ink washes. Completed early in the artist's career, it reveals Carracci's concern for drawing exactly what he saw. Firm but sensitive lines are accented by areas of soft light and dark washes that help define three-dimensional forms and create the illusion of depth.

Colored washes can also be obtained by thinning various types of paint with water. Although less frequently associated with drawing, paints can be extremely effective when used in combination with dry media and inks.

Paints

Watercolor paints consist of transparent pigments in a medium of water or gum and are available in tubes or sectioned pans (Figure 4.8). Watercolor pigments are ground extremely fine, resulting in a transparent effect that distinguishes this medium from other, more opaque paints. It should be noted that watercolors are not suited for use in covering large areas with heavy layers. *If an opaque effect is desired, any opaque water-based white paint can be mixed with watercolors. The type most frequently used is known as Chinese white. When mixed and used in this way, watercolors* are known as **gouache**.

Bridget Riley made use of gouache to achieve subtle color variations in a series of drawings completed in preparation for a large work installed in a New York bank (Figure 5.11, page 88). These gradual color variations are used to form a "V" in the center of this symmetrically balanced composition. Can you find it?

Several manufacturers offer opaque watercolors or gouache paints in tubes or pans. It is often referred to as designer's gouache and can be found listed in catalogs under watercolor paints. When properly mixed and applied, it covers areas opaquely with no streaks. However, when thinned with water the resulting wash often appears less clear than washes made with watercolors.

Tempera paint (also known as poster paint) is a water-soluble gouache paint that can be secured in liquid form or as a powder to be mixed with water.

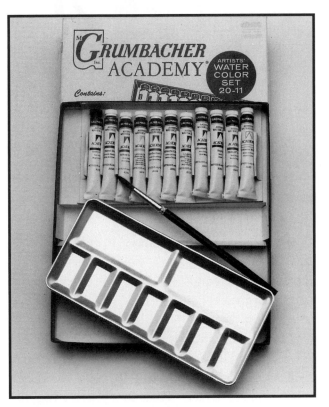

▲ **FIGURE 4.8 Watercolor paints**

When properly mixed it becomes opaque after it is applied. However, it is somewhat brittle when dry and requires a heavy paper to prevent cracking.

Acrylic paint is *the most commonly used name for synthetic pigments and media.* All paints consist of two basic parts: pigment and medium. The pigment provides the color and the medium provides the liquid in which the pigment is mixed. There are both natural and synthetic pigments and media. Compared with the natural paints, the synthetic acrylics are more versatile. They can be cleaned from brushes easily with soap and water and thinned with water, although they resist water after drying.

Because acrylic paints dry rapidly, it is necessary to place brushes not in use in a container of water. If this is not done, the paint in them will dry in a few minutes making them difficult to clean.

Surfaces painted with acrylic paints resist cracking or peeling and can be drawn upon with pen and ink once they are dry. Unlike other water-based paints, there is no danger of blotting, bleeding, or spreading because the synthetic binder forms a hard surface that prevents other absorbable

Artists at Work

■ **FASHION DESIGNER**

Wearable Art for the Future

"Clothing and style have always been important to me, yet I'm not into 'high fashion.' I like clothing that's functional yet stylish. Are there jobs in fashion design for people like me?"

There certainly are. Contemporary consumers come from a wide variety of backgrounds and lifestyles, and apparel designers must reflect this diversity in the designs they create. Fashion designers are key people in the garment industry. They must constantly ask: Who are my customers? What do they want their clothes to say? What materials do they want and how much do they want to spend?

Designers keep extensive research files and stay abreast of current trends by attending fashion shows, reading trade publications and consulting with merchandising experts. They combine this research with their own ideas in an attempt to create new designs that people will find appealing.

Although some fashion designers have their own studios and staffs or work free lance, selling their ideas and sketches, others are employed by manufacturers of apparel lines or related businesses. Many of the over twenty thousand designers and assistant designers working in the United States are employed by manufacturer's of paper patterns. Working as a fashion designer for a clothing pattern manufacturer would allow you to combine your skill in drawing and interest in fashion. Your job would be exciting and challenging.

The design process begins with a new idea for a garment. These ideas may be suggested by the merchandising director, who has the latest news about styles, or by you, the designer.

As an apparel designer, you need to have a creative imagination that can produce fresh, exciting fashions. You should be familiar with past designs and be an interested observer of contemporary trends, fads, and ethnic influences. Fashion design is competitive and you must meet demanding deadlines.

Although a college degree is not necessary to work as a fashion designer, it assures employers of your substantial training and background. Many specialized schools devoted to design have intensive programs.

In addition to art courses such as drawing, painting, sculpture, design, printmaking, and art history, classes like home economics, English, and world and American history can prove helpful for someone interested in fashion design. To gain experience with various fabrics and textures, you could work with your school or community theater, designing costumes, fashions, and period clothing. Working part time in a retail store would give you experience.

In addition to fashion design, many other careers in the fashion industry require abilities and interests like yours. Drawing talent, a sense of fashion, an understanding of the construction process, and design training are important to accessory designers, fashion consultants, fabric designers, fashion specialists, sports clothing designers, and fashion display directors. Whichever fashion career you choose, your job can be as important and exciting as next year's fashion statement. ■

media from penetrating. However, this also means that no other wet medium, including oil paint, can permanently bond with an acrylic surface. It can only rest on the surface rather than mix with the acrylic for a lasting hold.

Perhaps this discussion of wet media has left you somewhat confused since it includes mention of media often associated with painting rather than drawing. Indeed, some works of art are difficult to categorize as paintings or drawings. This could certainly be said for several works illustrated in this book including the watercolor by Paul Cézanne in Figure 2.3, page 23.

Like most wet media, watercolors can be used as a drawing medium or as a painting medium. The manner in which they are used is often regarded as the determining factor. If the work exhibits a decided linear quality and has been fashioned with drawing techniques, it is usually regarded as a drawing. This is true even if colored media were used in some way in its creation. However, it would be a mistake to place too much faith in hard and fast rules to distinguish between paintings and drawings. In the final analysis, artists creating works of art are only limited by their imagination and skill in using any type of media or technique to express their ideas, images, and feelings. If the artworks that result succeed in doing this, is it important if we cannot determine for certain if they are paintings or drawings?

Mixed Media

Combining several media (*mixed media*) to obtain desired effects in a work of art is an approach employed by contemporary artists as well as artists in the past. For example, Richard Lindner used colored crayons, brush and watercolor, and gouache over pencil to create what some interpret as a magician performing an escape trick from handcuffs (Figure 15 in Color Section I). Over 350 years earlier, Peter Paul Rubens combined pen and brown ink with black chalk accented with white, gray, and green paint to produce *The Garden of Love* (Figure 1.8, page 9).

Using several different media in the same work often enables an artist to achieve effects that cannot be obtained with a single medium. When those effects enhance the artist's efforts to communicate a specific idea, capture a particular image, or express a certain mood, they can be justified. This is not the case when they interfere with those efforts. Consequently, be certain when using mixed media that you have a clearly identified purpose in mind—to create a more visually rewarding image or to express more clearly an idea, mood, or feeling.

SHARPENING YOUR SKILLS

Try Mixed Media

Experiment with various combinations of dry and wet media on different surfaces. Which seem to have the greatest potential for you? Are you more comfortable working with a single medium? Do these experiments alter in any way how you perceive and respond to artworks created with mixed media?

CHAPTER 4 REVIEW

1. Why is experimentation important to develop skill in drawing?
2. Name three types of dry media and explain the advantages and disadvantages of each.
3. Name three types of wet media and explain the advantages and disadvantages of each.
4. What are the advantages in using mixed media in drawing?

STUDIO 1

Create A Mixed Media Still Life

SUPPLIES

- Pencil
- Sketch paper
- One sheet of white mat board, 12 x 18" (30 x 46 cm)
- Black felt marker with medium tip
- Crayons
- Chalkboard eraser
- India ink
- Brush
- Nail or some other pointed tool

1. On the mat board, complete a line drawing in pencil of a still-life setup consisting of several familiar objects. Draw the objects as accurately as possible and add an interesting background. Use a black felt marker with a medium point to outline the most important shapes and add details. Color the entire composition with crayons making certain to press down heavily as you apply each color.

2. With a chalkboard eraser, apply a light layer of chalk dust to the surface of your crayon drawing. (Talcum powder can be used for the same purpose.) Paint over the entire composition with india ink—the chalk dust will prevent the waxy crayon surface from resisting the ink.

3. While the ink is drying, use a pencil and sketch paper to create several interesting patterns composed of closely spaced lines. These lines can be straight or curved. Select the most intriguing pattern and etch it onto the inked surface with a nail or some other pointed instrument. By carefully scratching through the ink, you will bring out the crayoned still life composition beneath.

STUDIO 2

Silverpoint Drawing

SUPPLIES

- Graphite pencil
- Drawing paper
- Acrylic gesso
- Soft brush
- Heavy illustration board
- Fine sandpaper
- Drafter's mechanical pencil (lead holder)
- Silver wire

1. In this exercise, you will create a drawing using silverpoint. Begin by completing a preliminary pencil drawing of any scene you like.

2. Apply several light coats of gesso to a sheet of illustration board measuring about 20 x 15" (51 x 38 cm). Thin the gesso with water before you apply it. Use a brush about 2" (5 cm) wide. Sand the board thoroughly between coats with fine sandpaper. Gesso dries rapidly, so wash your brush between coats.

3. After you have prepared the illustration board, transfer your preliminary drawing to it, and render the design in silverpoint. Silver wire can be purchased from a jeweler. You will need about 2" (5 cm) of wire, about 1 mm thick. Remove the sharp point on your piece of wire with fine emery paper or a nail file, and insert the wire into a drafter's mechanical pencil (or lead holder).

4. Leave a border of about 2" (5 cm) around the drawing for a mat, and use a 16 x 11" (41 x 28 cm) working area.

Develop Your Portfolio

SUPPLIES

- ➜ **Three-ring binder or zippered portfolio**
- ➜ **Acetate page covers**
- ➜ **35mm Camera**
- ➜ **35mm Slide holders**

1. What is a portfolio? Why is it important? How does one go about developing one? If you are serious about drawing and think you might like to continue your art studies in the future, it is not too early to begin considering answers to questions like these.

   A **portfolio** is *a selection of drawing and/or other artworks that demonstrates your artistic interests and skills.* It is indispensable when you are:

   - Making application to universities or art schools in order to further your education in the visual arts.
   - Seeking a position that will enable you to put your training in the visual arts to practice.

2. Obviously, it is to your advantage to prepare a portfolio that will capture the interest of people who will review it. To do this, it should effectively showcase your artistic talent. It should include examples of your work that most clearly demonstrate:

   - Your command of the visual vocabulary.
   - Your familiarity with a range of art media and techniques.
   - Your ability to record images and express ideas, feelings, and emotions in a highly imaginative manner.

   Artworks that do this should be carefully selected from the body of work that you create while you are involved in this and other art courses. Begin this process now by examining the drawings you complete for the activities in *Creating and Understanding Drawings.* Continue the process as you finish each of the units in this book. You will find that the art criticism operations discussed in Chapter 2 will help you make your selections. Keep in mind, however, that final decisions can be reserved for later, when you have a greater number of artworks from which to choose.

3. Perhaps you will find several drawings that might be seriously considered for inclusion in your portfolio. Set these aside with a note card attached to each that provides:

   - Your name.
   - The title of the work.
   - The date (year) it was completed.
   - The medium or media used.

4. Later, after carefully matting (See Studio 7, page 102.) the artwork to be included in your portfolio, you will need to complete and attach to each an identification label that provides this information.

5. You may want to take photos of your oversize artwork; 8 x 10" (20.3 x 25.4 cm) color or black and white prints (glossies) work well for a three-ring binder. If you have three-dimensional art, you may want to consider 35mm color slides. Be sure to photograph each art piece from all four viewpoints—front, back, and left and right sides. Be sure the lighting is set up to enhance your work through effective shadows and highlights. (You may want to seek advice from your teacher on how to go about setting up the lighting.)

6. Keep adding to your portfolio, and review it often to track your own progress as you develop your drawing skills.

☞ TECHNIQUE TIP

Basics to Remember

- Clean your work area and tools thoroughly before you begin.
- Work in a well-lighted area.
- Wash your hands well before starting work and wash them frequently as you work.

▲ Were you able to determine what the boy was doing before you read the title?
Did you take into account the artist's keen sense of perception? How is this skill
exhibited in the drawing?

FIGURE 5.1 Giovanni Battista Piazzetta. *Giacomo Feeding a Dog*. 1739. Black chalk with stumping, and
traces of charcoal, heightened with touches of white chalk, on blue-gray laid paper (discolored to cream).
53.5 x 42.2 cm (21 x 16⅝"). The Art Institute of Chicago, Chicago, Illinois. Helen Regenstein Collection.

Entering the Studio

When you enter the studio to make a drawing, your pencil is not the most important thing to take with you. Neither is your paper or your drawing board.

The most important thing is not even a strong and honest desire to make a drawing. Your wish to have a good likeness of someone or something won't help you. In fact, this wish can get in your way unless you really enjoy taking part in the process of drawing.

The one thing you need to be successful is the desire to draw. Your attitude is your most important equipment.

This doesn't mean that the drawings you make aren't important. They are—but they are important to a large degree because they are the record of an act. People have considered the act of drawing important since the dawn of history.

The other things that make drawings important are their physical characteristics, aesthetic qualities, and uses. We talk about these subjects in other parts of this book. Your first concern, however, is your involvement in the act of drawing—the process.

objectives

After reading this chapter and doing the activities, you will be able to:

- Name the most important factor in making successful drawings.
- Make gesture and contour drawings.
- Illustrate the use of different drawing tools and media.
- Demonstrate basic drawing techniques.

Terms to Know

blind contour drawing
cast shadows
contour drawing
cross contour
form shadows
gesture drawing
highlights
outline contour
still life
thumbnail sketches
vertical axis

You Can Learn to Draw

Do you find that it matters only a little what you are drawing? Does it seem that the time you spend drawing goes much too fast? If so, you can probably become a successful artist. A bit of talent helps, of course, but it isn't nearly as important as most people think. A moderately talented student with self-discipline and a genuine desire to draw will be much more successful than an extremely talented student without self-discipline or much interest in the drawing process. If you are willing to practice and enjoy the process, the product will take care of itself. You don't need outstanding talent. Anyone who can write can learn to draw—in fact, it may even be easier because drawing is less abstract.

Drawing media, or materials, and how to use them were explained in Chapter 4. The activities in this chapter introduce basic drawing techniques.

■ GESTURE DRAWING

Drawing gestures or movements of the body is called **gesture drawing**. Since gestures require movement, you have to operate like a camera when you draw gestures and freeze the movement. You also need a person to make the gesture. At this point, you aren't expected to draw the figure, the human form. You are just expected to draw what the figure is doing. This is called the gesture. In Figure 5.1 on page 80, the artist captured the gestures of a boy feeding his dog.

▲ This drawing was done as a preliminary study for a painting. Notice how the erased lines—which are still visible—add to the sense of movement.

FIGURE 5.2   Hilaire Germain Edgar Degas. *The Violinist*. c. 1879. Black and white chalk, blue-gray paper. 48 x 30.5 cm (18⅞ x 12"). The Museum of Fine Arts, Boston, Massachusetts. William Francis Warden Fund.

It is impossible, of course, to draw an action without indicating the person doing the action. You will probably show the figure somehow. Even so, let that happen as a result of the drawing process—not because you are trying to draw the figure. Your attention should remain focused on capturing the gesture or action of the subject (Figure 5.2).

Doing lots of gesture drawings will help improve your drawing skills in four ways:

1. Gesture drawing forces you to see the model and the model's movement as a single image, not one detail at a time.

2. Gesture drawing helps you forget your childhood habit of outlining all of the shapes in a

---

Did You Know?

Seeing the thing you are drawing as a whole rather than just as a collection of parts results in more successful drawings. The fact that we naturally see things as a whole was discovered in Germany in 1912 by a psychologist named Max Wertheimer. He founded a branch of psychology called *Gestaltism*. The German word *gestalt* means pattern or form. According to Gestalt psychology, we only recognize objects by seeing total patterns or forms, not by adding up the individual parts we see. In making most drawings, do the large shapes first. Add the details later. Think in terms of the *gestalt* view of life.

drawing. You probably think that outlining is always the right way to begin a drawing. On the contrary, outlining isn't used for gesture drawing. Outlining can be slow, stiff, and frustrating. Persuade yourself to ignore the outlines, and make the shapes by "scribbling" them.

3. Gesture drawing helps you overcome your fear of the blank page as you immediately put expressive marks on paper.

4. Gesture drawing is a good way to become acquainted with various art-making media. You will try several in the gesture drawing activities.

If you have an easel in your *studio*, or art room, use it and work standing up. Standing will free you to make the almost athletic movements required in gesture drawing. It is a good idea to put the easel slightly to one side of what you are drawing. This is true any time you are drawing at an easel. You don't want to have to stand on tiptoe to peer over the top of the paper at the objects or *model*, the person who poses for a drawing. When you place the easel at an angle so the model is observed by looking across your drawing arm, the paper will be high enough to reach easily. You won't have to turn your head very far to see your drawing.

Also, don't hold the drawing instrument as if you were writing. See Figure 5.3 for the correct grip. You can't do gesture drawings with the small muscles in your fingers, as if you were writing a letter. You must use the large muscles in the whole arm. Using your whole arm helps you become involved in the action of drawing. It also removes the temptation to start out drawing details instead of looking for the single image.

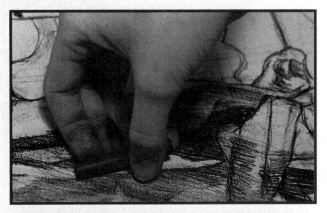

▲ **FIGURE 5.3   Note that the drawing instrument isn't held like a writing tool while drawing large shapes or doing gesture drawings.**

■ CONTOUR DRAWING

Drawing the edges, or contours, of figures or objects is called **contour drawing**. While gesture drawing is quick, contour drawing is slow and painstaking. While gesture drawing records an action all at once, contour drawing is more concerned with shape and structure. While gesture drawing may capture the entire image, contour drawing also explores the smallest details.

Outline Contour Drawing

The first kind of contour drawing we will explore is outline contour drawing. The **outline contour** is *the line around the outer edge of an object that shows the overall shape of the person or object that you are viewing from a particular spot.* Of course the shape's outline would change as you move around the object, viewing it from different angles.

▲ **FIGURE 5.4** **This pile of boxes has both outline and interior contours. Both the exterior and the interior contours are shown by the lines drawn on the drawing.**

The only kind of object whose shape wouldn't change in an outline contour drawing is a sphere. Imagine or look at a sphere, such as a globe or a smooth rubber ball. If you drew the outline contour from three different views, what shape would all three be? This shape could be drawn with the compass you use in geometry class.

When you are drawing more than one object, outline contours are more complex. For example, the shape formed by the pile of boxes in Figure 5.4 has an exterior contour line that defines the shape of the whole pile. The pile also has interior contour lines that outline the shape of each box. Outline contour drawings show the outline contours of a subject as a whole and of all the shapes within it.

A good way to learn to draw outline contours is to practice **blind contour drawing** in which you *concentrate on the contours of the object you are drawing and avoid looking at your paper.* Blind contour drawing is an exercise in a valuable but limited way of seeing things. It is perhaps the only kind of drawing that doesn't use the gestalt principle of drawing the overall image first.

As you know, in gesture drawing you disciplined yourself not to outline. In blind contour drawing, you should discipline yourself *never* to look at the drawing until it is complete. This is why it is called *blind* contour drawing.

If you cheat by looking at your paper out of the corner of your eye while you draw, you will defeat the purpose of blind contour drawing. When comparing your drawing with those of your classmates, everyone will know that you cheated. This won't be because your drawing will be any more accurate than theirs, but it will be stiffer, less detailed, and less sensitive.

While you are drawing, imagine the point of your drawing instrument actually moving slowly, like an ant crawling over the giant landscape of the model or objects. Move inch by inch along the edge of the shapes, over the bumps and hills, and into the cracks and valleys. Don't lift your drawing instrument from the paper until you finish. In most cases, this shouldn't be for at least ten or fifteen minutes. If you finish sooner, you have not been observing as closely as you should.

Blind contour drawing helps you accomplish two things. First, you will be closely observing the structure of the object or person you are drawing by feeling your way around all of the shapes with your drawing instrument. This observation will make you more sensitive to detail. Second, as you capture proportions, you will develop a connection between your drawing hand and the part of your brain that causes you to see the whole image of your subject. You will be trying to estimate the size, direction, and arrangement of all of the parts of what you are drawing.

Cross-Contour Drawing

Up to this point, we have been talking about the outline contours of shapes. The other kind of contour line is often called the cross contour of a form. An outline-contour line follows the shape of a form, flattening it. A **cross-contour** line *runs across the form or around it to show its volume or to give it depth.* This kind of line creates the illusion of a third dimension, depth, in addition to width and height.

One of the best examples of cross-contour lines is found in geological survey maps. The fragment of the Wheeler Peak Quadrangle shown in Figure 5.7 allows you to peer down like an eagle on the highest point in New Mexico.

By reading the contour lines on the map, you can see the highest point—the peak of the mountain.

SHARPENING YOUR SKILLS

Blind Contour Drawings of a Model

SUPPLIES

- Charcoal pencil
- Graphite pencil
- Fiber-tipped pen
- Newsprint

After you have practiced drawing inanimate objects, find a model who is willing to sit still for fifteen minutes while you practice some additional blind contour drawing. Use charcoal pencil, graphite pencil, and fiber-tipped pen on newsprint. Do some blind contour drawings of a model each day for the whole semester.

Blind contour drawings of people will produce some humorous results. When you look more closely, however, you will also see the beautiful line quality and the searching analysis that gives these drawings character.

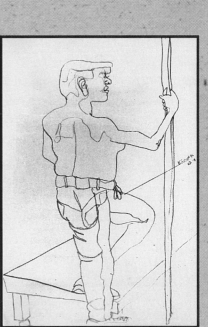

▲ **Figure 5.5** Student blind contour drawings from a model are often humorous, but like this one by Sharon Wagner, they can also reveal character.

▲ **Figure 5.6** Blind contour drawings like this student effort by Kristie Smith have effective formal qualities due to the diversity and analytical character of the line.

Figures 5.5 and 5.6 illustrate some good blind contour drawings created by students. Note how facial features, clothes, and clothing wrinkles are all treated as outlined shapes.

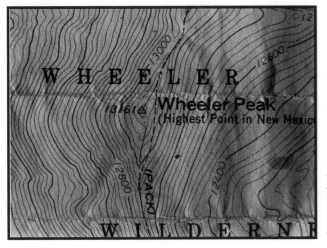

◀ **Figure 5.7** If you have ever hiked in the wilderness, you may have used a map like this one. A geological survey map is basically a cross-contour drawing of the wrinkles on the earth's surface.

Then you can see the shape of the mountain by looking at the cross-contour lines. These lines show levels that are each about 40 feet (12 m) lower than the previous one. They look like rubber bands slipped down over the peak or bandages around a mummy, each parallel to the one above it.

Now look at the drawing in Figure 5.8. The student who created this drawing did more than show the hollow outline of the objects. She also wrapped the objects with cross-contour lines to show the ins and outs, bumps and bulges of all the forms. Notice where darker values are located. How did the artist use cross-contours to create these areas? What purpose is realized by doing this?

The Sketchbook

A first-rate art critic once said, "There can be no end to drawing. It is the fundamental and continuing activity of the artist." Part of that activity takes place in a sketchbook. A *sketchbook* is a small pad filled with a moderately good grade of drawing paper. It can range in size from 4 x 5 inches (10 x 12.5 cm) to four times this size, or larger. It comes in every form from a simple, unbound notepad to an elegant, hardbound volume.

Most serious artists and many people who only make art for recreation keep sketchbooks. Sketchbooks are also used by artists such as architects, interior designers, illustrators, graphic designers, and industrial designers. One way artists use sketchbooks is to try out ideas before making works of art (see Figures 3.11, page 46 and 3.23, page 59). This type of drawing is called *sketching* or *making a rough*.

The sketch in Figure 5.9 was done by the student who completed the oil painting next to it (Figure 5.10 and Color Section I, Figure 16). The preliminary sketch helped the student in several ways. For instance, it allowed her to make a trial composition to see how much of the drawing surface she wanted the images of the still-life objects to cover. Obviously she decided to fill the space more fully with the objects when she made the painting.

The sketch also allowed her to practice drawing the objects and to draw them faster than she could

▲ **FIGURE 5.8** Student Cylinda Baker did this charming backporch still life using cross-contour lines to analyze the threedimensional shapes.

reproduce them with paint. As a matter of fact, she probably did several sketches for practice before even starting the painting.

Finally, the sketch helped her decide about the light and dark values for the objects in the still life.

Did You Know?

When commercial printers speak of the dimensions of a page, they usually give the width first and then the height (the opposite of fine art dimensions, where the height is always first), even if the page is wider than it is high. They also list the width first when they speak about illustrations to be printed on these pages. This is useful to know if you want to become an illustrator or a photojournalist.

In the last two activities, you made *horizontals*—drawings that are wider than they are long. Drawings that are taller than they are wide are referred to as *verticals*.

Printers in the United States usually give page sizes in inches, though this measurement may be changed as the international metric system becomes more widely used. When printers talk about widths of columns of printing, however, they usually refer to printing measurements, using the word *picas*. There are six picas in an inch, and each pica can be broken down into tiny measurements called *points*.

12 points = 1 pica; 6 picas = 1 inch; 72 points = 1 inch.

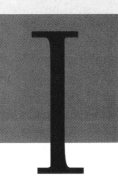

COLOR
SECTION

FIGURE 1
See pages 4–6 for discussion.

Vincent van Gogh. *Café Terrace at Night.* 1888. Reed pen and ink over pencil. 62.5 x 47.6 cm (24⅝ x 18¾"). The Dallas Museum of Art, Dallas, Texas. The Wendy and Emery Reves Collection.

FIGURE 2
See pages 6–8 for discussion.

Georgia O'Keeffe. *My Heart.* 1944. Pastel on paper. 69.9 x 54.6 cm (27½ x 21½"). The Museum of Texas Tech University, Lubbock, Texas. Collection of the West Texas Museum Association and the Museum of Texas Tech University.

FIGURE 3

Just as in music, a work can be restyled in as many ways as there are artists, depending on the way each artist employs the elements, principles, and media of art. See page 19 for discussion.

Mary Cassatt. *Girl Arranging Her Hair.* 1886. Canvas. 75 x 62.3 cm (29½ x 24½"). National Gallery of Art, Washington, D.C. Chester Dale Collection.

FIGURE 4   Student Work.

FIGURE 5   Student Work.

FIGURE 6
See page 20 for discussion.

Lynwood Kreneck. *Hot Day at Cardboard Cottage.*
1985. 55.9 x 48.3 cm (22 x 19").
Courtesy of the artist.

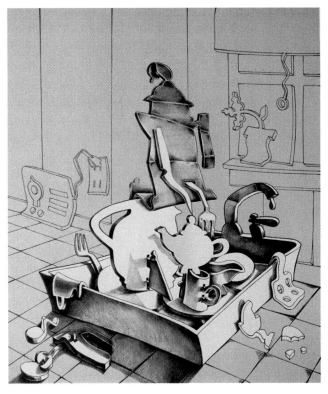

FIGURE 7
See page 49 for discussion.

Rogier van der Weyden. *Portrait of a Lady.* c. 1460. Oil on panel,
painted surface. 34 x 25.5 cm (13⅜ x 10¹⁄₁₆"). National Gallery of Art,
Washington, D.C. Andrew W. Mellon Collection.

FIGURE 8
See page 56 for discussion.

Edouard Manet. *The Plum.* c. 1877. Oil on canvas.
73.6 x 50.2 cm (29 x 19¾"). National Gallery of
Art, Washington, D.C. Collection of Mr. and Mrs.
Paul Mellon.

FIGURE 9
See discussion on page 57.

Berthe Morisot. *The Harbor at Lorient.* 1869. Canvas/oil on canvas. 43.5 x 73 cm (17⅛ x 28¾").
National Gallery of Art, Washington, D.C. Ailsa Mellon Bruce Collection.

FIGURE 10
See discussion on page 57.

Berthe Morisot. *In the Dining Room.* 1886. Canvas/oil on linen. 61.3 x 50 cm (24⅛ x 19¾").
National Gallery of Art, Washington, D.C. Chester Dale Collection.

FIGURE 11
See discussion on page 59.

Vincent van Gogh. *Landscape at Saint-Rémy (Enclosed Field with Peasant)*. 1889. Oil on canvas. 73.6 x 92 cm (29 x 36¼"). ©1993, Indianapolis Museum of Art, Indianapolis, Indiana. Gift of Mrs. James W. Fesler in Memory of Daniel W. and Elizabeth C. Marmon.

FIGURE 12
See discussion on page 61.

Wassily Kandinsky. *Improvisation 28 (Second Version)*. 1912. Oil on canvas. 111.4 x 162.1 cm (43⅞ x 63⅞"). Solomon R. Guggenheim Museum, New York, New York. Gift, Solomon R. Guggenheim.

Figure 13
See discussion on page 68.

Edgar Degas. *The Theater Box*. 1885. Pastel. 56 x 41.9 cm (22 x 16½"). The Armand
Hammer Collection. The Armand Hammer Museum of Art and Cultural Center, Los Angeles,
California.

FIGURE 14
Artist Terry Morrow's *Tejas Kid* is a fine example of a formal fantasy rendered in colored pencil. See discussion on page 71.

Courtesy of the artist.

FIGURE 15
See discussion on page 77.

Richard Lindner. *Charlotte.* 1963. Colored crayons, brush and watercolor and gouache over pencil on heavy white wove paper. 55.3 x 57.8 cm (21¾ x 22¾"). The Baltimore Museum of Art, Baltimore, Maryland. Thomas E. Benesch Memorial Collection. Gift of Mr. and Mrs. I. W. Burnham II and Friends.

Figure 16
See discussion on page 86.

Rebecca Naegnik. Courtesy of the artist.

FIGURE 17
This whimsical construction of wood and clay, *The Serpent's Portal*, is by Keith Owens. It is about two feet tall. Compare the finished work with the sketch in Figure 5.16 on page 90. See discussion on page 89.

Courtesy of the artist.

Figure 18
Ken Dixon's work called *Origin of the Evening Star* uses gum bichromate. The artist drew on the sensitized surface with colored pencils. See discussion on page 93.

Courtesy of the artist.

FIGURE 21
Note the formal use of cone-shaped objects in this student work titled *Teeth* by John Wilson. These objects were derived in part from the teeth of a killer whale. See page 93 for discussion.

Courtesy of the artist.

FIGURE 22
Using directional repetition and variation for interest, John Wilson introduced some musicians into his composition calling it *Teeth and Musicians*. See page 93 for discussion.

Courtesy of the artist.

FIGURE 23
See page 111 for discussion.

Edward Hopper. *Gas.* 1940. Oil on canvas. 66.7 x 102.2 cm (26¼ x 40¼"). Collection, The Museum of Modern Art, New York, New York. Mrs. Simon Guggenheim Fund.

FIGURE 24
See page 118 and 119 for discussion.

Elizabeth Layton. *Self-Portrait Holding Rose with Thorns.* 1985. Pastel with pencil on paper. 45.8 x 18 cm (18 x 7"). National Museum of Women in the Arts. Gift of Wallace and Wilhelmina Holladay.

FIGURE 25
This lion was engraved on the crystal bowl by Paul Hanna. See page 123 for discussion.

Courtesy of the artist.

FIGURE 26
See page 124 for discussion.

Marc Ferrino. Courtesy of the artist.

FIGURE 27
See page 127 for discussion.

Grant Wood. *Sketch for the Birthplace of Herbert Hoover.* 1931. Charcoal, chalk, and pencil. 74.3 x 100.3 cm (29¼ x 39½"). The University of Iowa Museum of Art. Gift of Edwin B. Green.

FIGURE 28
Student Angela Farris employed the stippling technique to create this tempera painting. Name at least one artist who made use of this same technique. See page 131 for discussion.

Courtesy of the artist.

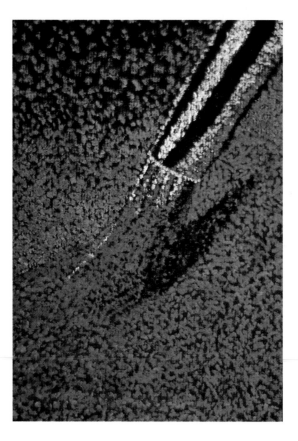

▲ FIGURES **5.9, 5.10** What changes did student Rebecca Naejgnik make from the sketch (above) to the finished painting (at the right)?

It was important for her to know what values to use. Even though the objects are painted in color, a large part of their contrast depends on the amount of light reflected by the colors.

Edgar Degas completed various sketches when preparing to paint a picture of a ballet rehearsal, and he did so for the same reasons as the student who created Figure 5.10. His sketch of a violinist helped him capture the actions and amused expression of a musician who plays the same music endlessly for young ballet dancers (Figure 5.2, page 82).

A sketchbook can also be used to record information in the form of diagrams of things you see. The visual notes need not be objective, either. You can probably imagine the sketches that Bridget Riley produced in her preliminary studies for the work that appears in Figure 5.11 on page 88. It can

be used as a visual diary of your ideas for compositions and design problems or it may just be used for drawing practice.

The illustrations in Figures 5.12 through 5.17 are examples of student sketches made for various purposes. Figures 5.12, page 88 and 5.13, page 89, are both shadow studies. The students used a strong light on the model to help them define the shadows. Figure 5.12, the study of a whole human form, was done rapidly with vine charcoal. Figure 5.13, the head study, is larger and more detailed than the study for the whole form. It still qualifies, however, as a sketch used for practice and for recording shadow information to be used in more finished works. It was done with a charcoal pencil. Why do you suppose the sketch of the whole body is smaller than the study of the woman's head?

SHARPENING YOUR SKILLS

Find and Discuss Pure Imitationalist Art

Very few works of art fall into a single style category. For instance, a mainly imitational painting may also have powerful formal characteristics as well as strongly expressive qualities. The student painting in Figure 5.10, page 87, however, comes about as close as any work can to pure imitationalism.

The student's intent was to do nothing more than reproduce what was in front of her as faithfully as possible. She didn't make the setup. She had little choice of the angle from which she viewed it, and she wasn't allowed to alter or move any of the objects in the composition. This is an art school painting made over thirty years ago as an exercise in the careful copying of shapes, colors, values, and texture. Look at the illustrations in this book. Can you identify any other works that can be described as pure imitationalism? Compare your selection with those made by other members of the class. Be prepared to defend your selections.

A fiber-tipped pen or fine-line marker was the instrument used in the sketchbook drawing of the stereo headset in Figure 5.14. Like the head drawing in Figure 5.13, it is almost life-sized. It also was probably done for practice and to save information. In this case, though, the structure and the relationship of hard and soft forms were more important to record than the light and shadow pattern. Why do you think the artist selected a pen to do this drawing?

The tiny sketches in Figure 5.15 are called **thumbnail sketches** *because they are almost small enough to have been drawn on a thumbnail.* Thumbnail

▲ What was your first impression of this work? Why did you react to it that way? How is the principle of gradation demonstrated in the work? What type of balance does Riley use?

FIGURE 5.11   Bridget Riley. *Study for "Deny."* 1966. Brush and gouache on heavy white wove paper. 50.6 x 66.8 cm (19⅞ x 26⁵⁄₁₆"). The Baltimore Museum of Art, Baltimore, Maryland. Thomas E. Benesch Memorial Collection.

▲ **FIGURE 5.12**   Nothing gives a more rapid or graphic indication of overall form than a bold, flat shadow study like this one by art student Sharon Wagner.

► **FIGURE 5.14** Many common objects have shapes worth sketching. This sketch by student Jeff McMillan clearly reveals the interesting qualities of a stereo headset.

▲ **FIGURE 5.13** This head study by student Richard Wood also deals with shadows, but in a larger, more detailed form.

▲ Jane Cheatham's tiny thumbnail sketches were done in ink for a group of paintings to be hung as a unit. The paintings are concerned with animal symbolism.

FIGURE 5.15 Courtesy of the artist.

sketches are small sketches drawn quickly to record ideas and information for finished drawings. Actually each little drawing is about 5 x 5 inches (13 x 13 cm). They were done with pen and ink. Jane Cheatham, the artist who did these expressive little sketches, used them to plan a series of paintings of animal totems, or symbols of ancestry.

Because they are thumbnail sketches, the artist could record many ideas rapidly. They reminded the artist of visual images and creative combinations of subjects on which to base her finished art. Graphic designers and illustrators use thumbnail sketches to record their ideas and also to show these ideas to other artists, art directors, and executives. If you would like to see a finished painting by the artist who did the thumbnail sketches in Figure 5.15, look at Figure 24 in Color Section II.

Artists who create three-dimensional works also use sketches. The sketches in Figure 5.16 on page 90 were done by Keith Owens, the artist who made the

whimsical sculptural construction in Figure 17 in Color Section I. Note how Owens visualized the sculpture from several viewpoints. Are all his sketches exactly like the finished construction?

Let's return to the questions about the examples you have examined thus far in this chapter. The student

▲ This sketch in graphite pencil was drawn by Keith Owens for his wood and clay construction called *The Serpent's Portal*. Note the tiny multiple-view studies.

FIGURE 5.16   Courtesy of the artist.

▲ How does the artist's use of texture and value add to this work's realistic appearance? Would this drawing be as effective with symmetrical balance? Why or why not?

FIGURE 5.17   Jeanette Leroy. *Scarf on a Coat Rack.* 1976. Pencil on paper. 56 x 38 cm (22 x 15"). National Museum of Women in the Arts, Washington, D.C. The Holladay Collection.

who sketched the shadows on the model shown in Figure 5.12, page 88, was interested in speed. She worked on a small scale since this was one of several practice sketches she made. This sketch showed the overall shadow pattern she hoped to use to define the form. She was practicing the good habit we mentioned of working with the general, large areas first and saving the details for later.

Did You Know?

Too impatient to carry a sketchbook, the English painter William Hogarth often used his thumbnail as a sketchpad to record an expression, a gesture, or a scene.

The student who did the almost life-sized head in Figure 5.13, page 89, was also concerned with shadows. He, however, needed more detail since he had already practiced general shadow structure. So he had to work larger and spend more time.

The student who drew the stereo headset in Figure 5.14, page 89, probably selected a pen for aesthetic reasons. He may have liked the way the pen lines expressed his emotions about drawing or about the object at that time (emotionalism). Or he may have liked the way the pen lines had to be overlapped into a dense texture to make the light-to-dark gradations (formalism).

Artists at Work

■ **SKETCH ARTIST**

Communicating with Charcoal and Paper

"I sketch all the time, but I'm not really into 'fine art.' My pad is like my instant camera. I try to capture everything I see. Who does that for a living?"

*A*ctually, there are many positions where your ability to sketch would be a powerful tool for communicating or working out ideas. Visual communication is the essence of graphic design. Some art directors of corporations and advertising firms began their careers as sketch artists or graphic designers. Sketch artists working in these industries seldom see their work published because it is done mainly on comprehensives, layouts, or storyboards. Many work as free-lance artists, hiring in when the staff is overloaded with work or unfamiliar with the subject. Others work full-time for a single agency.

Many artists use sketchbooks to record information quickly for a variety of purposes. Cameras are often not allowed in courtrooms, and the news media must rely on sketch artists to record the drama of the proceedings for use in their broadcasts. This type of work requires the artist to draw small thumbnail sketches very rapidly, capturing the mood of the scenes and the personalities of the participants.

Police also use sketch artists to capture the images of people they are interested in. Police artists work with the descriptions provided by witnesses to crimes to develop drawings of suspects and those wanted for questioning. Drawings provided by police artists are also useful for helping to locate missing persons.

Some quick sketch artists use pencils, charcoal, pastels or other media to create portraits for the general public, often accentuating the best or most prominent features. Because of their novelty and widespread appeal, many of these sketch artists are employed by theme parks and recreation companies.

Sculptors, architects, and other artists who work in three-dimensional mediums use sketching to develop perspectives of potential creations. Sketches drawn from different perspectives help them visualize the completed work as it would appear from different angles and distances.

Artists working in many commercial fields use sketches to communicate ideas and information to team members or customers.

As you can see, there are countless positions where your sketching ability will be an important asset. Sketch artists must have the ability to size up a situation quickly and bring the significant aspects of their subject into clear focus.

You should take all the drawing and fine art classes that you can. Don't be afraid to investigate and experiment. You may find another medium that allows you to use your talent for sketching while stretching your artistic capabilities.

For some of the positions that have been mentioned, a college degree or specialized training will be essential. For others, you will need only your pad and pencil along with a strong belief in your abilities. ■

▲ Ken Dixon's three-panel work is called *Passing Through*. Where do you think he came up with ideas for this drawing?

FIGURE 5.18 Courtesy of the artist.

Many art teachers consider the sketchbook to be an important tool that students should take with them everywhere, along with a drawing instrument. You may find that one of your first assignments is to keep a sketchbook and practice in it every day. Look for things you like that are also interesting to draw.

Try to stay away, though, from drawing what everyone else draws. Nearly all beginning artists draw their teddy bear, or their tennis shoe, or a comic book character. Instead, why not find the city's oldest manhole cover for a portrait, or draw a square foot of earth with leaves and twigs, or go to an import shop and sketch wicker furniture? Make every effort to capture the fleeting ideas suggested by your daily experiences or observations—subjects that are suggested by contact with the world around you as well as subjects that are born and nurtured by your imagination.

After you have sketched for several weeks, you will have accumulated quite a few pages of drawings in your sketchbook. You can use those ideas for the drawing activities in this book.

Make Your Drawings Original

In addition to the more-or-less mechanical application of skills, the drawing process involves ideas. If you are like most art students, you are already aware of the importance of creative ideas in the drawing process. Many art students aren't aware, however, that creative thinking is a skill that can be learned just as students learn to manipulate drawing tools and to closely observe what they draw.

Where do our ideas come from? They come from our experiences and our unique personalities. The people we know, the places we have seen, the books we have read—all our experiences generate ideas. For an artist, the experiences that he or she has had experimenting with various media are especially important in the creative process, see Figure 5.17, page 90, by Jeanette Leroy.

Look at Ken Dixon's three-panel drawing in Figure 5.18. As you look at this work, think about how Dixon's personal experiences might have led to his original idea for this work. Can you see that even something as personal as his handwriting is an important factor in the design? Figures 18 and 19 in Color Section I are other drawings by Dixon. The fact that he has used gum bichromate (a photographic printing medium) in all these works indicates how his experiences with media have contributed to his ideas. The use of the gum bichromate along with the more standard media, such as colored pencils, gives Dixon's work distinctive surface qualities.

For most people, family backgrounds can provide a rich source of drawing material. For example, Jeff McMillan had an idea for portraying his father as a fantasy character as much unlike his father's actual personality as possible. Figure 20 in Color Section I shows McMillan's father as an underworld figure from Central America, while in real life McMillan's father is a college administrator.

The multimedia drawings in Figures 21 and 22 in Color Section I are part of a series based on the personal images of John Wilson. An art student who is also a musician, he is interested in giant cetaceans (especially, as you can see in the drawings, the killer whales). Wilson rendered the threatening teeth of the killer whale in brightly colored, stuffed fabric in the first composition. In the second composition, he used a group of jazz musicians to repeat the direction of the row of whale's teeth to make a visually exciting and amusing drawing.

You can stimulate your own creative thinking in several ways:

- Be curious about everything and develop many strong interests. Take drawing ideas from things that interest you.

- Research your subject extensively. The library, your friends, government agencies, and professional societies are just a few of the many sources of information.

- Make many sketches to obtain information and experiment with a composition.

- Discuss your ideas with friends and your teacher.

- After experimenting with a new idea, leave it alone, "sleep on it" for awhile. Then come back to the idea with a fresh approach.

Your best ideas will probably come to you when you are alert but relaxed—and probably when you least expect them.

In looking for ideas, do you think it is ever good practice to draw what someone else has already drawn? There are only three reasons for reproducing anyone else's drawing. One reason is to explore a technique to discover how the artist did it. Another reason is to record information that the work was meant to give; for example, from a technical illustration in an encyclopedia. The third reason is to honor a famous work with commentary or an extension of the artist's idea.

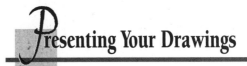

Presenting Your Drawings

Once you have produced several good drawings by completing the studio activities in this chapter, you will want to give attention to the presentation of your drawings. *Presentation* means how your finished artwork is prepared to be shown to someone else. You may be showing it to your teacher or to the public at an art gallery. If you become a designer or an illustrator, you will show your work to an art director or a client. If you present it as if you care about it, most people will give your art close attention. You can prevent your drawings from being overlooked by presenting them well. Matting is a good way of doing this. Studio 7 on page 102 explains the procedure.

CHAPTER 5 REVIEW

1. In a half-page paragraph, explain the difference between gesture drawing and contour drawing.
2. What is the technique you use when creating a blind contour drawing?
3. On what kind of a map do you find cross-contour lines? What can you tell by looking at the lines?
4. Name at least four reasons for keeping a sketchbook.
5. Why is it important to present your drawings well?

STUDIO 1

Gesture Drawings of a Still Life

SUPPLIES

•➔ Vine charcoal

•➔ Newsprint pad, 17 x 22" (43 x 56 cm) or larger

•➔ Drawing board and spring clips

•➔ Easel

1. Look at the figure drawings in Figures 5.19 and 5.20. Soon you will try to make drawings like these, but first practice the gesture drawing technique on a **still life**, *a group of nonmoving objects.* Make several drawings of a three-object still life from various positions around it.

2. For these drawings, use vine charcoal and newsprint. Vine charcoal, you may recall, is a black drawing medium made by cooking sections of vines in a kiln, or drying oven, until nothing remains but carbon sticks. The newsprint pad on which you will work is a pad made of the same paper as newspapers.

3. The pad should be large enough in size so you can get two or three drawings on a sheet. Use spring clips to hold the pad on a Masonite or wooden drawing board. Set the board on an easel. If there is no easel available, you may use books or anything stable as a make-shift easel by propping your board against them. Some artists simply hold the top of the board with one hand, balancing it on

▲ **FIGURE 5.19**   These small gesture drawings by student Damon Six were created in fifteen seconds each.

▲ **FIGURE 5.20**   These larger gesture drawings were finished by student Rob Wilson in about twenty seconds each.

STUDIO 1 | *Continued from page 94*

▶ **FIGURE 5.21**   Objects can be put together in many ways for a still-life drawing setup.

▶ **FIGURE 5.22**   The start of an expressive gestural approach to still-life drawing.

▶ **FIGURE 5.23**   Finished version of Figure 5.22. Note that the artist treated all objects as though they were transparent. This is necessary in good gesture drawing and desirable in all preliminary drawings.

STUDIO 1   *Continued from page 95*

one hip, while they sketch with the other hand.

4. Since the still life can't move, you will have ample time to draw it. Even so, spend only about twenty seconds on each drawing. With three objects in the composition, the time divides into five seconds on each object and a little over two seconds to change from one object to another. Try to define the stance, or direc-

tion, and the shape of each object without outlining it. Do this in a single, continuous series of strokes without raising your charcoal from the paper except between objects. See Figure 5.21 for a typical still-life *setup*, or group of objects arranged for drawing. See Figures 5.22 and 5.23 for a look at the drawing process.

5. Notice in the drawing in Figure 5.23 that every object

in the composition is drawn as though it were transparent. Drawing objects this way is a good idea, not just in gesture drawing but in all drawing. It will help assure that the objects you are drawing will be recorded accurately.

In gesture drawings, always try to exaggerate the differences in size, shape, and direction. Remember, *don't outline*.

STUDIO 2
Make Gesture Drawings of a Model

SUPPLIES

➺ **Vine charcoal**

➺ **Newsprint**

➺ **Drawing board**

1. After you have practiced gesture drawing with a still life, you should be ready to tackle the real gesture drawing of a person. Have a model assume five poses for twenty seconds each. Draw the gestures in the same way you drew the still life.

2. The first thing you need is a person to make a gesture. Dancers or athletes are good models for gesture drawing, or class members can take turns. The model should take active poses. Each action

should look as if it were interrupted or photographed in mid-motion with a still camera. Actions such as:

- the more active dance motions,
- bending to tie a shoe,
- lifting a heavy load,
- making a baseball umpire's "safe!" sign, or,
- placing something on a high shelf

are all good ones for your model to try. You can request some of the more difficult poses for this activity since the model will need to hold them for only twenty seconds.

3. Remember: *no outlines*. Don't think about the figure—draw

what the figure is doing. A good way to start your drawing without using outlines is shown in Figure 5.24. Start with the vertical axis of the overall motion of the figure. This **vertical axis** is *an imaginary line dividing the figure in half vertically*. Then get the tilt of the shoulders and hips (Figure 5.25). Finally, fill out the shapes by scribbling across the axis (Figure 5.26).

4. Make each drawing at least 8 inches (20 cm) high. This will enable you to place three or four on a page of newsprint. Do at least ten of these drawings a day.

STUDIO 2 | *Continued from page 96*

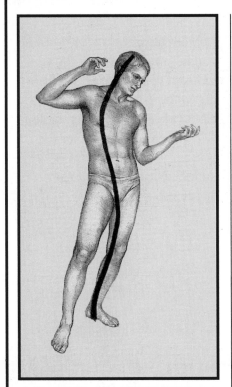

▲ **FIGURE 5.24**   Start the gesture drawing by quickly drawing the gesture of the axis line through the figure.

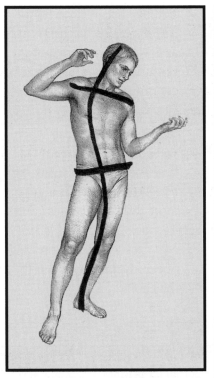

▲ **FIGURE 5.25**   A good second step in gesture drawing is to locate the position and tilt of the hips and shoulders.

▲ **FIGURE 5.26**   Finish your gesture drawing by scribbling lines around and across the form.

STUDIO 3

Do Brush and Ink Gesture Drawings

SUPPLIES

➛ **Brush**

➛ **Black india ink**

➛ **Watercolor paper**

1. Make several gesture drawings of a model in black india ink, which is a wet medium. Make each drawing the same size used for the vine charcoal drawings, 8 inches (20 cm). You can put three or four of these on a single sheet. To apply the ink, use a soft, round brush, Number 2 to Number 5.

2. The most commonly used ink for drawing with a brush is called *india ink*. This ink is almost waterproof, so avoid getting it on your clothes. The pigment or colored powder may separate from the liquid in the bottle, so shake the bottle before you start. (Be sure the cap is on tight!)

   You want the ink to make dark marks when you draw with it and this requires that the ink is thoroughly mixed.

3. You will need a working surface heavier than newsprint for ink drawing. The best paper is probably a moderately good grade of watercolor paper that isn't too rough. A watercolor block is easy to use for gesture drawing.

STUDIO 3   *Continued from page 97*

A *watercolor block* is a pad of watercolor paper for sketching. The sheets are glued down on all four edges so that the paper will stay flat. The pad is stiff enough not to need the backing of a drawing board. To remove a sheet, run an object such as a plastic ruler around the block underneath the sheet's edge. If you don't use a watercolor pad, attach watercolor paper to a drawing board.

4. Drawing with a brush and ink is unlike drawing with dry media. Practice some straight and curved strokes and some squiggles with your brush until you learn how to control it. Some of the strokes may look like oriental calligraphy or hand-

writing. This is not surprising; the brush has been used as a writing instrument for centuries in various Eastern countries.

5. You can make an expressive drawing with a brush when you are working rapidly to describe a gesture. Learning to control a brush is a little more difficult than learning to control a pencil or charcoal stick, but the extra range of expression is well worth the effort.

☞ TECHNIQUE TIP

Caring for Brushes

Before you use a new brush, wash out any glue placed on the tip to protect its shape.

While you are drawing, stop often to swish your brush around in water so that the medium you are using won't dry in the brush hairs. Then blot the brush with a rag, tissue, or paper towel. If you blot the brush, the medium won't be diluted when you dip your brush into it again.

When you are through with the brush for the day, wash it with soap and water until the rinse water comes out clear. Rinsing the brush will keep the medium from building up under the metal ring that holds the hairs. If ink or paint collects there, the brush hairs will fan out. Brushes should always be stored in a container with the brush hairs up.

STUDIO 4

Do Blind Contour Drawings of a Still Life

SUPPLIES

➡ **Charcoal pencil**
➡ **Graphite pencil**
➡ **Fiber-tipped pen**
➡ **Newsprint**

1. Make blind contour drawings of a still life in three media: charcoal pencil (a soft one of the wooden kind), graphite ("lead") pencil (also soft), and a fiber-tipped pen (sometimes

called a *fine-line marker*) that makes a medium-weight line.

2. The charcoal pencils recommended for this activity are the wooden kind, just like graphite pencils. Don't confuse them with the charcoal pencils wrapped in paper that is peeled off before they are sharpened. These paper-wrapped pencils are similar

to the large compressed sticks you used in gesture drawing.

3. Blind contour drawings are usually used to practice figure drawing, but, like gesture drawings, they can be made from any object or setup. Start by drawing some objects that have interesting shapes, such as chairs, fire-plugs, or perhaps a section

STUDIO 4   *Continued from page 98*

of an old, gnarled tree. Set up your easel and drawing board just as you did for gesture drawing in Studio 1.

👆 TECHNIQUE TIP

Sharpening Pencils

To get the most from pencils, proper sharpening is important (whether the pencil is graphite, charcoal, or colored). Ordinary pencil sharpeners don't leave enough lead exposed. Some studios have a drafter's pencil sharpener that removes only the wood and none of the lead. If your studio doesn't have one of these, sharpen the pencil by grasping the pencil and knife as

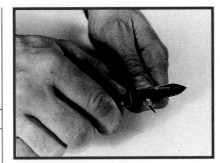

▲ FIGURE 5.27   Hold the knife in one hand to guide it. Push the knife with the thumb of the hand holding the pencil.

shown in Figure 5.27. Use the muscles in the hand holding the knife to guide the knife, not to push it. Push the knife with the thumb of the hand holding the pencil. Using this thumb will give you more control as you

remove the wood. Shape the exposed lead to a sharp point or any other shape you need with fine sandpaper.

➕ SAFETY NOTE

Sharpening Pencils Safely

For better control and safety, use a small, sharp knife, such as a mat knife, an Exacto knife, or a penknife, to sharpen pencils. A small, sharp knife is always safer than a large, dull one. Never use a kitchen knife or razor blade to sharpen pencils. Always push the knife blade away from your fingers or body.

STUDIO 5
Cross-Contour Drawing of Natural Forms

SUPPLIES

➡ **Graphite pencil**

➡ **Fiber-tipped pen**

➡ **Any paper except newsprint or other absorbent paper**

1. When doing your own cross-contour drawings, start out simply. Remember, unlike a blind contour drawing, you may look at your drawing as often as you wish.

2. Make a cross-contour drawing of natural forms, such as two

carrots and a potato. The contour lines can be drawn either vertically or, as on the mountain in the map, horizontally. In either case, contour lines will define the form and shape of what you draw. Look at Figure 5.8 on page 86 again and at Figure 9.14 on page 180. Observe the cross-contour techniques used by the artist.

3. It's a good idea to start by drawing the objects full size with a hard pencil. Later you

can go over the light pencil lines you want to keep with a fiber-tipped pen. After that, you can easily erase the pencil lines, leaving only the ink drawing. Make the drawing about 15 x 11 inches (38 x 28 cm).

4. Start by holding an object in your nondrawing hand close to the paper on which you are working. Do you remember making a drawing of your hand when you were a child?

STUDIO 5 *Continued from page 99*

You laid your hand on a sheet of paper and traced around it. You can't trace around most objects, but you can hold an object close to the spot where you will draw it and reproduce its size and outline fairly accurately. Remember not to press too hard with your pencil. You need to keep the lines light.

5. After you have drawn the outline of one form lightly in pencil, draw the others. Make certain that at least two of the three objects overlap. This overlapping will help tie your composition together.

6. Now that you have your composition outlined, you can add cross-contour lines with the pencil. Feel free to draw these as close together or as far apart as you wish. The spacing of these lines can be used to create different values. For example,

draw the lines closer together for the dark potato and wider apart for the light carrots. Of course, if the lines are too widely spaced, you will lose the image altogether.

7. After you have roughed in the cross-contour lines in graphite, darken them with a pen, making any necessary corrections. Darken only the cross contours, not the outlines of the shapes. Don't forget to follow the details closely just as you did in blind-contour drawing. Each little "hill" or "gully" is an important feature.

8. After you have inked the cross contours, erase all of the pencil lines, including the outlines. The cross-contour lines should be spaced closely enough to define the form making an outline unnecessary.

Computer Option

Select an object to draw. Choose a tool that will create freehand lines, such as a Brush or Pencil tool. With the mouse, draw the outline of the object as accurately as you can; do not worry if there are rough spots or distortions. Now, starting near one edge of the outline, draw a contour line. Use the Duplicate command or Copy/Paste commands to make copies of the contour line, spacing the copies at regular intervals. If necessary, use a Shape tool or Zoom tool (bitmap editor) to redraw portions of some of the lines so that they suggest the form of the object. Erase or Select-and-Delete the original outline.

STUDIO 6

Cross-Contour Drawing Using Shadows

SUPPLIES

- ➡ Charcoal pencil
- ➡ Graphite pencil
- ➡ Brush
- ➡ Black tempera paint, designer's gouache, or acrylic paint
- ➡ Drawing paper

1. In this cross-contour activity, you will be drawing shadows. Since this drawing is a bit more involved, you might wish to make it a little smaller than the one in the last activity to save time in finishing it. Leave a margin

for matting the drawing if you wish. Directions for matting begin on page 102.

2. Use a hard pencil for the preliminary work on this drawing. Select something interesting outdoors to draw. Work on your drawing in

STUDIO 6   *Continued from page 100*

early-to-mid-morning or mid-to-late-afternoon sunshine. This will provide distinct shadows, both on the forms and on the ground. In your pencil drawing, lightly outline the shapes of the shadows on your paper. You can return to the studio to do your *rendering*, or finished artwork.

3. If it isn't practical to do your preliminary drawing outdoors, set up something interesting in the studio. Put a strong light on it from above and on one side. If your studio isn't equipped with floodlights, you could use a clip-on light and reflector. The light and reflector can be purchased for a few dollars at a local supermarket or discount hardware store.

4. Look at the shadows in the pencil rendering in Figure 5.28. There are two kinds of shadows: form shadows and cast shadows. **Form shadows** are *the shadows on the side of forms away from the light source*. Form shadows on curved surfaces have soft or fuzzy edges. This is because a curved form turns gradually away from the light. The sharp corners of angular forms, of course, define the edge of the shadows at the corners where the forms turn abruptly away from the light.

5. **Cast shadows** are *the shadows cast by shapes onto other surfaces*. They have hard, distinct edges unless the surfaces are rough or fuzzy. Look at Figure 5.29 to see how to define the edges of the two different kinds of shadows with contour lines.

6. Before rendering this drawing in paint, do a small shadow study. Do this *rough*, or practice drawing, with charcoal pencil to establish the gray-to-black values of all of the major shadows. To make it easier, treat the cast shadows as if they were uniformly black. Actually, some areas of cast shadow are darker than others.

7. Rough in the overall value of each object. Try to show a clear separation between lighter and darker objects. Finally, darken the form shadows. Make their values consistent with the overall values of the objects on which they are found. After completing these steps, you should have a useful plan for your finished drawing.

8. For this drawing, you can try using black tempera paint, designer's gouache, or acrylic. Any of these paints produces a flat, black surface with fewer coats than most inks do. Do the finished rendering as a cross-contour line drawing. Allow the lines to thicken noticeably in the shadows. The white areas will be squeezed into narrow bands.

▲ **FIGURE 5.28**   Demonstration of careful shadow rendering that shows the soft edge and core of form shadows and the hard edge and value change in cast shadows.

▲ **FIGURE 5.29**   Although it is hard to show very subtle value changes with cross-contour lines, edge differences between form and cast shadows are evident in this drawing.

STUDIO 7

How to Mat a Drawing

SUPPLIES

- Mat knife with replaceable blades
- Metal ruler
- Hard graphite pencil
- Art gum or Pink Pearl eraser
- Mat board
- Backing sheet
- Masking tape

1. *Matting* means framing a picture with a border. Matting of drawings is usually required even in exhibitions whose rules don't require framing of artwork. Drawings included in an artist's portfolio are also matted. The artist, you may remember, shows the portfolio to people who might buy the art or pay for the artist's services. See Studio 3 on page 79.

2. The standard form for presenting drawings for both exhibitions and portfolios is a hinged mat (or border) on a backing with outside dimensions equal to those of the mat. Look at the mat in Figure 5.30. You can see how it is hinged to the backing with a strip of masking tape at the top on the inside.

3. There are various methods for mat cutting, but the following procedures seem most useful. (See Figures 5.32 and 5.33.)

4. First, clean the drawing surface with a soft eraser to take away any remaining pencil

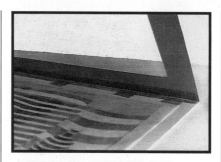

▲ FIGURE 5.30   Student Genevieve Smead made this neatly hinged mat. It is obvious that she wanted to present her work effectively.

lines or fingerprints. Use your pencil to mark on the mat board where the corners of the mat window or frame will be (Figure 5.32). A standard-sized sheet of mat board is 40 x 32 inches (102 x 81 cm). Use pebble-grained, double-sided (gray and white) board.

5. The size of the window will vary with the size of the drawing. The width of the frame around the drawing may vary, but in general the frame should not be less than 3 inches (8 cm) wide. The frame should be equally wide on all sides unless you want a slightly wider bottom margin for more visual stability. The inner edge of the mat window should usually cover about ¼ inch (6 mm) of the ragged outer edge of the drawing.

6. If the edge of the drawing isn't ragged, you can leave this amount of space—or a little more—between the

outer edge of the drawing and the inner edge of the mat. This practice adds interest to the framing without being too visually competitive with the drawing.

7. Use a *matknife* (sometimes called a box knife or utility knife) to cut through the mat board. It is important to keep a sharp blade in the knife. Paper dulls blades rapidly, so be sure to replace the blade when necessary. You will cut the lines on the inside edge of the mat window. Remember to put a piece of scrap cardboard under each line before you cut. The cardboard will protect the table top and keep the blade from being turned by the wood grain when you cut through the mat.

8. Lay the ruler along the outside edge of the first line. Hold it with your thumb and

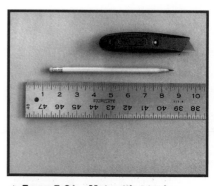

▲ FIGURE 5.31   Mat cutting tools include a mat knife (or utility knife) like this one, a metal ruler, and a pencil. Don't use a T square or triangle as a guide for cutting these lines.

STUDIO 7   *Continued from page 102*

two fingers of one hand. With your cutting hand, hold the knife blade against the ruler. Don't let it lean left or right. Cut the board with several strokes in the same groove. (See Figure 5.33.) Don't try to cut the mat in one or two strokes by using muscle. Cut the other three lines in the same way. (See the Safety Note below.)

▲ **FIGURE 5.32**   Mark only the corners of the mat window to save erasing unnecessary pencil lines.

9. Erase any marks left on the surface of the mat. Then trace around the outside of the mat onto the backing sheet and cut the backing sheet the same size as the mat. You can use corrugated box board as backing for your classroom drawings. A sheet of Fome-cor, a thin sheet of styrofoam sandwiched between two layers of cardboard, makes an even better backing board. You could also use another sheet of mat board as backing for a small drawing. Common poster board or card stock isn't stiff enough.

10. Lay the mat facedown, and hinge it to the top of the backing board with masking tape as shown in Figure 5.30. Place the drawing face up on the backing and close the mat on it. Then adjust the drawing to its best position. Hold it there while reopening the mat.

11. Fasten the drawing at the top of the backing with three or four short strips of tape so the drawing simply hangs loose against the backing. Leaving the drawing loose will prevent it from warping when the humidity of the air changes. (If you cut the strips of tape first and stick them lightly to your shirtfront, you won't need a third hand while you are trying to hold down the drawing.)

12. To protect your matted drawing, wrap it in some clear, thin acetate, a kind of plastic film. You can usually buy acetate for a few cents per foot at your local art supply or hobby shop. Cut the acetate a few inches larger than the drawing. Lay the acetate on a clean surface, and make sure there are no eraser shavings or bits of lint on the acetate or the drawing. Lay the drawing on it, facedown. Then fold the acetate over the back, and tape it to the backing board with masking tape. Fold it as if you were wrapping a package.

▲ **FIGURE 5.33**   Exert muscle power in the hand holding the ruler—not the one holding the knife. Use several strokes of a sharp knife, and don't cut on a bare tabletop.

13. The acetate wrapping will make your drawing look finished and will protect it in your portfolio or at home. It will, however, make the drawing a little harder to see because of reflections in the acetate. Ask your teacher whether you should wrap drawings before you hand them in or after they are returned.

✚ **SAFETY NOTE**

Cutting Mats

Don't use a razor blade to cut mats.

Don't try to cut mats by bearing down hard on a dull knife. Before you cut, make sure that the edges of your fingers on the hand holding the ruler don't hang over the edge of the ruler on the side where you are cutting.

Relax and be patient. More fingers are cut as a result of haste and impatience than anything else.

UNIT

1

Evaluation

■ APPLYING ART FACTS

On a separate sheet of paper, write the term or terms that best matches each definition given below.

1. The building blocks used by artists to express their ideas in visual form.

2. The element of art that refers to the surface feel of an object.

3. A drawing technique in which overlapping, parallel lines are used to create areas of differing degrees of darkness.

4. A kind of balance based upon the apparent weight of various objects included in the work.

5. The four art-criticism operations.

6. A theory of art that favors the use of the expressive qualities when judging artworks.

7. A nineteenth-century art movement in which artists tried to capture what the eye actually sees at a moment of time rather than represent what the mind knows is there.

8. A type of drawing in which the artist is concerned with capturing the movements or actions of the figure.

■ SHARPENING YOUR PERCEPTUAL SKILLS

CHAPTER 1

1. On a note card, list the elements of art and then select a work of art illustrated in Chapter 1 that makes use of at least three of these elements. Underline those elements on your list.

2. On the same note card, list the principles of art. Place a double line under those that are evidenced in the work identified above.

3. Identify a work of art illustrated in Chapter 1 that makes use of value gradation to suggest three-dimensional form.

CHAPTER 2

1. On a sheet of paper, make a list of the literal qualities observed in Figure 2.2 on page 22. Compare your list with those compiled by other members of the class. What things did you see that they missed? What did they notice that you missed?

2. Analyze Cézanne's use of the elements and principles of art in *Bathers Under a Bridge* (Figure 2.3, page 23). To do this, place checkmarks in the design chart (page 30) to indicate at least three design relationships linking an element with a principle. Compare and contrast your decisions with those of other students.

3. Write a short story based upon your interpretation of Francisco Goya's *Disasters of War* (Figure 2.4, page 23).

CHAPTER 3

1. Discuss in class the reasons why a knowledge of art history can help students hoping to improve their drawing skills. Were reasons presented that were not mentioned in the book?

2. Select a period or style of art discussed in this chapter. Use the resources of your school or community library to prepare an in-depth report on this period or style. Present your report in class.

3. Write the names of the following artists on a sheet of paper: Giotto, Jan van Eyck, Jacopo Tintoretto, El Greco, Antoine Watteau, Eugène Delacroix, Berthe Morisot, Käthe

Kollwitz, Andrew Wyeth. After each name, indicate the period or style associated with each. Which of these artists is of particular interest to you? Explain your choice in class.

CHAPTER 4

1. On your classroom chalkboard, list the dry media discussed in this chapter. Discuss the advantages and disadvantages of each.

2. Identify a work of art illustrated in any of the first three chapters that you consider to be especially successful. Discuss in class how the artist's choice of media contributed to the success of this work.

3. On a note card, indicate:
   a. The drawing medium you are most comfortable using.
   b. The drawing medium you are least comfortable using.

   Save this card.

CHAPTER 5

1. Complete a gesture drawing of a posed figure in action using the first medium listed on the card prepared above.

2. Complete another gesture drawing using the second medium listed on the card. Compare and contrast the two drawings. Write a paragraph in which you describe your reactions to working with each medium.

3. Complete a cross-contour drawing in which you use both media indicated on the note card.

4. Make a hinged mat and mount the most successful of the three drawings completed above.

■ MAKING CONNECTIONS

1. **FINE ARTS.**   Select any of the historical periods discussed in Chapter 3. Working with one or two other students, conduct the research and write a report that discuss the artwork created in the Far East (India, China, Korea, or Japan) at the same time period.

2. **SCIENCE.**   Select an object from the natural world (flower, fruit, vegetable) and bring it to class but keep it concealed. Play a game of 20 questions in which students attempt to identify the object by asking questions focusing on the elements and principles associated with the object. (Examples: "Is it a round, symmetrically balanced form?")

■ THINKING CRITICALLY ABOUT ART

1. **DESCRIBE.**   Find and cut out a large photograph showing the face of a well-known person seen from the front. Prepare a detailed description of this individual and, along with other members of the class, turn your description and the photograph in to your teacher. The teacher will select two descriptions and read them out loud after telling students that they will draw the face being described. If your description is read, wait for the second.

2. **COMPARE AND CONTRAST.**   Exhibit the completed drawings from the above assignment, noting similarities and differences. Are students able to identify the individuals they drew? Compare the drawings with the magazine photographs of them.

3. **ANALYZE.**   Look through magazines for photographs that demonstrate the principles of harmony and variety. Cut out the best examples and bring them to class. Along with other members of the class, design two colorful montages titled "Harmony" and "Variety."

4. **JUDGE.**   Select the drawing from this first unit that you regard to be the most successful. What aesthetic qualities did you take into account when arriving at your decision? Which drawing did you consider to be the least successful? Did you judge this work in terms of the same aesthetic qualities?

Realistic Drawings

CHAPTER 6
Understanding and Judging Literal Qualities

CHAPTER 7
Making Imitational Drawings

In Unit 2 you will learn about drawings done in a realistic style. You will focus on the literal qualities, which are considered the most important aesthetic qualities by imitationalists. To learn how other artists have used the literal qualities, you will imagine that you are attending an opening of an exhibition at a local art gallery. No matter which of the theories of art you personally prefer, in Chapter 6, "Understanding and Judging Literal Qualities," you will assume the role of an imitationalist critic. You will use the art-criticism process to describe and judge several drawings. Basing your decision on how well they imitate reality, decide how successful they are.

In Chapter 7, "Making Imitational Drawings," you will use what you have learned in earlier chapters to create your own realistic drawings.

▲ **Why do you think the artist chose this pose for the figure? What does the figure seem to be doing? The musculature of the figure is highly defined and shows masculine qualities. Why do you think this is so?**

Michelangelo. *Studies for the Libyan Sibyl.* c. 1511. Red chalk on paper. 28.9 x 21.3 cm (11⅜ x 8⅜"). The Metropolitan Museum of Art, New York, New York. Joseph Pulitzer Bequest. (Detail at left.)

▲ What has the artist done to make the objects in this drawing look so lifelike? The light comes from two different sources. Can you point out the direction of those light sources?

FIGURE 6.1 Charles Sheeler. *Of Domestic Utility*. 1933. Conte crayon. 63.5 x 49.2 cm (25 x 19⅜"). The Museum of Modern Art, New York, New York. Gift of Abby Aldrich Rockefeller.

Understanding and Judging Literal Qualities

In Chapter 2, you learned about three theories of art: imitationalism, formalism, and emotionalism. Each of these ideas about what makes an artwork successful focuses on different qualities. You discovered that:

- An imitationalist measures drawings by their literal qualities or subject matter.
- A formalist measures drawings by their qualities or the elements and principles of art.
- An emotionalist measures drawings by their expressive qualities or how well they express meaning or feelings.

In this chapter we want you to think like an imitationalist. Responding to literal qualities in drawings will contribute to an appreciation of realistically rendered artworks such as Figure 6.1 and help prepare you to create drawings of your own. As an imitationalist, you will describe everything you see in drawings.

objectives

After reading this chapter and doing the activities, you will be able to:

- Explain how an imitationalist judges drawings.
- Describe the literal qualities in drawings.
- Judge drawings based on their literal qualities and give reasons for your judgment.

Terms to Know

linear perspective
Realists

an Imitationalist

You may find that acting like an imitationalist isn't difficult. In fact, you may already be an imitationalist without knowing it. If you are, that should make the role even easier to play. All you must do is respond to works of art the way you always have—by focusing attention on their literal qualities. As an imitationalist, you are convinced that literal qualities are the most important ones in drawings. They are the standard by which you judge all art.

If you aren't an imitationalist, you are asked to act like one while you read this chapter. This pretending may seem awkward at times, but it will direct your attention to the literal qualities in art. You will play other roles in later chapters, and these may be more to your liking. For now, remember that you aren't concerned with the design qualities or the expressive qualities found in drawings. You are much too busy judging works of art by how real their subject matter looks.

As you read, you will encounter questions that you should ask yourself as you examine drawings in your role as an imitationalist. Often these questions won't be followed by answers.

You can react to these unanswered questions in one of two ways; ignore them and read on, or try to answer them before reading further. If you want to develop your understanding and knowledge of drawing, you will try to answer the questions. They serve several important purposes: to sharpen your perception, to stimulate your thinking and, more importantly, to bring out your personal opinions, feelings, and ideas.

■ THINK YOUR WAY THROUGH

A final comment is needed about responding to drawings. As you read and reread this chapter—and the rest of the book—don't become alarmed if you find yourself wanting to change some of your answers to the questions. Changing your mind shows that you are thinking your way through this book instead of just flipping through the pages to finish your assigned reading.

▲ **FIGURE 6.2** Do you often visit art museums and galleries? What kinds of artworks do you enjoy seeing there? Do these visits help you discover ideas for your own art?

It is now time for you to take on the role of an imitationalist. Remember, you are to respond most favorably to drawings rendered in a realistic style. Among the works displayed at a local gallery opening are drawings done in this style. Having learned this fact, you look forward to seeing the drawings and make plans to attend the opening.

SHARPENING YOUR SKILLS

Look at the Details

Complete a thorough description of the drawing *Gas* in your role as an imitationalist. To do this, make a list of everything you see in the work.

▲ Does this appear to be a modern service station? Why or why not? Is there anything odd about its location? What time of day is it? Do you think this is important to the mood of this drawing?

FIGURE 6.3   Edward Hopper. *Study for Gas.* 1940. Conte and charcoal with touches of white on paper. 38.1 x 56.2 cm (15 x 22⅛"). Whitney Museum of American Art, New York, New York. Josephine N. Hopper Bequest.

Gas by Edward Hopper

The gallery is jammed with people. They are all voicing their opinions about the wide assortment of artworks on display (Figure 6.2). The room becomes silent when you enter; everyone is eager to see how you will react to the drawings. People edge closer as you pause before a black conte crayon drawing by the American artist Edward Hopper (Figure 6.3). They all watch as you study it closely.

Several of the more impatient onlookers interrupt your examination. They urge you to give your opinions about the drawing. What will you mention first? Will you begin by describing the work in a general way and then point out the details? If so, you might say that the drawing consists of a gas station

▲ Did you immediately notice the attendant in this drawing? Do you think he is important to this scene? Why did the artist change this figure in the painting? (See Color Section I, Figure 23.)

FIGURE 6.4   Edward Hopper. *Study for Gas.* (Detail).

located at the side of a narrow country road. Maybe you describe the dreary station, the three gas pumps, and the solitary figure in the foreground.

Will you also mention the road? It looks hardly wide enough for two cars to pass each other. A row of dark trees keeps the eye from moving back into the distance. This barrier emphasizes the isolation of the small gas station.

The figure at the gas pumps seems to be performing some kind of job (Figure 6.4, page 111). What is he doing? It is impossible to say for certain. There is no car waiting for service, and there is none in sight on the road that might need attention. So there seems to be little need for the attendant to be doing anything at the moment.

Someone in the group interrupts to ask if you think the drawing is successful. Remember that you think the literal qualities just described are the most important in the drawing. How will you respond? Does the drawing show this scene in a realistic way?

You might answer that the drawing is quite descriptive, even though there aren't many details. The artist held his imagination in check. He must have been determined to include only the most important features and details. He wanted to portray a specific place at a certain moment in time. Several people listening to your comments look again at the drawing and then nod in agreement. They also are convinced of the drawing's success. (Look at Hopper's painting *Gas* in Figure 23 in Color Section I to see how many changes there are.)

Gross Clinic by Thomas Eakins

Another drawing across the gallery (Figure 6.5) catches your attention. You make your way through the crowd to look at it more carefully.

Any discussion of Eakins must begin with his firm commitment to realism in his works. This commitment prevented him from becoming a popular painter during his lifetime. It isolated him from everyone but his family, students, and a few friends.

Eakins was twenty-seven years old when he returned to his native America after studying art in France. He found that the most financially successful American artists were producing dull landscapes and sentimental scenes of daily life. He certainly had the skill to paint similar pictures and if he had painted them, he would probably have been popular and wealthy. Yet Eakins stubbornly insisted on painting life exactly as he saw it.

What could have inspired such loyalty to an artistic style? Why did Eakins choose a life of disappointment and frustration? While in Europe, Eakins had seen and been impressed by the works of Gustave Courbet (Chapter 3, page 56) and other leading contemporary French artists. These artists, known as

---

SHARPENING YOUR SKILLS

Ask Questions

Before reading further, make a complete list of everything in the drawing *Gross Clinic*.

Continuing in your role as an imitationalist critic, look at this drawing and answer the following questions:

- Where is this scene taking place?
- How many people are pictured?
- What is each person doing?
- How do the actions of the single female figure set her apart from everyone else in the drawing?
- Who is the most important person in the drawing?
- How is this person's importance emphasized?
- To whom is this person speaking?
- How are the people dressed? Are their clothes appropriate for the occasion?
- Where does the light come from? What is its purpose?
- Finally, is this a successful work of art?

▲ Point to the most important figure in this drawing. How has the artist directed the
viewer's attention to this figure? How is the standing surgeon linked to the patient
and the surgical procedure he is explaining?

FIGURE 6.5   Thomas Eakins. *Gross Clinic*. 1875. India ink wash on cardboard. 60 x 48.6 cm
(23⅝ x 19⅛"). The Metropolitan Museum of Art, New York, New York. Rogers Fund.

Realists, had *rejected subject matter that glorified the past or romanticized the present. They painted everyday events the way these subjects really looked.*

However it was the work of the masters of the seventeenth century—Diego Velázquez, Franz Hals, and Rembrandt van Rijn—that Eakins never forgot. These master artists were his teachers. The lessons he learned from their works affected every drawing and painting he did during a career of forty years.

The realism valued by imitationalists is clearly shown in the drawing *Gross Clinic* that Eakins completed in 1875, four years after his return to the United States. The subject fascinated him so much that he did a large painting of it as well. It is often called his greatest work. The clinic was a natural subject for Eakins since he was fascinated by a study of anatomy and knew many of the staff at the clinic. He even required his students at the Pennsylvania Academy of Fine Arts to dissect human corpses as a way of learning how to draw and paint the human figure accurately.

The drawing shows a hushed operating room filled with attentive students. They are listening to a highly respected physician explain a surgical procedure. There is a momentary pause in the lecture. A woman, shielding her eyes with an arm, starts sobbing. She is a relative of the patient. The law at that time required a relative to be present during surgery. The doctor, ignoring her, stands with his back to the patient, still holding the scalpel with which he made the incision.

Many people objected to the blood on the scalpel and on the surgeon's hands. They said that showing the blood was tasteless and unnecessary. They didn't listen when Eakins explained that the blood was a vital part of the scene. The blood had to be shown exactly as he saw it. Eakins also studied geometry and perspective in order to draw accurately.

In one drawing that he did in preparation for a painting, he used perspective to reproduce as accurately as possible the reflections in rippling water (Figure 6.6).

Self-Portrait at the Age of Twenty-Two by Albrecht Dürer

As you continue to stroll through the crowded gallery, you are fascinated by what you can learn from drawings by studying their literal qualities.

Did You Know?

Eakins was humiliated when his painting of the *Gross Clinic* was rejected by the Philadelphia Centennial Exhibition. The painting was eventually put on display, but not with the other works of art. Instead, it was included with the Centennial's medical exhibits!

The realism that was responsible for isolation during his lifetime still sets Thomas Eakins apart, but in a completely different way. Today, he is widely regarded as one of America's most important artists.

You pause a moment to look at a small ink self-portrait by Albrecht Dürer (Figure 8.6, page 161). This drawing looks so lifelike that it must have been completed while the artist was studying his own reflection in a mirror. This fact would explain the unusually large hand delicately balanced as if he were holding a mirror in front of his face.

While you are admiring the precision in this drawing, you suddenly notice something quite surprising. Unless you had carefully studied the drawing, you would have missed it. You tell the people standing next to you to look at the drawing of a pillow included on the same sheet of paper.

They look puzzled, so you urge them to look at it more closely. "What do you see?" you ask. As they, too, see something in the pillow, they begin to smile. There, hidden among the wrinkles and shadows, are several strange facelike images.

Head of a Girl with Braids by Henri Matisse

What's this? Some people are waving to you and pointing to still another drawing. They want your opinions about it, so you hurry over to examine it. Clearly this drawing (Figure 8.8, page 164) is unlike any of the others you have looked at so far. As an imitationalist, how will you respond to this work? Can you say that it is lifelike, accurate, or detailed?

It is a drawing of a girl with braids, but it is hardly lifelike. It is little more than a simplified outline. The artist has made little effort to show volume or realistic detail.

▲ **What does this drawing tell you about the artist's approach to art? What can you learn from it that will be helpful in your own efforts to create art?**

FIGURE 6.6   Thomas Eakins. *Perspective Studies for John Biglin in a Single Scull.* Date unknown. Pencil, pen, and wash. 69.5 x 114.8 cm (27⅜ x 45³⁄₁₆"). The Museum of Fine Arts, Boston, Massachusetts. Gift of Cornelius V. Whitney.

You are disappointed with the drawing. It obviously lacks the literal qualities that you think are necessary in a successful drawing. It isn't surprising, then, that you reject it as unimportant.

The Last Respects by Henri de Toulouse-Lautrec

The next drawing on display (Figure 10.6, page 202) also seems unsuccessful to you. Although it is more realistic than the last work, it lacks the detail needed to make it look lifelike. Even so, you pause a few moments to look it over. Parts of the picture at least hint at reality. The face, for example, with its furrowed brow, heavy eyelids, and drooping mustache, belongs to a specific person who is clearly grieving. However, the face hasn't been drawn with light and dark values. As a result, it lacks the three-dimensional form of a real face.

You find another drawing in the gallery that is appealing because of its exciting use of literal qualities (Figure 6.7, page 117). However, glancing at your watch, you find that it is still quite early. If you hurry, you will have enough time to return to your studio to work on drawings of your own—imitational drawings, of course.

Did You Know?

In geometry, we learn that parallel lines will never meet, no matter how far they are extended. In **linear perspective,** *they meet at the horizon.* We consider the horizon to be at an infinite distance from the viewer. So we allow parallel lines to converge at an infinitely distant vanishing point. This idea works with some accuracy in drawings, but in real life the horizon is seldom far away. With your eyes about 4 feet (1.22 m) above the ground, the horizon is only about 2½ miles (4 km) away.

Artists at Work

■ INTERIOR DESIGNER

From Aesthetic Idea to Functional Space

"I've redecorated my room three times in the past two years and I'd love to design the interior of a big beautiful home, but are there really many job opportunities in interior design?"

Actually, the profession of interior design has grown rapidly over the past few years and promises new job opportunities in the future. Residential interior design is not the only outlet for your abilities. As a trained interior designer, you might be employed by one of a variety of companies and institutions to solve problems related to the function and quality of an interior environment. Architectural firms, furniture and department stores, design firms, and even government agencies are among the companies that hire full-time designers. Or, you might decide to be self-employed, working independently from your own studio.

Some designers choose to work exclusively with new buildings while others specialize in revitalizing existing spaces. Designing efficient and pleasant interiors usually involves more than simply redecorating walls and rearranging furniture as you did in your room. You might be asked to design a space using a feature such as a fountain, atrium, artwork, or unique piece of furniture as a focal point. Other jobs might require planning and coordinating all the interior arrangements of a building complex.

On larger projects, you would be involved with project evaluation, space planning, layout, work flow, and comprehensive design.

As a residential designer, you would work with individual clients, creating interiors for rooms, apartments, condominiums, or homes that fit each client's tastes, personality, and lifestyle.

To be successful as an interior designer, you must have a strong sense of design, color, form, and scale as well as an understanding of materials and methods. You need patience and an imaginative and creative approach to problem solving. Well developed communication skills and the ability to work with a wide variety of people are also necessary qualities. You must be sensitive to the tastes of your clients, yet sure of your own instincts. Also, you must be businesslike and well-organized to deal with mounds of paperwork: specifications, orders, esti-

mated costs, catalogs, contracts and administrative details. Lastly, you must have a full understanding of what it means to provide a service to others.

You must have a formal education from an accredited school to begin a successful career in interior design. Graduation from an accredited school with a degree or major in interior design, or graduation and diploma from a three-year professional school is necessary to become an associate member of the American Society of Interior Designers (ASID). Full membership requires a two-year apprenticeship under a professional designer after graduation.

Part-time positions in interior design studios are usually filled by college students. However, you can gain valuable experience by working in the home furnishings section of any department store. ■

▲ How does the expression of the woman at the far left suggest that the grandfather is only pretending to be angry? Does this make her an important part of this drawing? If your answer is yes, why do you think the artist did not emphasize her more?

FIGURE 6.7 Jean-Honoré Fragonard. *Grandfather's Reprimand.* c. 1770–1780. Gray-brown wash over black chalk on laid paper. 34.8 x 44.8 cm (13¹¹⁄₁₆ x 17⅝"). National Gallery of Art, Washington, D.C. The Armand Hammer Collection.

SHARPENING YOUR SKILLS

What Do You Perceive?

Before reading further, describe and judge the drawing in Figure 6.7. Share your description with classmates. In what ways are your descriptions similar and different?

CHAPTER 6 REVIEW

1. How do imitationalists judge drawings?

2. What are the literal qualities?

3. What clues in the drawing *Self-Portrait at the Age of Twenty-Two* (Figure 8.6, page 161) would lead you to believe that this artwork was completed while the artist was studying his own reflection?

4. Name three skills required of an interior designer.

▲ In what ways is the principle of variety demonstrated here? How has contrast of value been used to emphasize an important feature in this drawing? Compare this image with Figure 24, Color Section I.

FIGURE 7.1 Elizabeth Layton. *Self-Portrait Holding Rose with Thorns.* 1985. Pastel with pencil on paper. 45.8 x 18 cm (18 x 7"). National Museum of Women in the Arts. Gift of Wallace and Wilhelmina Holladay.

CHAPTER

Making Imitational Drawings

What most of us think of as realistic drawing is far from real looking (Figure 7.1). The term *imitational* drawing is more accurate because it refers to drawing that tries to *imitate* the way things actually look.

We would probably choose a photograph instead of an imitational drawing if we wanted a picture to show exactly how something looks. However even a photograph doesn't display things as we really see them. Why is this true? A photograph can show only two-dimensional shapes. It creates the illusion of objects in space only because we make judgments about their depth from clues such as perspective and shadows.

We also judge depth or distance by what biologists call **binocular vision**. *People and some animals look at things with two eyes, each of which sees distant objects from a slightly different angle.* Also, this angle changes as the objects move closer to us or farther away (Figure 7.2, page 120).

The brain translates information from these different angles into a distance or depth comparison. As a result, we see three dimensions—width, height, and depth—while a camera "sees" only two.

Like a photograph, imitational drawing creates an image on a two-dimensional surface; it can't make something look completely real. Yet the artist can create the illusion of depth by using his or her knowledge of proportion, negative space, perspective, and shadows to make the viewer "see" distance and volume. You will learn how to use these techniques in this chapter.

Objectives

After reading this chapter and doing the activities, you will be able to:

- Make drawings in which all shapes and spaces are in correct proportion to each other.
- Make freehand drawings in both one-point and two-point perspective.
- Make drawings that create the illusion of atmospheric perspective.

Terms to Know

binocular vision
caricature
center of vision
freehand drawing
heroic figure
one-point perspective
parallel perspective
station point
stippling
two-point perspective
wash drawing

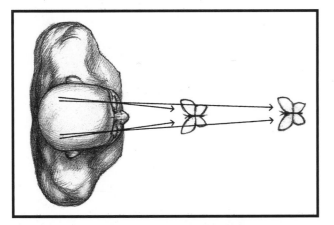

▲ **FIGURE 7.2** This diagram isn't biologically accurate, but it shows how stereoscopic vision helps us judge distances.

▲ **FIGURE 7.3** This drawing was done in rubbed graphite pencil by student Kevin Gentry.

roportion

In making drawings that look real, one of the first things to consider is proportion. We say that items in a composition are *proportional* if their sizes appear to be accurate when we compare them. Each object in a drawing must be the correct size in relation to all the other objects.

The size of a person's hands should be correct in relation to the face. The size of a brick in a wall should be correct in relation to the wall's height. The size of a house on a distant hill should compare correctly with the size of a daisy that is right in front of us.

Though we may not immediately recognize all of the items in the still life in Figure 7.3, we decide it shows a real setup because the popcorn popper, the pitcher, and the branch seem to be the right size in comparison with each other. That is, the proportions look correct. The shapes and forms are the correct size. The girl in the student sketch in Figure 7.4 looks believable because most of the proportions are correct.

How can we make things in a drawing look the right size? We measure their proportions, and then we place the objects or figures in the right positions.

Did You Know?

No photographic technique has been able to duplicate the human brain and eyes in creating images of objects in space. Stereoscopic photography, which combines two images into one, captures some of the illusion, but this photography is limited because it requires a controlled viewing position. The principle of binocular vision has also been used to design optical range finders for mapmaking and tank gunnery. Your local camera dealer will have stereoscopic cameras and viewers and books on double-image photographs.

Double-image (or 3-D) movies are another example of the use of the principle of binocular vision. These movies are produced by making one print of the film in warm colors and one print in cool colors. These prints are shown side by side. The audience is given glasses that filter out the warm colors for one eye and cool colors for the other eye. Because of binocular vision, the brain imposes one image on top of the other so that viewers see a third dimension, depth.

Did You Know?

Holograms, three-dimensional pictures produced by lasers, also try to duplicate human vision. They succeed to a degree because the image changes as the viewer moves from side to side. Holograms are still limited, however, because they can't capture images of moving objects or adequately portray natural color.

▲ **FIGURE 7.4**   Although art student Bryon Stamets drew this figure rapidly in charcoal, he didn't neglect correct height proportions.

Negative Space

Besides measuring, another effective way to determine correct proportions is to carefully study the negative space around and between the shapes of things you want to draw.

Examine the photograph of a typical still-life setup (Figure 7.5). Then look at the tracing of the negative spaces in the picture. If you can accurately draw the spaces where there are no objects, you can easily fill in the objects using correct proportions and placement. In fact, even if you don't fill in the objects, it will often be obvious what they are. When you start figure drawing, using negative space to check proportions can be particularly helpful. Start now making a habit of checking the negative spaces. Remember that space is an element of art, and it is important in all drawings.

▲ **FIGURE 7.5**   The drawing over the photograph of the still life outlines some of the negative areas.

SHARPENING YOUR SKILLS

Draw Negative Spaces

SUPPLIES
- Soft charcoal pencil
- Sketchbook

Practice drawing negative spaces in your sketchbook for a still-life setup. Make each drawing fill a page. Working too small will cause you to overlook important details. Do five or six drawings.

▲ FIGURE 7.6 Even an outdoor scene like the one in this student drawing can be rendered by drawing the negative shapes first.

SHARPENING YOUR SKILLS

Do a Large Drawing of Negative Spaces

SUPPLIES
- Vine charcoal
- Newsprint

Do a large drawing of the negative spaces from (for) a collection of objects or an outdoor scene. If the negative shapes between some objects near at hand overlap those between objects farther away, don't worry about it; draw all of the negative shapes transparently (as though you could see through them). Now go back to find the outlines of the positive shapes of the objects in the picture, and darken them. They should emerge clearly from overlapping negative shapes.

The purpose of this exercise is to practice proportion and placement for making imitational drawings. However, if you do the exercise carefully enough, you can produce an interesting formal drawing like the one in Figure 7.6.

Perspective

Another major technique to use when making imitational drawings is linear perspective. It is often called simply *perspective*.

As you will recall from Chapter 1, Renaissance artists developed the technique of perspective because of their increased interest in making drawings more lifelike. The goal of perspective drawing is to portray objects and figures the way they appear to the viewer's eye—to re-create the way the viewer actually sees what is being drawn. As you learned in Chapter 1, perspective is one way artists suggest the element of space. It creates on a flat surface the illusion of depth or volume for three-dimensional objects.

In Chapter 12, you will learn details about making accurate perspective drawings using special measuring tools. Architects, industrial designers,

---

Did You Know?

On the viewing deck at the top levels of the World Trade Center in New York City, the windows overlooking the city have small perspective drawings like the ones Albrecht Dürer made. The drawings are on clear sheets fastened to glass and help viewers locate the outlines of points of interest like famous buildings and bridges.

and engineers use perspective to make plans, sketches, and technical drawings. In this chapter, you will learn how perspective works so that you can make realistic drawings using careful estimation instead of exact measurements.

■ PERSPECTIVE DRAWING

When you create a perspective drawing you act as a magician of sorts. Like a magician, you create an illusion. A perspective drawing is the illusion of three-dimensional objects and spaces on a two-dimensional plane—the picture plane. Although some beautiful three-dimensional drawings have been done by etching or scratching a design on glass (See Figure 25 in Color Section I), your goal is not to create the illusion of space in this manner. Instead your goal is to create a similar illusion on paper. The paper becomes the picture plane.

For **freehand drawing**—*drawing done without measuring tools*—you must know how to estimate proportions the way you did in the still-life drawings you made. You also must know how to relate objects to the horizon.

■ THE HORIZON

As you know, the horizon is that line in the far distance where the earth and sky seem to meet. From most station points, or points of view, the horizon is hidden from us by trees, hills, or houses. You may have seen the horizon, however, while you were at the beach looking out to sea or when you were in the country on flat land. We see the horizon only because the earth is a ball and always curves downward away from where we are standing. Look at the diagram in Figure 7.7.

One important thing to remember about the horizon is that it always seems to be at eye level—that is, at the height of our eyes above the ground. If you move, it moves. You can prove this simply by looking at something outdoors that is a bit taller than you are and has no obstructions around it. The horizon will seem to pass behind the object. If you step up on a ladder and look over the object, the horizon will seem to move up to a point above the object. The horizon will always be *at your eye level*. That is why another name for the horizon line is *eye level line*.

▲ **FIGURE 7.8**   This picture was shot with a fairly low horizon or eye level so that you can see the underside of the eaves on the house.

If your eye level (the horizon) is above an object, you will see the top of the object. If your eye level is lower than the top of an object, you will be unable to see its top. You might however, see the underside of some sections, such as the eaves of a house (Figure 7.8). If you are drawing a person from a low eye level, you would see the undersides of the eyebrows, nose,

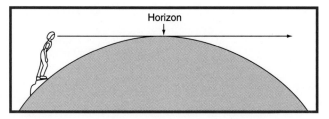

▲ **FIGURE 7.7**   This little figure on a greatly reduced earth shows the curvature that causes us to see a horizon.

▲ FIGURE 7.9 The shaded areas in this wash by art student Marc Ferrino show that you can see the undersides of nose, chin, and eye sockets because the horizon is low.

lips, and chin (the darkened areas in Figure 7.9). See the same work in Color Section I, Figure 26.

The second important thing about the horizon is that it passes behind every person and every object in a scene *at the same height above the ground*. To create a believable illusion of deep space, you must be consistent in placing people and objects in relation to horizon height. In the example in Figure 7.10, the horizon is about one yard (1 m) above the ground. This is the eye level of viewers who are squatting down and, in this case, the height of the camera taking the picture.

Did You Know?

In geometry, we learn that parallel lines will never meet, no matter how far they are extended. In linear perspective, they meet at the horizon. We consider the horizon to be at an indefinitely distant vanishing point.

This idea works with some accuracy in drawings, but in real life the horizon is seldom far away. If you are sitting in a chair at the beach with your eyes about 4 feet (1.22 m) above sea level, the horizon is only about 2½ miles (4 km) away. If you are on a mountain and your eyes are one mile (1.61 km) high, on a clear day you can see about 96 miles (163.6 km) before the horizon cuts off your vision.

▲ FIGURE 7.10 The horizon in this flat countryside is about 36" (1 m) high because that was the height of the camera that "saw" it.

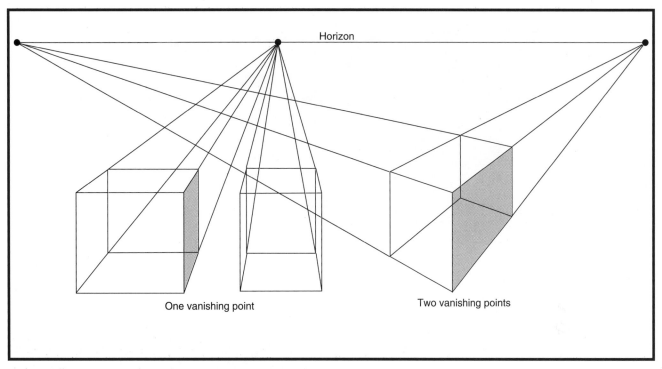

▲ **FIGURE 7.11**   **Two of the boxes are in one-point perspective, so they vanish to the same point on the horizon line. Turned at an angle to the picture plane and the viewer, the third box is in two-point perspective.**

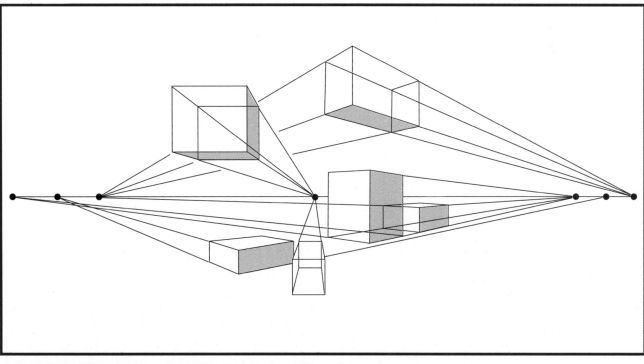

▲ **FIGURE 7.12**   **There can be as many different sets of vanishing points as there are objects at different angles to the viewer.**

◀ **The completed interior of this building looks very much like this perspective drawing of it.**

FIGURE 7.13 Paul Stevenson Oles, for I.M. Pei and Partners, Architects. East Building. National Gallery of Art, 1970. Courtesy of the artist and the Department of Architecture, Texas Tech University, Lubbock, Texas.

Vanishing Points

Study the diagram in Figure 7.11 on page 125. You will see that the lines defining the front edges of the box in the center of the drawing are parallel to the picture plane. They are also parallel to the horizon, so they are called *horizontal* lines. These lines, if they were extended, would never come together or vanish at any point on the horizon.

On the other hand, the lines that form the right and left edges of the box, moving away from us at a ninety-degree angle to the picture plane, would come together at a central vanishing point on the horizon. This *central vanishing point* is also known as the **center of vision**. The box to the left of the center box is sitting parallel to it, so its receding lines will vanish to the same vanishing point.

The receding lines of the box on the right, however, vanish to a set of *two* vanishing points because none of this box's sides are parallel to the horizon. Neither of its two vanishing points can be the same as that of the first box. There can be as many sets of vanishing points in a drawing as there are objects set at different angles to the picture plane or horizon. See Figure 7.12 on page 125 for an example of a drawing using several vanishing points. Which two boxes have edges that recede to only one vanishing point? Which two other boxes are sitting at the same angle?

Although many artists like to play with perspective to create special effects, it is a basic tool for making imitational art. As we mentioned earlier, perspective is often used by designers to show how a finished product will look. Figure 7.13 is an example of an architect's

▲ **Rebecca Berry showed the exterior of this home with a dramatically exaggerated perspective.**

FIGURE 7.14 Courtesy of the artist.

▲ **FIGURE 7.15** Student Holly Holt's fantasy features a house with exaggerated perspective and a gigantic brush. It was done in charcoal pencil.

perspective drawing of interior space. This rendering shows an addition to the National Gallery of Art in Washington, D.C. Designing interiors requires that concern be directed to the effective and satisfying use of space. An architect also relies on perspective to draw building exteriors like the one in Figure 7.14.

Perspective is also used in fine art drawings like the one in Figure 7.15. In this student drawing, the perspective is exaggerated, and an out-of-proportion object (the brush) is included to create an imitational fantasy drawing. How many vanishing points do you think this artist used?

■ ONE-POINT PERSPECTIVE

The simplest kind of perspective is the kind you see if you are standing in the middle of a long, straight road, sidewalk, or railroad track. Known as **one-point** or **parallel perspective**, *the lines formed by the sides of the road, walk, or track seem to come together at a vanishing point on the horizon also called the center of vision.* Notice how the lines converge in the drawing of the center box in Figure 7.11 on page 125. Notice also how the lines of the road in Grant Wood's drawing (Figure 27, Color Section I) converge in the same way.

In a one-point perspective drawing, all receding lines meet at one vanishing point. One-point perspective presents a dramatic view of deep space. The sides of objects facing the viewer are parallel to the picture plane. The sides of these same objects that move back into space seem to converge at a central point on the horizon directly in front of the viewer.

One-point perspective was popular during the Renaissance (Chapter 3, pages 46–51) and later with a group of twentieth-century artists called Surrealists (Chapter 3, page 62). It is also popular today with interior designers because it allows them to make renderings for their clients that show three walls of a room's interior. See this kind of rendering in Figure 7.13.

Look again at Figure 7.14. Is this architectural rendering done with one-point perspective? If not, how do you know this? Is the drawing in Figure 7.15 done with one-point perspective?

SHARPENING YOUR SKILLS

Draw a One-Point Perspective Scene

SUPPLIES
- Hard graphite pencil
- Art gum or Pink Pearl eraser
- Higher contrast drawing medium of your choice
- Ruler
- Lightweight bristol board

For a more advanced exercise in one-point perspective, pick a section of a street or the interior of a room you want to draw. Stand a bit behind a point you have chosen as your picture plane.

Put your horizon at a height you think is appropriate. A low horizon will make more objects overlap and cause objects to tower over the viewer, making a more dramatic picture. A high horizon will keep some objects from overlapping, sometimes making them harder to combine in a unified way, but it will allow for a larger view of the ground area being drawn. For an example of a student's one-point perspective, see Figure 7.16 on page 128.

■ TWO-POINT PERSPECTIVE

Look again at Figure 7.12 on page 125. Note that each box that isn't parallel to the horizon and picture plane has *two* vanishing points. Also, these vanishing points can't be used for any other box unless the two boxes are parallel to each other. Each of these boxes is drawn in what we call two-point or angular perspective.

Two-point perspective is often used by illustrators. *It lets them show things the way we usually see them—at odd angles, from various points of view— rather than squarely at a ninety-degree angle.*

◀ FIGURE 7.16 This is a one-point perspective of an interior art gallery space done by art student Cody Bush.

Two-point perspective uses all of the rules of perspective discussed thus far. The parallel edges or sides still come together at common points. These points are still on the horizon, and they are still called *vanishing points*. The horizon is still at eye level and still has the center of vision on it, but the center of vision is no longer a vanishing point, as it was in one-point perspective.

The best way to observe two-point perspective is to look at the corner of a rectangular box that is sitting diagonally to your picture plane. The box at the far right in Figure 7.11 on page 125 is a good example. Figure 7.17, however, is a rare three-point perspective of a box on which even the lettering is in perspective.

SHARPENING YOUR SKILLS

Draw a Building in Two-Point Perspective

SUPPLIES
- Charcoal or soft graphite pencil
- Drawing paper

For a more challenging two-point problem, draw a house or some other building that interests you—maybe your own home. Make sure the building is based on rectangles. You should be able to see enough of the building to have some idea of its plan. You will need to estimate and draw an outline of where the building rests on the ground.

After drawing the house, add trees, shrubs, fireplugs, and anything else in the environment you would like. Include as many interesting details as you wish, but remember to keep them in correct perspective.

Remember, work from the ground up, put everything in a basic box, and work transparently. Start lightly, and darken the visible lines later. Note that the top of the basic box for the building will be above your eye level (the horizon). The lines from the top of the nearest corner will angle down to the vanishing points instead of up (as for the box you drew in the previous activity).

Note: Leave a margin because you may wish to mat this drawing.

▲ **FIGURE 7.17** This box is on a sign in front of a store in Plainview, Texas. Can you find three vanishing points?

■ ATMOSPHERIC PERSPECTIVE

Atmospheric perspective creates the illusion of decreasing contrast in colors, values, and intensities across areas of deep space or distance. It can be achieved in an imitational work of art by gradually reducing the contrast in drawing objects that are farther away from the viewer.

For an example from nature, think about the way distant mountains look. They seem to be blue-gray and almost disappear into the sky. This effect is caused by layers of atmosphere that exist between the viewer and the mountains.

For an example of an atmospheric perspective, look at the detail of the Peter Rogers mural (Figure 7.18). This mural in the foyer of the Museum of Texas Tech University is one of the largest india ink and wash drawings we know of. A **wash drawing** is *made*

▲ This detail of Peter Roger's remarkable ink and wash mural shows the atmospheric perspective in the fading contrast of the distant mesas.

FIGURE 7.18 Courtesy of the Museum of Texas Tech University, Lubbock, Texas.

they seem to fade. The mesas appear blurrier and less distinct than the objects in the foreground. This kind of perspective is combined with linear perspective, created by reducing the size of the man and horse in the left middle ground.

You can also make atmospheric perspective work in drawings that don't involve deep space. Look at the student rendering of two blue-jean-clad figures in Figure 7.19. Observe how the nearest figure contrasts in value with the background as well as with the figure behind. This value contrast seems to move the figure forward.

Stippling is one technique used to create atmospheric perspective. **Stippling** means *rendering light*

with a brush and ink or paint thinned with water. This drawing is an excellent example of imitational art making use of both linear and atmospheric perspective. Note the reduction in value contrast as the eye moves from the foreground logs, rocks, and grass to the distant mesas at the right side. This change in value helps create the illusion of distance. The more air between the viewer and distant objects, the more

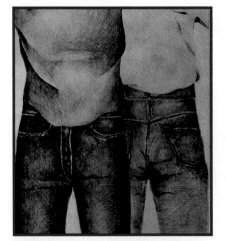

▲ FIGURE 7.19 Atmospheric perspective can be used even for short distances. Art student Ann Pikoraitis decreased the contrast for the more distant figure.

▲ FIGURE 7.20 Art student Mike Cherapek chose stippling to render atmospheric perspective in this evening snow scene.

◀ **Stippling is an appropriate technique for reproduction in newspaper advertising.**

FIGURE 7.21   Courtesy of *The University Daily*, Texas Tech University, Lubbock, Texas.

▶ **FIGURE 7.22**
**This patterned rendering
is by art student Christina Konen.**

and dark gradations in a drawing by making a pattern of dots. The dots are spaced closer together or farther apart to show value changes used to suggest space. A variation of stippling is called *patterned rendering*. In this case, tiny shapes are used instead of dots.

Figure 7.20 is an example of a stippled drawing by a student. Notice how the man in the foreground stands out because he contrasts in value with the background bushes. Also notice the lack of contrast when comparing the background building with the snowy evening sky. This lack of contrast is another example of atmospheric perspective.

Stippling makes it easy to render atmospheric perspective because you can work all over the drawing at once, adding more dots where they are needed. Remember, though, that it is easier to add dots than to remove them, so it is a good idea to make sketches just to decide where to place darker values.

Of course, the stippling technique is not limited to drawings in which the artist is concerned with creating the illusion of space. For example, examine the stipple drawings in Figures 7.21 and 7.22. The first drawing is a detail from an illustration for a newspaper advertisement. The drawing in Figure 7.22, while not totally realistic, is a student's drawing of a female head. It is a good example of patterned rendering. Another example, completed with tempera paint, can be found in Figure 28 in Color Section I.

Shadow

Light and shadow allow us to see objects as three-dimensional shapes that have volume—a vital ingredient of imitational art. (We see objects as volumes because there are no true lines in nature. Lines are considered one-dimensional, and in our three-dimensional universe, objects must have width and depth as well as length. What we call *lines* that define the edges of shapes actually have width, even if it is only the width of a pencil lead, and depth, even if it is only the depth of a grain of carbon dust.) We don't see people and objects because they have lines around them as they do in

SHARPENING YOUR SKILLS

Draw an Open Paper Bag

SUPPLIES
- Soft graphite or charcoal pencil
- Drawing paper

Wad up a paper bag and lay it on the floor with its mouth facing the light. Now draw the receding space inside it in values of shadow.

▲ Peter Hurd's sketch of publisher James Lorenzo Dow is a preliminary drawing for a large fresco. A fresco is a painting on the wet plaster of a wall.

FIGURE 7.23 Courtesy of the Museum of Texas Tech University, Lubbock, Texas.

▲ In this sketch of pioneer rancher, oil producer, and philanthropist Dora Nunn Roberts, Peter Hurd adheres to correct head and height proportions.

FIGURE 7.25 Courtesy of the Museum of Texas Tech University, Lubbock, Texas.

◀ In Peter Hurd's sketch of Dow's head, which shadows are form shadows and which are cast?

FIGURE 7.24 Courtesy of the Museum of Texas Tech University, Lubbock, Texas.

Make Value Studies of Crumpled Paper

SUPPLIES
- Soft graphite or charcoal pencil
- Drawing paper

To practice drawing shadows, crumple a large piece of paper and do some sketches of it from various angles, showing the different values. Now do a more finished rendering using a floodlight. See Figure 7.26 for an example.

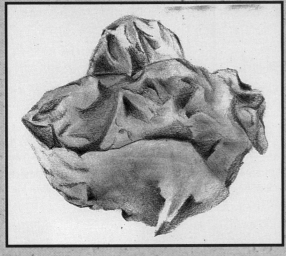

▲ FIGURE 7.26 Art student Alison Howze defined the planes and curves of crumpled paper in this shadow exercise.

drawings. We see them only because they reflect light. The amount of light they reflect from a particular side tells us which side is toward the light and which side is in shadow, or turned away from the light. Shadow gives us a clue about the thickness or volume of objects or the space they occupy.

In this text, we won't try to deal with the effects produced by multiple light sources. For most imitational drawing, a single light source like sunlight is adequate for a convincing illusion. Once you learn to use light from a single source to create shadows, using more than one light source is fairly easy to learn.

As you discovered in Chapter 5, there are two basic kinds of shadows: form shadows and cast shadows. Form shadows appear on any form on the side that is away from the light. Cast shadows fall on a surface that is shielded from the light by another object.

For shadow structure, look also at the sketches by Peter Hurd in Figures 7.23, 7.24, and 7.25. In Figure 7.23, the light source is in front of the model. You can see the broad treatment of light and shadow on the model's left arm.

Drawing the Human Figure

In any chapter about imitational drawing, there needs to be a section on the human figure because so many imitational drawings have people in them. On the other hand, there are many good figure drawing texts and books on the structure of the human form already available. For any detailed study, we recommend these. In this section, we will tell you how to get started drawing human figures and explain the most important human proportions.

When measuring proportions of figures, it is both traditional and practical to use the head as a unit of measure. This doesn't include the hair or a beard. In real life, most of us are about 7½ heads tall.

(Remember using a book as a unit of measurement when you sighted along your pencil? To draw figures, you will use the head to make similar length and width measurements to determine proportions.)

Look at Peter Hurd's sketch of Dora Nunn Roberts in Figure 7.25, and measure the model's head. Divide her overall height (head to toe) by the head measurement. You will find that she conforms to the 7½-head standard.

Even though the real-life human figure is 7½ heads tall, we suggest that you take a hint from ancient Greek sculptors and use an 8-head figure. Using eight heads as the standard would make only about a ½ inch (12 mm) difference in the head size of the model. This amount translates to less than ¼ inch (6 mm) on the head size of an 18 inch (46 cm) figure in a drawing.

The Greeks used eight heads to make what art historians call the **heroic figure**, *a figure that appears a little taller than life-sized.*

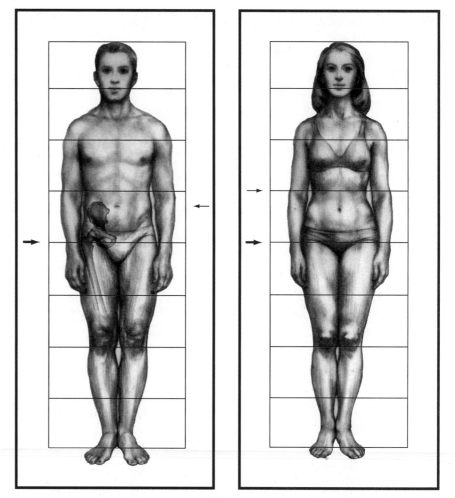

▲ **FIGURE 7.27** These figures are eight heads tall. The greater trochanter (indicated by the large arrow) is at the halfway point. The woman's waist is higher than the man's (see the smaller arrows).

Their sculptures of human figures represented their ideal of a body with perfect proportions. The heroic figure is an example of using exaggeration to express an idea. The other reason for using an eight-head figure is that eight is an even number. The halfway point between the top of the head and the ground becomes four heads. You can see the measurement on the chart with the sketch in Figure 7.27.

You can find this halfway point on your own body by pushing a finger into the side of your hip, low on the pelvis, at the point where the big bone of the leg, called the *femur*, is fastened. The projection you feel at the top of this bone is called the *greater trochanter.* It is the midpoint of your body. Knowing the midpoint of a standard figure is useful when you are drawing. Many people mistakenly think the waist is the middle of the figure.

On the other hand, if you want to put a man of about average height (72 inches or 182 cm) in a drawing with a horizon or eye level line 32 inches (80 cm) high, you know exactly how to place him. The horizon will pass behind him about 4 inches (10 cm) below the projection of his hip, the great trochanter. One-half of 72 inches (182 cm) is 36 inches (91 cm), and 4 inches (10 cm) above the horizon at 32 inches (80 cm).

Another look at the chart in Figure 7.27 will tell you that on the mature female figure the center of the chest is 2 to 2½ heads down from the top. On the mature male, the line below the large, flat chest muscles called the *pectoralis majors* is down about two heads, or slightly more, from the top.

Although the waist averages about three heads down from the top of the figure, its location varies.

◀ FIGURE **7.28**   The horizon is about 3 feet (91 cm) high. No. 5 is about 5'8". The referee and background players are on the finished drawing. No. 5 started as a gesture drawing on a tissue overlay just like the player guarding him.

When we refer to some people as *long-legged* or *short-legged*, we are usually referring to the height of their waists. People with high waists look as if their legs are long, but the fact is that legs take up about the same proportion of the figure on all of us. Check the comparison in Figure 7.27.

When a person's arms are hanging naturally at the side of the body, the tips of the fingers are somewhere near mid-thigh. This location varies, though, because people with high waists often have slightly shorter arms. The elbows usually line up with the waist.

Again, refer to the chart in Figure 7.27. Measure the legs from the bottom of the figure to the point where the knees bend. That point is just below the *patella*, or kneecap. The knees are about halfway between the greater trochanter and the ground, six heads down (or two heads up) on the classic figure.

Most of these vertical figure measurements are averages that can vary slightly from person to person. The two measurements that seem to be constant are the 7½ head height of the figure (which is exaggerated to eight heads in drawing) and the midpoint location of the greater trochanter.

Width proportions vary so greatly that averages are almost meaningless. They depend on such things as the shoulder muscles (*deltoids*), the mus-

cles that wrap around the sides of the rib cage (*latissimus dorsi*), and the amount of fat on the body. Individual differences in body width can always be measured by using the head as a proportional unit.

When standing erect a person's neck is not vertical; it extends forward. The head and face are vertical, but the axis of the neck will tilt, sometimes as much as thirty degrees.

There are subtle differences between male and female figures. Even though many women now concentrate on muscular development, the average male skeleton and muscles are heavier, and the male is somewhat more angular. On the whole, men are typically taller than women. Also, the male figure's hips are narrower than shoulder width, while the female's hip and shoulder widths are often about the same.

Figures to be placed in drawings can be drawn first on an overlay. They can then be refined while being reproduced on another overlay. Finally, they can be transferred onto the working surface in correct relation to eye level. (See Figure 7.28.)

Working on overlays instead of making corrections with an eraser allows you to draw more freely. You won't put anything on the surface of your finished drawing until you think it is ready, so you can start with a free, expressive sketch.

■ DRAWING THE HEAD AND FACE

Study the drawing of the woman in Figure 7.29. It is marked with the basic proportions of the head and facial features. The basic structural proportions of the head don't vary much from one person to another. The surface features, however, vary a great deal.

First, you must draw the basic proportions and the gesture of the head correctly. The gesture of the head is the way the person holds it. Drawing the surface features—eyes, nose, mouth, ears—will be easier after you have drawn the basic proportions of the head. You have probably seen cartoons of famous people that we instantly recognize. These cartoons are called **caricatures**, *portraits that humorously exaggerate people's features and ignore the basic structural proportions.*

When you measure the vertical proportions of a face, you may be surprised to find that the nose isn't at the halfway point. The *eyes* are. Between the highest point on the head and the underside of the chin, the center of the eyes is the halfway mark. Remember, we don't count the hair on top of the head or any beard.

Look at Figure 7.29 for illustrations of the following dimensions.

Forgetting the whole head for a moment and considering just the face, let's look at vertical dimensions. The face extends from the hairline to the bottom of the chin. The place we are talking about when we refer to *hairline* is the place where the top of the head turns downward to become the facial plane. The hairline isn't always the actual starting point for the hair.

The face divides vertically into three equal areas. One is from the hairline to the browline (the

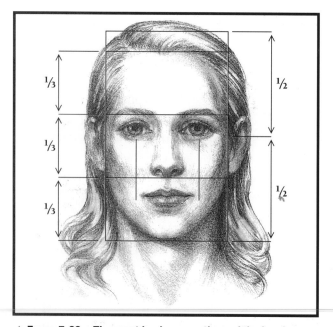

▲ **FIGURE 7.29** The most basic proportions of the head are usually the same. The facial plane is divided into thirds, with the brow and the base of the nose as dividing lines.

---

bony ridge over the eyes where the eyebrows are). The middle area is from the browline to the bottom of the nose, where it joins the upper lip. The bottom third is the rest of the face. These measurements hardly ever vary from face to face.

The length of the ears and the distance between the eyes don't vary, either. Ears are the length of that center third of the face between the brow and the base of the nose. (There are exceptions, of course. See the Did You Know? feature on facial dimensions.) The distance between the eyes is the width of one eye opening, corner to corner.

The rest of the face measurements do vary from one person to another, but we can at least give averages. One of the varying measurements is the

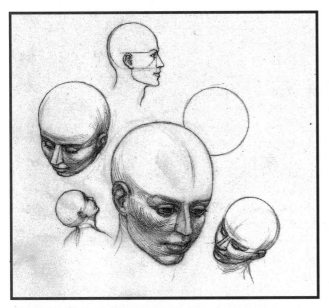

▲ **FIGURE 7.30 Starting the sketch with a ball for the cranium is a good way to capture the head gesture.**

SHARPENING YOUR SKILLS

Make a Full-Color Head Drawing

SUPPLIES
- Pastel chalks or pencils
- Drawing paper
- Felt pad, paper stumps, or tissue

For a more advanced head drawing, do a self-portrait or a portrait of a model in full color. Try the Impressionists' stippling technique, or blend colors by rubbing them with a felt pad, paper stumps, or tissue. Pick an appropriate paper for pastels. Be sure to spray your drawing when you are finished.

width of the mouth. On the average, the corners of the mouth are directly under the center of the eyes. The mouth opening is often a third of the way down between the nose and the bottom of the chin. It is also often lower than this, but seldom higher.

The distance between the outer corner of an eye and the outer point of the cheek bone is usually no greater than an eye's width. Of course, this distance varies with the size of the eyes and the width of the skull across the cheek bones.

The shape of the eye opening varies, but it is usually not shaped like an almond or like a football with points at both ends. On the average, the eye opening is arched at the top. The bottom line is somewhat straighter and usually turns up a little at the outer end.

The upper eyelid covers about the top third of the iris, the colored portion of the eye. The bottom of the iris meets the line of the lower lid. The upper lid often overlaps the lower lid at the outer corner, and the little notch of the tear duct may be seen at the inner corner. (In extremely old or ill people, the lower lid droops, exposing white beneath the iris. In amazement, joy, or fear, the eyes may be opened enough to expose white all around the iris.)

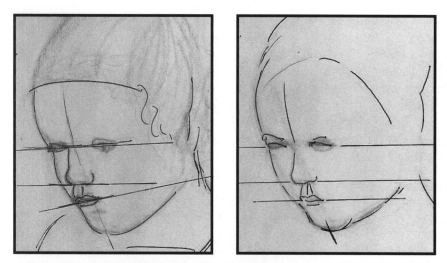

▲ **FIGURE 7.31**   To construct the final drawing at the right, student Julie Miller used preliminary sketches to correct the important alignments of eyes, nose, and mouth. She used graphite and white conte on toned paper.

Although the method isn't entirely accurate, a general way of constructing the head and capturing its gesture is to draw a ball for the cranium, the portion of the skull enclosing the brain, then hang frontal and lateral (side) planes on it. You can see examples in Figure 7.30.

Once this is done, the horizontal guidelines are added. They indicate the location of the eyes, from outer corner to outer corner, the base of the nose, and the mouth, from corner to corner. These lines pass through the skull—not around it—and they must all be parallel to each other. Otherwise the head you are drawing will look bent.

Notice that these horizontal lines seem to get closer together when the head is tilted forward or backward. In Figure 7.31, the first sketch of the child's head is corrected by the second one, which makes the horizontal lines parallel to each other. The finished drawing shows how close the lines are to each other and how the nose overhangs the upper lip because the head is tilted forward. The characteristic smallness of a child's features in relation to the cranium is also evident.

■ DRAWING PORTRAITS AND SELF-PORTRAITS

Before starting a portrait or self-portrait, look at the following examples made by students.

The student who drew the girl in Figure 7.32 certainly had the inspiration of a beautiful model. The drawing is an excellent example of a graphite and white conte rendering on gray charcoal paper. Also, you can see the careful measurement of proportion in the features and the parallel alignment of the eye axis, base of the nose, and mouth.

Steven Haynes's graphite rendering (Figure 7.33) is a Scholastic Art Award winner. He earned this award for the richness of surface, the emerging character of the form, and the interaction of line and value. It is definitely a portrait made to look like someone. However it also makes use of some deliberate distortions. We show it here in a chapter on imitational drawing so you can compare the basic head structure of a realistic head with this one with its slightly misaligned features, widely spaced eyes, and shortened forehead.

▲ **FIGURE 7.32** This drawing was done by student Ken Bussard with graphite and conte on toned paper

▲ **FIGURE 7.34** Christa Moser is the art student who did this sketch for a self-portrait. It is expressive but accurate.

Christa Moser's sketch (Figure 7.34) is another drawing that has as many expressive qualities as imitational ones. Note in these drawings that even with the exaggerations and expressive pastel chalk strokes, the anatomical proportions of the head are correct.

▲ **FIGURE 7.33** Art Student Steven Haynes distorted certain structural aspects of the head to make an expressive portrait.

CHAPTER 7 REVIEW

1. What illusion can the artist create to make the viewer "see" distance and volume?
2. Besides measuring, what is another effective way to determine correct proportions of a subject?
3. What is another name for the horizon?
4. Define the terms one-point perspective and two-point perspective.
5. What is stippling?

STUDIO 1

Measuring Proportions

SUPPLY

↠ **Pencil**

1. Let's try checking the proportions of some things in the room using a pencil as a measuring tool. Look at Figure 7.35. The student artist is using the pencil as a ruler to measure height or width. She is holding the measurement by using a thumbnail as the marker. Note that she holds the pencil at full arm's length from her eyes.

2. Lean a large book against the studio door, and step back a few feet. Using your pencil to measure, find out how many "books" high the door is when it is seen from where you are standing. Start by sighting down your arm and holding the pencil just as the student in Figure 7.35 is holding it. Be sure to extend your arm fully. Place the top of the pencil in line with the top of the book; then slide your thumbnail down the pencil without moving the pencil until the thumbnail marks the bottom of the book. Hold this measurement.

3. Extend your arm again. Now start at either the top or bottom of the door, and see how many books high it is.

4. Suppose you were making a drawing of the book and the door from where you were standing. You could decide

▲ **FIGURE 7.35**   Making comparative measurements with a pencil is a helpful technique. Remember always to keep your arm straight when sighting along the pencil.

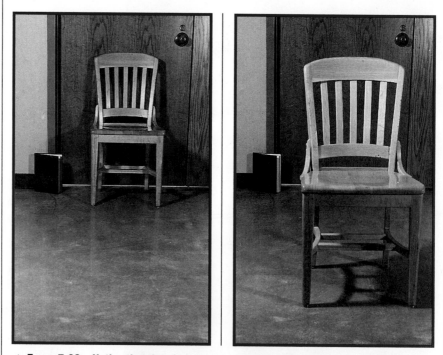

▲ **FIGURE 7.36**   Notice that the chair is much closer in the second photograph. You can tell this because the chair seems much larger and has moved downward in the picture.

STUDIO 1   *Continued from page 140*

how much of your paper you wanted the door to cover. Then, by dividing this height by the number of books it contains, you would know how tall to make the book. Of course, width comparisons may be made the same way. In fact, you can use the measurement of one object in a drawing (like the book's height) as a unit to measure everything in the drawing. As long as you are consistent in using it, you can even make up your own unit of measure and mark it on a pencil or brush.

5. Now put a chair next to the book and door. Return to

your drawing **station point**, *the viewpoint from which you made your first measurements*, and find out how many books high the chair is. Then move the chair to a point halfway between your station point and the door. What happens to the measurement?

If you changed the proportion (number of books of height) of the chair in a drawing, you would change the element of space by moving the chair closer. See Figure 7.36 for a photograph of how the chair changes proportions and placement in the drawing when it is moved closer.

6. Notice that you could also use the book to measure the distance between objects. For example, when the chair was moved closer, it became taller, but it also had to be moved down on the page.

7. You can use your pencil as a measuring stick whenever you draw. However, you must remember: *always remain at the same station point while you are measuring, and always measure with your arm fully extended.* Ignoring these two rules will make your estimates meaningless.

STUDIO 2

Proportional Drawings of a Still Life

SUPPLIES

➥ **Soft graphite or charcoal pencil**

➥ **Newsprint**

1. Make a still-life setup of three simple objects on a table. Using the measuring technique you have just learned, make an outline drawing of the shapes. Make them no bigger than 6 inches (15 cm) in their largest dimension.

2. Then make a drawing of the same objects after moving one of them much closer to you. Now move one of the other objects much farther

away, perhaps to another table, and make a third drawing. See the examples in Figure 7.37.

▲ **FIGURE 7.37** Making several drawings of a group of simple objects with some of the objects moved to different distances will help you learn to draw illusions of deep space.

STUDIO 3

Eraser Drawing of Negative Spaces

SUPPLIES

- ➡ Compressed charcoal, vine charcoal
- ➡ Sand pad, felt pad, or tissue
- ➡ Kneadable eraser, chamois skin
- ➡ One-ply bristol board
- ➡ Drafting tape
- ➡ Drawing paper, 17 x 22" (43 x 56 cm)

1. For this negative space rendering you will cover an entire sheet with a middle value of gray and then erase the areas where the positive shapes would be, leaving only the negative spaces. Use a still-life setup or objects from an outdoor scene for your subject.

2. First, rub the compressed charcoal against the sand pad. A sand pad is a small paddle with sheets of fine sandpaper attached at one end. Tap the sand pad lightly against a sheet of paper or into a shallow dish. Repeat this process until you have a small pile of carbon dust.

3. Use a sheet of paper at least 17 x 22" (43 x 56 cm) for this drawing. Fasten your paper on the drawing board at the corners with drafting tape. Sprinkle the paper lightly with carbon dust, then smooth the dust to an even coating of gray with the felt pad, a small pad of felt cloth, or tissue.

4. Next, squeeze your kneadable eraser into a ball. A kneadable or dough eraser can be squeezed into any shape. Transfer the eraser to your non-drawing hand, and continue to knead or squeeze it occasionally to keep it soft while you draw.

5. Now start drawing with your finger wrapped in the chamois skin. Chamois is a soft, flexible leather. It will pick up carbon dust from the paper almost like an eraser. Feel out the shapes of the objects in your drawing. The chamois will leave only the negative areas dark gray.

▲ FIGURE 7.38   Here student artist Brock Lareau covered black paper with the media of white chalk, then erased negative space until the still-life images of machine parts and bottles emerged. Also notice how well he reveals form and cast shadows.

Computer Option

With the Rectangle tool, create a box that covers most of the screen. Switch to the Paint Roller or Fill tool. Fill the box with a medium shade of gray (about 30 percent) or, if your program includes pattern fills or filters, with a coarse, grainy pattern. Now set the line width of the Eraser or Pencil tool to medium-thick and the color to white. Carefully "carve" lines and shapes of objects out of the gray or patterned "background."

6. Focus on the positive shapes. Shape your kneaded eraser to a point and draw the lightest lights on the positive shapes. Pick up more dust on the corner of your felt pad, and use the dust to build up darker darks where you see them. Finally, use vine charcoal to fill in the darkest darks in your drawing. When your drawing is finished, spray it with fixative.

TECHNIQUE TIP

Using Spray Fixative

Spraying drawings with fixative protects them from smearing. Drawings in just about any dry medium will be damaged by

STUDIO 3   *Continued from page 142*

rubbing against other surfaces if they aren't sprayed.

Spray fixative is sold both in aerosol cans and in small bottles with atomizers. Fixative in a bottle is applied by blowing through the atomizer.

Test the spray first on a piece of scrap marked with the same medium used in the drawing. Don't hold the spray device too close to the drawing. Keep the spray device 12 to 18 inches (30 to 46 cm) from it. Move the sprayer continuously. Several light coats are better than one heavy one. Fixative dries rapidly.

For your purposes, spray fixative labeled *workable* is best. This term means that after you lightly spray an area of a drawing, you can still draw on it.

✚ SAFETY NOTE

Using Spray Fixative Safely

Always use spray fixative outside the studio in a well-ventilated area—outdoors, if possible. Breathing fixative over a long period of time can be lethal. Try to hold your breath during the few seconds of each spraying.

STUDIO 4

Perspective Drawing on Glass

SUPPLIES

↦ **Lithograph pencil or china marker**

↦ **Glass or acrylic plastic**

1. A German Renaissance artist named Albrecht Dürer (Chapter 3, page 51) made perspective drawings on a piece of glass. You can do the same thing. Go to a window, and pick a scene some distance away that includes constructed objects such as sidewalks, fireplugs, part of a building, or a parked car.

2. Position yourself so that you can see this scene without moving your head. Ask an assistant to stand behind you and place a hand on either side of your head to help prevent you from moving.

3. Now simply draw the scene on the glass with your lithograph pencil or china marker.

▲ **FIGURE 7.39**   This girl has drawn the outline of some steps she sees through the window. She could continue to draw the whole scene on the glass (or picture plane).

The result is a perspective drawing. (See Figure 7.39.)

4. If your studio has no windows, use a piece of glass or heavy acrylic plastic in a picture frame. Make a tabletop still-life setup, and have two people hold the "window" steadily in front of it while you draw.

STUDIO 5

One-Point Perspective Drawing of Boxes

SUPPLIES

- Hard graphite pencil
- Art gum or Pink Pearl eraser
- Fiber-tipped pen or technical pen
- Ruler
- Lightweight bristol board
- Drawing paper, 17 x 22" (43 x 56 cm)

1. For this first one-point perspective drawing, use some rectangular boxes of different sizes as your subject. You will need a sheet of drawing paper that is about 17 x 22 inches (43 x 56 cm). Tape it on your drawing board so that it forms a vertical rectangle 22 inches (56 cm) high.

2. Place the boxes on a table, grouping some together and separating one or two from the rest. Place them so that the sides of each box are parallel to the sides of the table. Do your drawing looking squarely at the middle of one of the four sides of the setup, but with your body and drawing board turned a little to the side. Then you won't have to peer over the top of the drawing board.

3. If you stand up to draw, stay back from the table about 10 feet (3 m). If you draw seated, leave only half of this distance between yourself and the table. In any case, make sure your eyes are at least 17 inches (43 cm) higher than the tabletop.

4. Raise the paper on your easel until your eyes are level with a point about two-thirds to three-fourths of the height of the paper (one-third or one-fourth of the way down from the top). Use your ruler and pencil to draw the horizon. Don't forget that the horizon line represents your eye level. In fact, in this case, it *is* your eye level. Mark a point in the center of it. This point will be your center of vision and also the single vanishing point.

5. You have used your ruler for the last time on this drawing. You need to learn about drawing in perspective freehand—without the use of instruments other than your pen, pencil, eyes, and brain.

6. Using your pencil, draw the horizontal line for the front of the table as far down on the paper as it seems to be below your eye level (or horizon line). Make it extend almost from edge to edge of your paper. From each of the ends of this line, which are the front corners of the table in your drawing, draw a line to the vanishing point (center of vision).

7. These are the lines of the edges of the table that are going away from you toward the other end of the table. You can think of these lines as going *to* the vanishing point,

but it will be easier to draw them if you pull them *from* the vanishing point downward toward the corners.

8. Even if you draw lines toward the corners, you will probably make them crooked the first two or three times. Just be patient; use a soft eraser, like an art gum eraser or a Pink Pearl eraser, and correct them until you have two lines extending like railroad tracks to the horizon.

9. Of course, your table doesn't extend to the horizon, does it? So where should you cut it off? You will need to measure proportions. Select a unit of measure (perhaps the height of one of the boxes), and measure the length of the table by the pencil-sighting estimation method. Then draw another horizontal line cutting off the table at the proper distance up on your paper. If you have been somewhat accurate, you should have a good representation of the rectangular tabletop in one-point perspective.

10. Now draw the boxes with your pencil, using your eraser to make corrections. Start by looking at the boxes as though you could see through them to their bottoms resting on the table; draw these rectangular bottoms just as you drew the tabletop.

STUDIO 5   *Continued from page 144*

11. Of course, these rectangles will be smaller and will be placed differently, but their edges that are parallel to the receding edges of the table-top will vanish to the same vanishing point. Again, use the proportional measuring technique to locate the corners of the boxes on the table. Draw lines to the vanishing point, and cut off the boxes to the right length.

12. Next, raise vertical lines from the front corners of the boxes. Measure the front verticals of each box, and cut them off with the horizontal top edge. Then extend the top receding edges to the vanishing point. These edges are parallel to the receding edges of the table. The lines will cross the verticals you raised from the back corners of the boxes, and the boxes can be completed with one more horizontal. Each line you draw may need some corrections.

13. Since you have been carrying lines to the vanishing point and drawing transparently, many of your light pencil lines aren't a part of the objects you have been drawing. They are part of the total drawing, however, and they make it more interesting. Leave them undisturbed.

14. To complete your drawing, locate all of the lines defining edges of the table and boxes that are actually visible from your point of view. Darken these lines with either a fiber-tipped pen or a technical pen, such as a Rapidograph. A technical pen is usually used for *mechanical drawing* (drawing done with measuring tools), but it is also becoming popular with artists. Technical pens are fairly expensive, so read the directions carefully before using one.

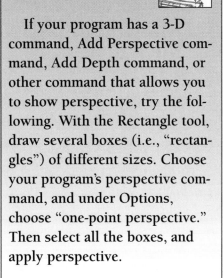

Computer Option

If your program has a 3-D command, Add Perspective command, Add Depth command, or other command that allows you to show perspective, try the following. With the Rectangle tool, draw several boxes (i.e., "rectangles") of different sizes. Choose your program's perspective command, and under Options, choose "one-point perspective." Then select all the boxes, and apply perspective.

TECHNIQUE TIP

Using the "Basic Box" in Perspective Drawing

Before doing any perspective drawing, you should learn three important procedures:

1. *Put each object in the drawing in a basic box.* This basic box should be square or rectangular and just large enough to contain the object that you want to draw. The farthest extended points of the object should just touch the sides of the box.

2. *Draw the shape of each basic box and each object on the ground or floor first.* You can raise vertical lines from the corners of the box, which you have drawn in perspective on the ground or floor. Put a lid on the top, and start drawing the object inside.

3. *Draw everything transparently.* Drawing the lines and shapes that would normally be hidden by other shapes is a good idea in any drawing because it makes you understand the structure of objects. This technique is required to make an accurate perspective drawing so that you can find correct proportions of objects defined by a basic box.

STUDIO 6

Two-Point Perspective Drawing of a Box

SUPPLIES

- Hard graphite pencil
- Art gum or Pink Pearl eraser
- Fiber-tipped pen or technical pen
- Ruler
- Lightweight bristol board
- Drawing paper, 17 x 22"
  (43 x 56 cm)

1. Make your own two-point perspective drawing, using a rectangular cardboard box as a subject. Put the carton on the table with one corner nearest to you. Remember that the horizon is at eye level. You will be able to see that the top and bottom edges of each side would seem to come together if they were extended to points on the horizon. There are two vanishing points—a right one and a left one—as in the diagram in Figure 7.40.

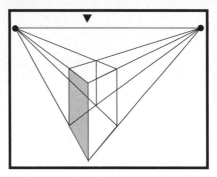

▲ FIGURE 7.40   This box is distorted because the vanishing points are too close together.

2. Can you tell what is wrong with the box in Figure 7.40? It is distorted. The parallel edges come together too rapidly. The front corner looks as though it is about to fall right out of the picture toward us.

3. This kind of distortion makes the drawing look like a photograph shot with a wide-angle lens. Sometimes you

will want to use this kind of exaggerated perspective for dramatic effect—but not if you are trying to draw imitationally. This drawing is distorted because each of the vanishing points is much too close to the center of vision—and to the other vanishing point.

4. In Figures 7.40 through 7.42, the center of vision is indicated by a small vertical mark on the horizon above the box. If you look again at the box you are drawing, you can tell that the vanishing points in your drawing should be much farther apart than the ones in Figure 7.40. Placing vanishing points too close together is a common error for beginners and, unfortunately, for some more experienced artists, also.

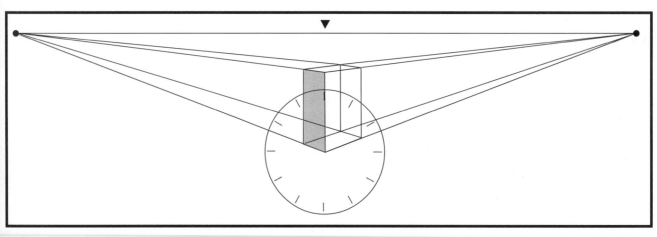

▲ FIGURE 7.41   It is helpful when sketching a basic box or rectangular object to use an imaginary clock face at the nearest corner. This technique is derived from a system recommended by artist Dick Freeman.

STUDIO 6   *Continued from page 146*

5. For your drawing, you will first draw the box in light pencil lines. Indicate the horizon and vanishing points, and in your first drawing place the box well below the horizon. If you turn the paper sideways, you may have enough space to get both vanishing points on the paper where you can see them. If not, tape two sheets together.

6. How do you know where to locate the vanishing points? If you look at Figure 7.41, page 146, you will see that the nearest corner of the box has a dial like a clock face over it. With the lower front corner of the box in the center of the clock, the right bottom line recedes toward the horizon at a point between two and three o'clock. The left bottom line goes back at an angle between nine and ten.

7. You can look at your box and make the same kind of estimate. Then draw the lines from a point where you have decided the corner should be all the way to the horizon. Now you have located the right and left vanishing points.

8. To help you estimate the proper angles, you can cut a 4-inch (20 cm) circle in a piece of cardboard and put marks along the edge of the circle like those on a clock face. You can then look through the circular hole, centering the corner of the

box in the circle, and estimate the angles at which the lower edges of the box recede. Remember to hold the circle straight up and down while you look through it.

9. Now check the drawing you are making, and ask yourself if you will be seeing the box at an angle you like. Will you be seeing enough of the side you want to see, or does it need to be turned a little? Finding the right angle would be important if you were drawing a house with doors, windows, and other details on the sides, or if the box you are drawing has lettering on one side that you want to be readable in the drawing.

10. The box in Figure 7.42 is the same size as the one in Figure 7.41, and the center of vision is in the same spot. The box

in Figure 7.42, however, has been turned farther to the right (or clockwise, if you were seeing it from above).

11. This angle has pushed the right vanishing point far out to the right. It went off the page, in fact. Of course, at the same time the left vanishing point came in closer to the center of vision. The right and left vanishing points are still the same distance apart, and the box is still seen in undistorted perspective. Now, however, we see a broader view of the right side of the box, while the left side has decreased in size. How has the angle of the front corner changed in the clock dial?

12. After you have decided that you have your box at the right angle and the horizon is at the height you want, draw

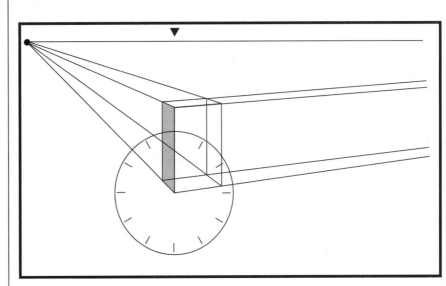

▲ **FIGURE 7.42** **When the box is turned at a different angle to the viewer, the edges "tell a different time" on the clock face.**

STUDIO 6 | *Continued from page 147*

the outline of the box where it rests on the table. Pick a spot for the front corner, and estimate the angle of the corner. Extend lines to the vanishing points.

13. Use your pencil to measure the proportional distance along the bottom edge of the box to the rear corners on each side. You can use any unit of measure you wish as long as you use it consistently. Stay in the same spot to measure everything.

14. Now raise verticals from the corners of your box in the drawing. Remember that you are making a transparent drawing. Measure the height of the front corner of the real box with your pencil. Cut off the vertical lines at the front corner of your drawing at the correct proportional height. From this height you can extend lines to the right

and left vanishing points that will automatically locate the top rear corners of the box in your drawing. Look at Figures 7.43 through 7.45 for step-by-step illustrations of this process.

15. When your drawing is complete, leave all of the pencil lines visible. Darken with ink the lines defining the edges that you can use on the real box.

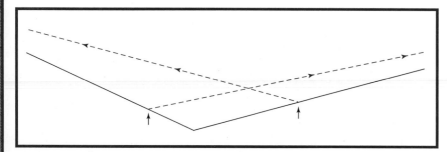

▲ FIGURE 7.43   To find the back of the box, cut off the lines that extend to the vanishing points.

▶ FIGURE 7.44   With the floor laid, verticals can be raised at the corners of the walls.

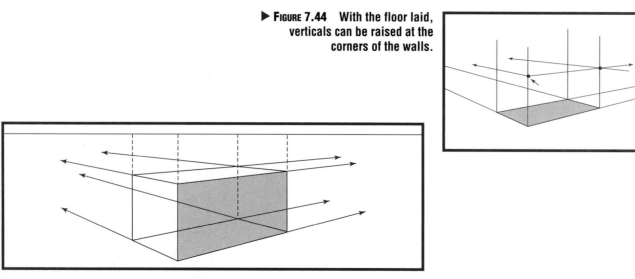

▲ FIGURE 7.45   Completed box in two-point perspective.

STUDIO 7

Atmospheric Perspective Using Stippling

SUPPLIES

→ **Graphite or charcoal pencil**

→ **See-through vellum**

→ **Drafting tape**

→ **Hard graphite pencil or ballpoint pen**

→ **Any wet drawing medium**

→ **Bristol or illustration board**

1. For this activity, choose a scene involving deep space, with objects or people in the foreground, middle ground, and background as subject matter. You will create atmospheric perspective by using stippling.

2. It is a good idea to do some sketches to practice showing values before starting the rendering. You don't have to use stippling in the sketches, though. A preliminary drawing on see-through vellum will also help you design your finished work. There should be no lines left in a stippled rendering because they would be out of character with the rest of the drawing. You can transfer the lines lightly from your practice drawing to bristol or illustration board (another type of heavy drawing paper) and erase them later.

3. To transfer your original artwork, turn the preliminary drawing into carbon paper by rubbing graphite or charcoal on the back. Or if you don't want to damage your preliminary drawing, you can rub carbon all over the back of a third sheet. Then slip the third sheet between the preliminary drawing and the paper to be used for the finished rendering.

4. In either case, tape the preliminary to the finished sheet firmly at the top with drafting tape. Use only a few strips of tape at the bottom so you can lift the preliminary occasionally to check the transfer. Trace the lines of the preliminary drawing with a hard pencil or a ballpoint pen. Remember to place the carbon-rubbed side *down* against the surface of the paper for the finished rendering.

5. After making the transfer, start rendering the lights, darks, and gradations with a wet medium. Stippling is usually done with ink, but almost any wet medium will work. Use a fiber-tipped pen or any instrument to apply paint or ink. Whatever tool you choose, practice stippling on the side to see how to make good light-to-dark gradations.

6. With single-sized dots, only the space between them controls the value. With dots that vary in size, the control of transition from light to dark is easier. Of course, when the dots get close enough to blend, you have white dots on a black ground—and, finally, solid black.

7. Don't make the dot pattern too important by letting the dots get too large and obvious. In that case, a formal element would overpower the subject matter. Look at the formal drawing in Figure 7.22 on page 131 (the patterned rendering) again. In imitational drawing, the subject matter shouldn't be overshadowed by any formal element.

8. When working with atmospheric perspective, remember that you can stipple in negative spaces as well as in positive shapes to control contrast. Look again at Figure 7.20 on page 130.

Note: You may want to mat this drawing, so leave a margin.

Computer Option

Draw a simple indoor or outdoor scene, or call up from disk such a scene that you previously created. If your program includes textured patterns either as fills or through Filter commands, apply a dense pattern to objects and shapes in the foreground. Choose a pattern where the dots or pixels are separated by more space, and apply this to objects further back in the picture. The shapes or objects furthest back in the picture should have a pattern in which dots are more widely spaced still.

STUDIO 8

Perspective, Shadows, and Reflections

SUPPLIES

⇨ Soft, medium, and hard charcoal pencils

⇨ See-through paper or vellum

⇨ Drafting tape

⇨ Hard graphite pencil or ballpoint pen

⇨ Medium-surface bristol board

1. Select a subject for a drawing with perspective, shadows, and reflections. You can use a setup with fruit, cylindrical objects, and drapery, like the one in Figure 7.46, or a single ordinary object like the toothpaste tube in Figure 7.47. Another possibility would be to draw a one-point perspective with furniture and figures, like the detail of a graphite pencil drawing in Figure 7.48 on the next page. Still another possibility would be to imagine your own subject matter. Use either a still life with different objects, textures, and reflections; a small object, enlarged to show details; or an interior with objects and figures in which you use low eye level and reflections on a floor, pool, or mirror.

2. Rough out your ideas first in thumbnail sketches using different points of view, placement of objects, and location of light sources. Make sketches even if you are working from a setup.

▲ FIGURE 7.46   Drawing student Annette Berlin showed unusual skill with the charcoal pencil in this drawing.

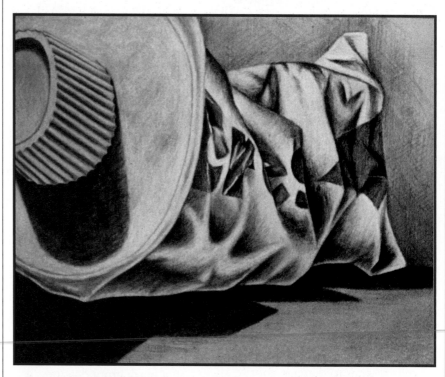

▲ FIGURE 7.47   A dramatic view of a small object made to fill the working area by art student Mike Cherapek.

STUDIO 8   *Continued from page 150*

3. Keep the design flexible until you are ready to start the final drawing. Be willing to move or change items to create a better composition. If you use overlays of see-through paper or vellum, you won't be tied to a certain composition. You can easily make changes until you are pleased with the design (see Figure 7.49).

4. When you are satisfied, transfer the overlays to the final drawing as you did for the stippling activity (see page 149). Render the design with shadows and reflections. Remember to work all over the rendering, doing large, major areas of shadow first, then the details.

5. To learn about reflections, bring a mirror to the studio, and place objects next to it or on it. Study their reflections. Then look at a curved reflective surface, such as the coffee pot in Figure 7.46 on page 150, or a rippled one like the floor in Figure 7.48. See how these surfaces reflect the objects. Don't try to draw reflections in window glass and showcases until you have had some experience with "pure" reflective surfaces such as the mirror. Glass partly reflects images, but it also partly transmits images of whatever is on the other side. The mixture of two images is harder to render.

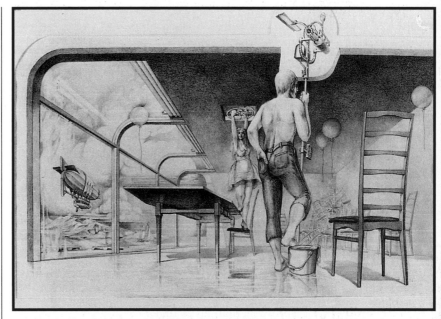

▲ **FIGURE 7.48**   Detail of a graphite pencil drawing on white vellum.

▲ **FIGURE 7.49**   Preliminary see-through paper overlay used in composing and correcting the drawing in Figure 7.48.

Evaluation

■ APPLYING ART FACTS

On a separate sheet of paper, write the term that best matches each definition given below.

1. The criteria used by formalists to determine the success or lack of success realized by a work of art.

2. The term used to indicate that the sizes of objects in a composition look correct and lifelike.

3. The viewpoint from which an artist makes his or her first measurements for a drawing.

4. A way in which artists create the illusion of depth or three-dimensional volume on a flat surface.

5. In a picture, the place on the horizon where parallel lines going away from the viewer would finally come together.

6. A type of drawing made with a brush and ink or paint thinned with water.

7. A technique used to create light and dark gradations in a drawing with a pattern of dots.

8. Shadows on any form that appear on the side that is away from the light.

■ SHARPENING YOUR PERCEPTUAL SKILLS

CHAPTER 6

1. Select a drawing in this or any other book and describe its literal qualities to the class as accurately as you can. Do not allow other students to see the drawing and do not repeat your description. Ask students to complete a sketch based on your description. Compare the completed sketches to the

drawing described. Do they provide evidence that you presented a thorough and detailed description of the literal qualities?

2. Examine Eakin's drawing of *Gross Clinic,* Figure 6.5 on page 113. What would you add, take away, or change if you were the artist? How would you defend your decision?

3. Find a realistic drawing in a library book and show it to the students in your class for 15 to 20 seconds. Ask each student to identify something noted in the work. Compile a list of these items on the board. Then produce the work again and determine if all the major items have been accounted for.

CHAPTER 7

1. Make a drawing of a room in your house or school. Use your comparative measuring skill to ensure that the doors, windows, and objects in the room are in correct proportion to each other.

2. Draw a one-point perspective of a scene you have observed in your neighborhood. Make sure that the horizon is at your eye level. Leave the lines for basic boxes and the lines going to the vanishing point lightly visible in the drawing. Darken the visible lines of actual objects.

3. Complete a drawing demonstrating two-point perspective using full color and variations of light and dark values. Use colored pencil or chalk. This perspective drawing must include at least one familiar manufactured object (vehicle, piece of furniture, farm machinery).

4. Do a stippled drawing that clearly illustrates atmospheric perspective. The scene you

choose to draw should include objects placed at different locations in deep space. Complete several preliminary drawings to help you design your finished drawing.

5. Do a drawing of a still-life setup. Use colored pencils to recreate the natural colors observed in the still life objects. Pay particular attention to the form and cast shadows.

6. Complete a drawing of a model using a proportional chart nine heads tall. Complete a second using a proportional chart of ten heads. Compare these drawings with the one you did using a chart eight heads tall. Can you think of any reasons why you might wish to make drawings with distorted proportions?

7. Do a two-point perspective drawing in pencil that includes at least three human figures. These figures should be in correct proportion and perspective. Develop the figures on a see-through vellum overlay and refine them on other overlays. Transfer them to the finished drawings in proper relation to the horizon.

■ MAKING CONNECTIONS

1. **FINE ARTS.** Examine the artworks illustrated in Chapter 3. Can you identify a work in which the artist clearly exaggerated the proportions of his human figures?

2. **LANGUAGE ARTS.** Use the drawing by Fragonard in Figure 6.7 on page 117 as your inspiration for a humorous short story. Make certain that Fragonard's drawing illustrates an important event in this story.

3. **HISTORY.** Fragonard's drawing (Figure 6.7, page 117) was completed at the same time important events were taking place in America (1770–1780). Visit your school library and prepare a report on this significant period in our history. Present your report in class.

4. **LITERATURE.** Look again at Eakin's drawing (Figure 6.5 on page 113) showing real people involved in an actual event. Can you think of a novel (or a short story) that makes use of this same realistic style? Prepare a short outline of the plot and present this orally in class. Explain why you think it would be appropriate to refer to the novel as "realistic."

■ THINKING CRITICALLY ABOUT ART

1. **DESCRIBE.** Look through magazines and cut out pictures that show deep space with one- and two-point perspective. Design a bulletin board display in which you provide a brief description of both types of perspective. Illustrate your display with the magazine pictures.

2. **ANALYZE.** Examine the illustrations in Chapter 3 with the art element of space in mind. Find a work that shows deep space. Find another that uses shallow space. Explain how the artist's use of space in these works contributes to its visual effectiveness.

3. **INTERPRET.** How could an artist's decision to use deep or shallow space affect the mood or feeling of his or her drawing? Find a drawing in this or any other book which demonstrates how the mood or feeling is enhanced by the artist's decision with regard to space.

4. **JUDGE.** Examine the drawings by Eakins (*Gross Clinic*, Figure 6.5, page 113) and Fragonard (*Grandfather's Reprimand*, Figure 6.7, page 117) in Chapter 6. Assume that you are an imitationalist and find yourself in a position to recommend that one of these works be purchased by a local museum. Which of these drawings will you recommend? What arguments will you use to defend your decision?

Structural Drawing

CHAPTER 8
Understanding and Judging Design Qualities

CHAPTER 9
Making Formal Drawings

▲ Compare this drawing with *Spanish Steps* created by Panini on page 10. What art elements and principles would you discuss if asked to analyze Guardi's drawing?

Francesco Guardi. *The Stairway of the Giants, Ducal Palace, Venice.* Eighteenth century. Pen and brown ink, brown wash, over red chalk, on paper. 26.4 x 18.6 cm (10⅜ x 7⁵⁄₁₆"). The Metropolitan Museum of Art, New York, New York. Rogers Fund.

Unit 3 emphasizes the design (also known as formal or structural) qualities, which are the aesthetic qualities valued most by formalists. As you learn to understand and create structural drawings, you will learn how other artists have used the elements and principles of art to produce drawings that are effectively organized.

In Chapter 8, "Understanding and Judging Design Qualities," you will play the role of a formalist critic. You will analyze several drawings and make judgments about them based on their design, or formal, qualities.

When you return to the studio in Chapter 9, "Making Formal Drawings," you will use what you have learned through art criticism and history to create structural drawings. All types of drawings—including those whose purpose is to imitate reality or express emotion—rely on an effective use of design qualities.

▲ Matisse completed a number of large pen and ink drawings of a Rumanian blouse embroidered with brightly colored threads. Note the line patterns on this drawing. How were those patterns created? Does this figure appear to be lifelike? If not, does this make the work unsuccessful? Why or why not?

FIGURE 8.1 Henri Matisse. *The Rumanian Blouse.* 1937. Pen and ink on paper. 63 x 50 cm (24¹³⁄₁₆ x 19¹¹⁄₁₆″). The Baltimore Museum of Art, Baltimore, Maryland. The Cone Collection, formed by Dr. Claribel Cone and Miss Etta Cone of Baltimore, Maryland.

Understanding and Judging Design Qualities

In Chapter 6 you were asked to assume you were an imitationalist. You were supposed to describe and judge several drawings you saw at a gallery opening according to their literal qualities. Were you comfortable in that role or did you experience some uncertainty as an imitationalist? You might have been uncertain because you knew that imitationalism overlooks many important qualities of art.

In this chapter, you are invited to become an inflexible formalist—and you may become uneasy again. You are asked to focus on certain aesthetic qualities and ignore others. A **formalist**, *considers only the design qualities—the elements and principles of art—to analyze and judge drawings.* (You might want to briefly review the discussion of these elements and principles in Chapter 1.)

objectives

After reading this chapter and doing the activities, you will be able to:

- Explain how a formalist judges drawings.

- Analyze drawings to determine how artists have used the elements and principles of art.

- Judge drawings based on their design qualities and give reasons for your judgment.

Terms to Know

design relationships
formalist
prototypes

You, the Formalist

Being a formalist won't be easy because analysis, the second of the art-criticism operations, is often difficult. Don't become discouraged, however. With practice, you will develop more skill at analyzing the elements and principles in drawings. Look at Figure 8.1 on page 156, and see how many elements you can distinguish and name the principles employed. You may even surprise yourself by being able to see how artists use these elements and principles to achieve an overall sense of unity in their compositions.

■ USE THE DESIGN CHART

The design chart below will help you examine drawings as a formalist would. You can use it to identify the elements and principles and the ways they are combined in drawings.

Of course because you are a formalist, you prefer works of art that emphasize the design qualities. From an article in the local newspaper you learn that drawings of this kind will be displayed at a nearby gallery. You decide at once to attend.

Gas by Edward Hopper

The gallery is jammed with people. They are voicing their opinions about the wide assortment of artworks on display. The room becomes silent when you enter; everyone is eager to see how you will react to the drawings. People edge closer as you pause before a black conte crayon drawing by the American artist Edward Hopper (Figure 6.3 on page 111). They watch as you study it closely.

Several of the onlookers are waiting for your reactions to the Hopper drawing. What will you

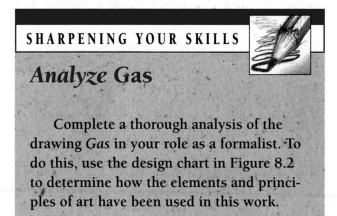

SHARPENING YOUR SKILLS

Analyze Gas

Complete a thorough analysis of the drawing *Gas* in your role as a formalist. To do this, use the design chart in Figure 8.2 to determine how the elements and principles of art have been used in this work.

▼ **FIGURE 8.2   Design Chart.**

DESIGN CHART		PRINCIPLES OF ART								
ELEMENTS OF ART		Balance	Emphasis	Harmony	Variety	Gradation	Movement/ Rhythm	Proportion	Space	
Color	Hue									
	Intensity									
	Value									
Value (Non-Color)										
Line										
Texture										
Shape/Form										
Space										

UNITY

mention first? Certainly you won't refer directly to the drawing's subject matter. No, as a formalist you are much more concerned with the way the drawing is put together, or how the artist made use of **design relationships**, *the way art elements and principles are combined.* You might begin your analysis by stating that the artist used the principles of harmony, emphasis, variety, and gradation to organize the elements of shape, value, line, and space.

Of course you are ready for the puzzled looks on the faces of some in your audience. After all, not everyone is familiar with formalism. So you decide to go into more detail. You will explain how different combinations of elements and principles create an overall sense of unity or wholeness in the drawing.

You begin your explanation by pointing out the three white circular shapes on top of each gas pump. These same circular shapes are repeated in the contours of the two dark areas (trees) to the far left. This repetition helps tie the composition together resulting in harmony (Figure 8.3). The artist has also enhanced harmony by repeating rectangular shapes in the gas pumps, curbs, sign, and building (Figure 8.4).

When everyone understands how the principle of harmony has been used to organize the element of shape, you ask if anyone can identify the most important shapes in the drawing. Most members of your audience find these shapes easily. Several immediately point to the gas pumps.

Then you ask how the artist emphasized these gas pumps. After a pause, one member of the group observes that their light and medium values contrast with the dark and light values behind them. Someone else suggests that the gas pumps are important because they are placed directly in the center of the composition. By emphasizing the gas pumps in this way, the artist pointed out the function of the isolated building beside the narrow road. It couldn't be mistaken for a grocery store, a fast-food restaurant, or a motel.

Next, you draw the group's attention to the different kinds of lines in the drawing. You make sure that everyone notices how the vertical lines that are repeated in the gas pumps, tree trunks, sign post, and building add to the picture's harmony. These lines, however, contrast with the diagonal lines of

▲ FIGURES 8.3, 8.4 Shown above are two diagrams of *Gas* by Edward Hopper. The repetition of circular shapes (top) and rectangular shapes (bottom) contributes to the harmony of this composition.

the road and curbs. The vertical and diagonal lines also contrast with the horizontal lines of the treetops, sign, and service station. The contrasting lines add variety and visual interest to the drawing.

Seeing that your audience is now involved in analyzing Hopper's drawing, you explain how the artist created the illusion of depth or space. To do so, you introduce the principle of gradation. Space is suggested by the gradual narrowing of the road's shape. You point out how the road gradually narrows as it extends back into the drawing until it disappears from view at the base of the trees. Space was also accented by the gradual change in the sizes of the circular shape at the top of each gas pump. (See the design chart with all of these design relationships in Figure 8.5 on page 160. Of course, there are more design relationships. Take time to look for them before continuing your reading.)

DESIGN CHART		PRINCIPLES OF ART							
ELEMENTS OF ART		Balance	Emphasis	Harmony	Variety	Gradation	Movement/ Rhythm	Proportion	Space
Color	Hue								
	Intensity								
	Value								
Value (Non-Color)			X						
Line			X		X				
Texture									
Shape/Form				X					
Space						X			

UNITY

▲ FIGURE 8.5   Refer to the text for an explanation of the design relationships in Edward Hopper's drawing *Gas*.

Since you have found most of the important design relationships in the Hopper drawing, you prepare to move on. Someone asks if you think the drawing is a good work of art. Before answering, you remind yourself that as a formalist you think the formal, or design, qualities are the most important of the aesthetic qualities. You then ask yourself if the artist used formal qualities effectively in this drawing. Were the elements and principles of art combined to achieve unity? If so, it is a successful drawing.

Maybe you believe that the drawing is something more than a collection of parts. You might believe that it will interest you after repeated viewings as much as it did when you first saw it. If so, you may want to classify it as a great drawing. Everyone is waiting. What is your decision? (You can see Hopper's painting *Gas* in Figure 23 in Color Section I.)

Gross Clinic by Thomas Eakins

You pass several other drawings before stopping at another that appeals to you (Figure 6.5, page 113). Several people urge you to analyze this drawing. Of course you agree to do so.

SHARPENING YOUR SKILLS

Ask Questions About Design Qualities

Complete a thorough analysis of the drawing *Gross Clinic* on page 113. To do this, use the design chart in Figure 8.2 on page 158. During this analysis, answer the following questions:
- What art element stands out?
- Which art principles were used to organize this element?
- You can see the outline of a large pyramid shape. What is at the top?
- Was the placement of that object at the tip of the pyramid a deliberate attempt to emphasize that object?
- Does the use of this pyramid shape contribute to the balance in this drawing? Is this balance symmetrical or asymmetrical?
- Is this drawing a successful work of art?
- What aesthetic qualities would you refer to if you had to defend your judgment?

Self-Portrait at the Age of Twenty-Two by Albrecht Dürer

Later you stop briefly before a drawing by Albrecht Dürer (Figure 8.6). You look at how certain elements of art such as line, value, and texture have been used in the face, hand, and pillow. Do these parts fit together to form a unified whole? Is this a finished work of art? Or is this work a series of detailed but unrelated drawings? Did the artist draw only to develop an idea, record certain information, or sharpen drawing skills?

Did You Know?

You might be surprised to learn that Dürer was the first artist to complete a true self-portrait. Your surprise may change to awe when you learn that he created his first one when he was thirteen years old!

Dürer was born in Nuremberg, Germany, in 1471, the second son in a family of eighteen. He was interested all of his life in reproducing his own sensitive and often troubled features with pencil and paint. Perhaps the worry often seen in his self-portraits was due to the religious conflict between Martin Luther and the Catholic Church. The artist became involved in this controversy. Finally Dürer sided with Luther and became a strong spokesman for change.

Dürer's concern for structure is apparent in his pen and ink drawing *Lamentation* (Figure 8.7, page 162), a carefully composed religious scene completed in 1521, seven years before his death. Skillful use of light and dark values draws attention to the figure of the dead Christ, gives roundness to all the figures, and creates the appearance of space.

The mourning figures crowded around Christ form a large triangle. It rises from a wide base to form a point where a ladder rests against the cross. (To the right of this ladder, you can see Dürer's famous signature and the date.) In addition, there is a second triangle in this composition. Can you find it? What important purpose does it serve?

▲ Is it possible to describe this work as having unity? Why or why not? Discuss with members of your class the different motives the artist may have had for creating these unrelated drawings on a single sheet of paper.

FIGURE 8.6   Albrecht Dürer. *Self-Portrait at the Age of Twenty-Two.* c. 1493. Pen and brown ink on paper. 30.3 x 20.2 cm (11¹⁵⁄₁₆ x 7¹⁵⁄₁₆"). The Metropolitan Museum of Art, New York, New York. Robert Lehman Collection.

This second, smaller triangle, with its base along the right edge of the drawing, overlaps the larger one. The top of this triangle is suggested by a series of heads and the bottom by the legs of the reclining Christ. This second triangle serves to emphasize the faces of the two main figures in this religious drama—Christ and his mother. Unlike most of the figures around them, some of whom gesture dramatically, they are quiet and still. The mother gently takes her dead son's hand in her own and seems to be whispering a last farewell. The finality of that farewell is subtly suggested by a woman to the mother's left. She holds a jar of ointment to be used for the burial.

▲ Notice how the details in this work, while impressive, take on a secondary importance. The artist is more interested in the overall arrangement or design of his drawing.

FIGURE 8.7 Albrecht Dürer. *Lamentation.* 1521. Pen and ink on white paper. 29.0 x 21.0 cm (11⅜ x 8⁵⁄₁₆"). The Harvard University Art Museums, Cambridge, Massachusetts. Bequest of Meta and Paul J. Sachs.

Artists at Work

Form Following Function

"Last fall I entered a science fair competition with a contraption that poaches an egg, makes a cup of coffee, and toasts a piece of bread all at the same time. How will studying art help me achieve my goal of becoming an inventor?"

Most people who want to take advantage of their inventive natures by developing marketable products seek a more secure career in the field of industrial design. Industrial designers must be part engineer, architect, drafter, sculptor, graphic designer, and salesperson. They combine artistic talent and skill in working with three-dimensional forms. With specific knowledge of production techniques and materials, they create new products and refine manufacturing procedures. Their awareness of function and aesthetic form helps them determine the "look" and "feel" of products ranging from automobiles to furniture, hair dryers to ballpoint pens.

After assessing your client's needs, drafting designs for approval, and rendering two and three-dimensional drawings, you would supervise as your drawings were made into *models* or **prototypes**. Now color and other graphic considerations such as labels would be considered. For example, black might not be the best choice for a new hair dryer because it makes the dryer appear too heavy. On the other hand, yellow is a color that appeals to both men and women.

As an industrial designer, you must enjoy research and sticking with projects from beginning to end. You need to be aware of current trends in styles and technology and up-to-date on the development of new materials and the applications of old ones. An awareness of public tastes is essential.

In addition to the ability to draw, you will need a strong background in color and design. You must be able to communicate visually as well as verbally. Also, you must be capable of working with administrators, engineers, and sales people as well as with other members of design and production teams.

College training is essential to obtain the broad background necessary for success as an industrial designer. Basic art skills such as drawing, painting, and sculpture are as important as the information obtained from courses in basic engineering, materials, manufacturing methods, model making and drafting. Many schools that offer major programs or degrees in industrial design requires that students take courses such as: drafting, drawing, airbrushing, sculpture, graphics, rendering, welding, model making, lettering, display design, experimental design, interior design, transportation design, and furniture design.

To get started now, you should take drawing, drafting, painting, and sculpture classes at every opportunity. Model making and photography can be useful hobbies that will also pay dividends later. Of course, part-time work in a drafting office, manufacturing company, carpenter shop, or design studio can provide useful experience. Even working in a retail store can help you become familiar with consumer psychology and public reaction to products. ■

Head of a Girl with Braids by Henri Matisse

Your curiosity is aroused by a group of people gathered before a drawing by Henri Matisse of a girl with braids (Figure 8.8). You decide to investigate. A lively discussion about the work is going on. A gentleman quietly informs you that an earlier gallery visitor said this drawing is unsuccessful. (He is, of course, referring to you in your previous role as an imitationalist in Chapter 6.)

▲ In 1910 Matisse saw an exhibition of Near Eastern art that had a lasting influence on him. He began to develop art that showed flat patterns with flowing linear decoration. Can you see any of that influence in this drawing?

FIGURE 8.8 Henri Matisse. *Head of a Girl with Braids.* c. 1916. Brush with india ink. 56.1 x 37.5 cm (22⅛ x 14¹³⁄₁₆″). The Art Institute of Chicago, Chicago, Illinois. Gift of an anonymous donor.

This statement is a challenge you can't ignore, so you step forward to inspect the controversial drawing. "What is wrong with this work?" you ask. Someone answers that the other critic said the drawing is unimportant because it doesn't look real. As a formalist, how will you reply to this charge? Will you reply that all works, especially abstract works like this one, should be judged by their design qualities instead of their literal qualities?

Referring to the drawing, you explain that what the artist has drawn is less important than how he decided to draw it. To understand and appreciate this work, a viewer should study how the artist used line variety in the hair, the curve of the shoulders, and the contour of the face. Instead of looking for details that aren't there, the viewer should notice how only the most essential lines were used to create a sense of rhythm. The repeated curved lines create harmony. Variety was achieved by changing the length, thickness, and direction of these lines.

You conclude by saying that this drawing wasn't meant to look exactly like a girl with braids. Instead, its appeal is due to a careful arrangement of lines—lines which the artist identified after studying a girl with braids. Once viewers recognize how the design qualities are used in this drawing, they should realize that it is a successful work of art.

The Last Respects by Henri de Toulouse-Lautrec

You are preparing to leave the gallery when several people lead you to a final drawing (Figure 10.6 on page 202) created by Henri de Toulouse-Lautrec. It shows a workman standing with bared head, holding his hat in his hands, staring at a funeral procession. After studying the work, you decide it is successful.

Like the Matisse drawing, *The Last Respects* uses only a few lines to suggest the different forms. The distant, dark, solid shapes of the funeral procession contrast with the light values and sparse lines of the foreground figure. This contrast emphasizes the importance of the funeral scene. The man's dark scarf, however, repeats the dark values in the funeral procession and ties these two parts of the picture together into a harmonious whole.

Distance is implied by the contrast in proportions between the man in the foreground and the much smaller figures in the background. The illusion of space is also created by the way the man overlaps the background scene. The artist used the principles of emphasis, harmony, and proportion to effectively arrange the elements of line, shape, and space. The result is a unified and visually exciting composition.

You find another drawing in the gallery exciting because of its effective use of the elements and principles of art (Figure 8.9). Take time to analyze and judge this work. Keep in mind that as a formalist you are mainly concerned with design qualities. (Don't read further until you have analyzed and judged the drawing in Figure 8.9.)

Noting the time, you are pleased to discover that it is still quite early. If you hurry, you will have enough time to return to your studio to work on drawings of your own—drawings, of course, in which you emphasize design qualities.

▲ **Explain how the principle of rhythm is demonstrated in this drawing. What adjective best describes the feeling communicated by this drawing? Compare your choice of an adjective with choices made by other members of your class.**

FIGURE 8.9   Vincent van Gogh. *Grove of Cypresses*. 1889. Reed pen and ink over pencil on paper. 62.5 x 46.5 cm (24⅝ x 18⁵⁄₁₆"). The Art Institute of Chicago, Chicago, Illinois. Gift of Robert Allerton.

Did You Know?

In some art historian's opinions, Toulouse-Lautrec's skill as a caricaturist and in capturing likenesses was greater than that of his contemporaries (Degas, Manet, Cézanne, Gauguin, Redon, and Seurat, to mention a few).

Much of Toulouse-Lautrec's work was inspired by Montmartre, a section of Paris known for its night life. In contrast to another contemporary, Monet, who painted mostly outdoor scenes, Toulouse-Lautrec preferred capturing the character of entertainers and their patrons in restaurants, cabarets, and theaters.

CHAPTER 8 REVIEW

1. What aesthetic qualities do formalists favor when judging and defending decisions about works of art?

2. How can a design chart help in identifying design relationships?

3. What does the term *design relationships* refer to in a finished work of art?

▲ How would you respond to someone who claimed this is a poor drawing? In order to arrive at a positive judgement of it, what aesthetic qualities should be taken into consideration?

FIGURE 9.1 Peggy Bacon. *The Painter.* Date unknown. Graphite on paper. 27.9 x 21.6 cm (11 x 8½"). McNay Art Institute, San Antonio, Texas. Bequest of Marion Koogler McNay.

Making Formal Drawings

A formal drawing may express an idea or a strong emotion, or may even be highly representational (Figure 9.1). The chief emphasis of a formal drawing, however, is on the visual experience created by the structure—the ways the elements and principles of art have been used. In other words, a formal drawing's main subject is itself. A formal drawing is art about art, although it may also communicate on other levels. In Color Section II, Figure 1, Jacob Lawrence employed design qualities to make a statement about skilled workers in his painting *Cabinet Maker*.

The formal, or design, qualities of a drawing—the ways the artist has used the visual vocabulary—are important in all works of art. This doesn't mean, however, that the literal and expressive qualities of drawings aren't important. They are. What it does mean is that an artwork that imitates reality or expresses emotion may be judged primarily on its use of the literal or expressive qualities. Still, it is unlikely that the work will be judged successful if it fails to use design qualities effectively.

In this chapter, you will learn ways to organize design qualities in drawings. You will also discover ways to arrive at the visual ideas needed for creating drawings based on design qualities.

objectives

After reading this chapter and doing the activities, you will be able to:

- Explain different ways that artists use design qualities in their drawings.

- Make drawings of objects and people, emphasizing the design qualities.

- Make abstract drawings.

- Use different media to enhance the effect of the design qualities in drawings.

Terms to Know

aberrant scale
bleed
cropping
engraving
formal drawing
frottage
illustration
rubbing
scratchboard
vignette

Understanding Design Qualities in Drawings

Even emotional drawings require the use of structure to express the artist's idea. The fascinating technical pen work by Frank Cheatham in Figure 9.2 is an example of skillful formal drawing. He has used the principles of art to organize the elements, creating an exciting visual experience. Whatever symbolic meaning this drawing communicates, its main impact is visual.

The work in Figure 9.3 is by Gary Edson. This fine art print is more imitational than Cheatham's work, but it still relies on strong design qualities for its impact. For instance, note the way the complex shapes are organized to suggest space, the way value contrasts emphasize important images, and how variety in line, texture, and shape adds to visual interest.

The drawing in Figure 9.4 is an illustration from a college newspaper. An **illustration** is *a*

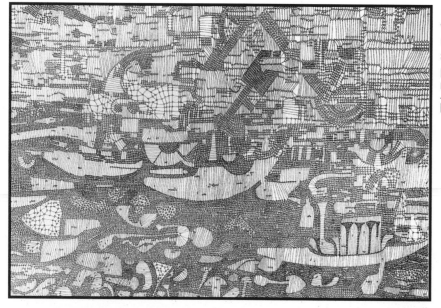

◄ Frank Cheatham's drawing, done with a Rapidograph technical pen, reflects his interest in primitive design and mysterious artifacts. How are the principles of variety and emphasis used here?

FIGURE 9.2 Courtesy of the artist.

◄ This intricate etching is by artist and museum director Gary Edson. While the images are imitational, they are used in a formal structure. How is variety exhibited in this work?

FIGURE 9.3 Courtesy of the artist.

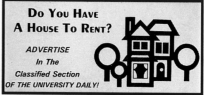

DO YOU HAVE A HOUSE TO RENT?
ADVERTISE In The Classified Section OF THE UNIVERSITY DAILY!

▲ The little illustration of the house from a newspaper ad is both symbolic and strongly formal. What two elements are emphasized here?

FIGURE 9.4 Courtesy of *The University Daily*, Texas Tech University, Lubbock, Texas.

drawing used to tell a story, give instructions, or make a product look attractive.

The artist drew this illustration to sell a service. To do this, the artist had to be at least as concerned with creating a visual experience for the viewer as with the need to advertise real estate in a newspaper. To serve the primary goal of the advertiser, the artist had to make use of strong design qualities in the illustration. Notice how the tiny illustration intrigues the viewer by the way it uses the element of line. The lines outlining shapes are broad enough to be shapes, also. These narrow shapes that outline other shapes are so strong that they become part of the image they define. The repetition of the three basic geometric shapes (circle, square, and triangle) creates harmony. The combined effect of these uses of the elements is a visual economy and overall unity in an image that is quickly recognized as a symbol for a home.

Even though the main reason for making an illustration is to promote a product or tell a story, the drawing must produce a visual experience for the viewer before it communicates the artist's message. To create this visual experience, the artist must use the principles of design to organize the elements in the drawing. The drawing must have a unified structure. The science fiction illustration in Figure 9.5 accomplishes this with its stippled rendering and overlapping and partly transparent shapes. The man's features suggest a particular emotion associated perhaps with the potential destructive powers of the rockets he may have helped develop.

▲ The design or structural qualities of this science fiction illustration by Marvin Moon are strengthened by the stippled rendering technique. What has been done to emphasize the important images?

FIGURE 9.5   Courtesy of the artist.

Did You Know?

In the history of American art, it is interesting that early commercial artists and illustrators of books came from the ranks of the fine artists. Most of them were trained as drafters and painters. This was also true in Europe where our traditions of painting and sculpture originated.

Now, however, there is a trend for some artists to participate in a number of professional activities during their lifetimes. Several artists featured in this book are multi-talented individuals whose work is nationally or internationally published and exhibited in a number of separate fields.

Design qualities can also be used to show viewers how subjects really look—but from the point of view of the artist. The drawing done with technical pens in Figure 9.6 on the next page imitates reality to the extent that at first we wonder if it is supposed to portray an actual farm scene from the 1930s. On second look, however, we notice strange things in the drawing. There is a baboon-like creature under the quilting frame with the little boy. Also we see the antique pistol and the floating transparent planes—to say nothing of the pterodactyls outside the window. Could this drawing also illustrate a science fiction story or a fantasy?

Actually, Figure 9.6 isn't an illustration. It is simply a fantastic drawing. Even so, it shows both real and imagined people and objects in a realistic way. The drawing's imitational qualities—the realistic people engaged in an everyday activity—are important because they give the fantastic images more impact. How has the artist employed proportion, perspective, and shadows to enhance the drawing's imitational qualities?

The drawing's success as a work of fine art, though, is due mainly to its design qualities—the manner in which it has been organized or put together. It is based on a one-point perspective with a vanishing point at the

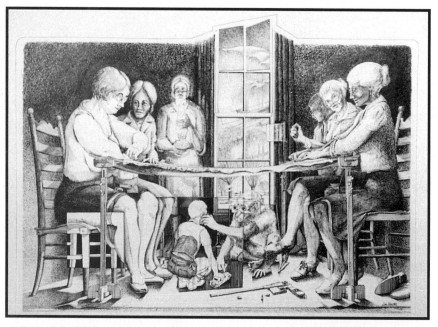

▲ FIGURE 9.6   While the images in this technical pen rendering are imitational, the overall structure is formalized. How has the artist used contrast of value to emphasize the important figures?

SHARPENING YOUR SKILLS

Using the Wash Medium

SUPPLIES
- Black watercolor
- Tempera, acrylic paint, or india ink
- Number 2 and Number 5 round brushes
- Shallow dishes or watercolor palette, small sponge
- Medium-rough watercolor paper or block

In this activity you will learn to use a wash, see Chapter 4, page 74. Mix two gray washes by adding paint or ink, a little at a time, to water in two bowls or a watercolor palette (a special board for mixing paints). You will recall that watercolor is a transparent paint consisting of pigment mixed with water. Test the washes by brushing them onto water color paper. Add pigment until the washes dry to the values you want to use.

Now follow these steps:

1. Dampen an area of paper with the sponge, and brush one wash into the damp area as smoothly as possible.
2. Do the same in another area, floating more pigment into one side to create a gradation of value.
3. Dampen another area, and float some of the other wash into it. Dry the brush and use it to pick up pigment from the wet area.
4. Outline an area with a brush, and color it with wash.
5. Draw some simple three-dimensional forms with the small brush, and add wash for shadow.
6. Experiment and, when finished, exhibit and discuss your work in class.

center of vision on a horizon that is somewhere outside the lower windowpane. Around this central vanishing point are distributed two groups of large figures. They share the darkness of the room and are connected by the quilting frame. The figures in each group overlap each other, unifying the groups into single shapes. These shapes, in turn, frame the window above and the boy and the fantasy creature below. Note also how the artist has used light and dark values and different textures to add visual interest to the composition.

All of the directions established by the axis (vertical dividing line) of each figure, the window, the chair backs, and the legs of the quilting frame are in line with each other and with the vertical sides of the drawing. The quilt, chair rungs, seats, and window crosspieces all align horizontally. The viewer perceives repetition, alignment, contrasts, and balance in the directions, shapes, lines, and textures. The drawing is unified, even though there is a great variety of figures and objects.

As you have seen from these examples, both emotional art and imitational art need structure. For a drawing to convey a complex message or tie together a variety of realistic images into a visually pleasing whole, the artist must effectively organize its design qualities.

Subject Matter in Formal Drawings

It is difficult to find a purely formal drawing. By definition, a **formal drawing** *reveals little concern for literal qualities or realistically rendered subject matter.* Often, the lack of concern for literal qualities results in artworks that are abstract or nonobjective.

Purely formal art exhibits a similar lack of concern for expressive qualities. However, finding a drawing without expressive qualities is almost impossible. It could be argued that even the coldness caused by eliminating any feelings is in itself the expression of an attitude.

The graphite drawing in Figure 9.7 by Grey Rigney is probably about as purely formal as any we could ever find. Rigney's drawing is a product of careful planning and many sketchbook drawings. Even

▶ Sometimes drawings become part of three-dimensional works. Grey Rigney has made a strong statement in graphite on a seven-foot column of wood and canvas. How is rhythm or movement suggested here?

FIGURE 9.7   Courtesy of the artist.

though it is almost totally abstract, its design elements were originally derived from nature and from shapes found in industrial scenes. The artist was very successful in putting together hard-edged shapes and an area of expressive lines in a drawing that actually becomes three-dimensional. This work of art is a combination of illusion and real three-dimensional form. Many fine artists are working with the mixing of illusory space and real space as well as mixing various media in the same piece of art.

A piece of fine art that would be considered simply imitational by many people is the drawing by Marvin Moon in Figure 9.8 on page 172. This is a sketch for a watercolor that was made to record facts. It was also created, however, as a compositional study to preserve strong design qualities in the finished work. Some of these qualities are the massive shapes and their repetition with variation. The shapes are related to the darkening sky by gradation through the values of the shadows and the dark trees.

Figure 9.9 is another drawing that is almost completely formal because of the way it was created. The approach to this drawing was to make several blind contour drawings from a model (recording contours without looking at the drawing). Then the artist developed shapes by overlapping the blind contour drawings as if they were transparent. Contrasting values were obtained by hatching, cross-hatching, and filling in areas with black ink. The original subject matter—the model—almost disappeared from the drawing.

Finding Design Ideas from Rubbings

You may have noticed from the last few activities that formal drawings often have their origins in real-life objects. Starting your sketch with a real object in front of you can stimulate your thinking and can help you arrive at a design idea. Of course, the identity of the original subject often becomes difficult to recognize as the visual statement takes shape. This is fine since it is the design qualities, not the literal qualities, that determine the success or failure of a formal drawing.

In addition to focusing attention on design qualities while sketching a real object, another way to find a visual idea is to take a rubbing from the surface of a natural or man-made object and to use parts of the rubbing in a design. A **rubbing** (also called a **frottage** (FRAW-tazh)) is *the image caused by putting a piece of fairly smooth, flexible paper over an object with a raised image or textured surface and rubbing a pencil lead or a graphite stick over it.* You can see examples of rubbings in Figure 9.10 on page 174.

▲ This sketch for a watercolor of the old St. Francis Church at Ranchos de Taos, New Mexico, was done on a piece of scrap paper. The artist, Marvin Moon, saw the design qualities in the church's structure.

FIGURE 9.8 Courtesy of the artist.

▲ **FIGURE 9.9** This student drawing was developed by overlapping three blind contour drawings and controlling values by hatching and cross-hatching. How are variety and harmony demonstrated here?

SHARPENING YOUR SKILLS

Learn to Make Rubbings

SUPPLIES
- Black or dark blue pencil
- Drawing paper
- Cropping Ls

Make ten to twelve pencil rubbings of various textured surfaces. Then crop interesting shapes from them and combine and mount these in interesting designs in your sketchbook.

Rub with the side of the pencil, not the tip. Use moderate pressure, and keep the strokes going in the same direction. Don't choose paper that is too thick or stiff. Also, remember that you will have to keep the paper and the object stationary. The shapes you crop from the rubbing should be placed and mounted in a visually satisfying design that takes into account the alignment of similar and contrasting shapes, a variety of textures, and an overall balance of the shapes and textures used.

Computer Option

This activity requires that your software program have an Airbrush or Spraycan tool. To begin, create or Open from disk an image of a scene or object similar to one of those shown in Figure 9.10. Select the Airbrush or Spraycan tool, and set the line width to extra-thick. Next, zoom in on your object so that its image fills most of the screen. Place the tip or nozzle of the Airbrush or Spraycan in the center of the image and, holding the mouse steady, press the left mouse button for about one second to leave an uneven pattern of dots. Move the mouse to another area of the picture and repeat the process. Continue until all areas of the image have been sprayed.

Selecting a small area of a picture to use as an independent design is called **cropping**. An easy way to visualize this area is to separate it and determine its proportions with a pair of cropping Ls. Again look at Figure 9.10. The two L-shaped pieces of white cardboard lying on the rubbing in the lower right corner are cropping Ls. As you can see, these Ls could be moved to isolate a square or rectangle of any size in the rubbing. After this, the area could be marked with a ruler, cut out, and mounted in a sketchbook.

Use Selective Vision

Since a camera records only the things at which it is pointed, photographers need good judgment about where to point the camera. There are many technical things that photographers can do to improve their pictures, but the people who practice photography as an art form know what, when, and how to shoot. They use selective vision to find design qualities—the elements and principles of art—in their subjects.

As you make drawings that are effectively structured and have exciting design qualities, you can also use selective vision. You can find an interesting scene and emphasize its design qualities. Or you can make a carefully organized setup and find a formal design within it to draw.

Annette Berlin's colored pencil drawing from a still-life setup in Figure 2 in Color Section II is a good example of the selective vision approach. Not

SHARPENING YOUR SKILLS

Drawing into a Rubbing

SUPPLIES

- Black or dark blue pencil
- Drawing paper
- Other drawing media of your choice

Make a rubbing of an area of texture large enough for a finished drawing, at least 12 x 18 inches (30.5 x 46 cm). Tape your paper to the surface on one edge only, since the paper will probably stretch a little in the rubbing process.

Then, instead of cropping to make a good design, draw into the rubbing. Emphasize some shapes and values. You might need to combine some shapes to unify the composition or restructure others for better alignment. Try to draw so that there are no obvious differences between the original rubbing and the added drawing.

▲ FIGURE 9.10 Rubbings from wood and stone. The one in the lower right is being condensed to a strong formal structure by the use of cropping Ls.

only was her judgment in cropping the drawing important, but also the structure of the setup itself was carefully thought out to emphasize the elements and principles of art. Of course, the unusual combination of a satin dress and a catcher's mask adds considerable interest to the composition, but that choice affects literal and expressive qualities more than design qualities.

Another type of selective vision that can be used to create a formal drawing is aberrant scale or abnormal scale. To use aberrant scale, you could enlarge something that is normally quite small to make it a major element in the drawing. Or you could draw something that is normally gigantic to look tiny. Using **aberrant (uh-BARE-unt) scale** *manipulates the element of shape to create emphasis.*

The drawing done by student Nicole Brints (Color Section II, Figure 3) uses aberrant scale in enlarging objects. The drawing features a fragment of a basket and a piece of barbed wire that have been enlarged several times. These items have become impressive subjects in a formal drawing.

Use Media to Add Design Qualities

Using certain media or tools can themselves produce strong design qualities in drawings, in addition to those qualities consciously emphasized by the artist. We can find examples of how media can affect design qualities in both fine art and illustration.

SCRATCHBOARD

Observe how the artist's choice of medium determined some of the design qualities evident in the drawing illustrated in Figure 9.11, page 176. Roger Beikmann's drawing is done on a surface called scratchboard. **Scratchboard** is *illustration board that has been coated with a chalk-like substance that can then be drawn on with ink.* Heavy, dark areas are usually filled in with a brush. Since the chalky surface can be easily scratched, white lines can be brought out by scratching into the dark areas with a *stylus* (a metal pen-shaped instrument), a Number 11 Exacto knife, or other special tools. Scratchboard is relatively expensive, but it provides an interesting drawing experience. Many illustrators who make black and white line drawings for newspapers and magazines prefer scratchboard.

Beikmann's drawing has design qualities similar to many wood or linoleum engravings. An **engraving** is *an artwork in which an image is cut into a surface.* Look again at Figure 1.1 on page 2. The design qualities result from what is often called value reversal or white-on-black rendering.

SENSITIZED SHADING SHEETS

Another black-and-white illustration and cartooning medium is sensitized shading sheets like Grafix Duoshade. (See the student drawing in Figure 9.12, page 177.) Applying chemical developers to the surface of this paper creates instant hatching and cross-hatching. As you have already discovered, hatching and cross-hatching can add the design element of a texture to shaded areas.

After the lines are drawn, one developer is brushed on the areas of light gray value to raise the hatching stripes to the surface. In the darker areas, another developer is applied that creates a cross-hatched pattern.

For professional examples of the use of shading sheets, see Figures 13.10 and 13.13 in Chapter 13, "Cartooning," pages 250 and 253.

SHARPENING YOUR SKILLS

Make a Drawing in Aberrant Scale

SUPPLIES
- Colored pencils
- Drawing paper

In your drawing, use aberrant scale to enlarge some objects that are even smaller than the ones in Brints's drawing. Use a magnifying glass if necessary to see details of the objects. For example, you could draw carefully placed rows of closed safety pins with a few jacks or marbles and one open safety pin where you want some emphasis. Remember that the formal statement made by the size emphasis must be supported by other principles of design.

Computer Option

Using freehand drawing tools, as well as the Rectangle and Ellipse tools, draw several everyday objects. Fill the objects with a variety of colors or, if your program features them, patterns. Experiment with positioning the objects with respect to one another so as to add interest; you can do this by selecting the objects one at a time with the Scissors, Pick, or Lasso tool and moving them about the screen. When you are satisfied with the composition of your picture, use the Zoom tool to magnify various areas of your work.

▲ **FIGURE 9.11** Scratchboard is usually associated with illustration, but student Roger Beikmann used it for an almost abstract drawing. Is texture an important element here? How is it realized?

▲ **FIGURE 9.12**   This rendering of a cup was done by drawing student Cylinda Baker using a shading medium called Duoshade. The cross-hatching occurs by painting a clear developer on the sensitized paper.

Media Affect Design Qualities

Figure 25 in Color Section I and Figure 4 in Color Section II are two different formal works by the same versatile artist, Paul Hanna. All of his works exhibit care directed to effective structure, but in these two the media enhanced the design qualities.

According to most people, Figure 25 Color Section I is a glass engraving and Figure 4, Color Section II is a painting. The first artwork is an image made up of lines that were cut into the surface of a glass bowl. The marks on the second were made with paint. We could, however, refer to both artworks as drawings. The engraving tool was used like a drawing instrument, and the painting consists only of lines.

Did You Know?

Traditionally, the Paul Hanna painting (Figure 4 in Color Section II) would be called a *tondo*. This term was often used to describe a painting that was round instead of square or rectangular. Today it would simply be called a round painting.

It is interesting to note that Paul Hanna, in addition to being skilled at drawing, painting, and glass engraving, is a nationally published cartoonist. Some of his cartoons appear in Chapter 13.

No matter what we call them, both of these works have powerful design qualities related to the media used to make them. A glass engraving is transparent and reflects light. These qualities cause the piece to take on some of the character of its surroundings. Shapes, lines, textures, and colors from the surroundings can be seen through the bowl or are reflected from its surface. These elements, in turn, blend with the engraved image to produce a constantly changing, often complex design.

Paul Hanna also gave his painting design qualities through the medium he used. Ignoring literal qualities, it is a visual statement made up of the elements of shape, form, space, color, texture, and value. All of these elements are organized by applying the principles of design to the single element of line.

This painting was done on a circular stretched canvas that is large enough to absorb the viewer's visual attention. Spatial illusions are realized by color and value overlapping. As a result, it seems to be an absolutely pure formal statement. Its use of design qualities creates a powerful visual experience.

Then, after looking more closely, we find ourselves caught up visually in an agitated mass of energetic lines going in hundreds of directions. Suddenly, we become aware that the piece is also extremely expressive. It communicates an idea about the actions of the artist when making art. *No New Tricks* (Figure 5 in Color Section II), a humorous miniature—3 inches (7.6 cm) in diameter—is a mixed media work with emphasis on design qualities and symbolism.

■ SILVERPOINT

Another medium that affects some of the formal elements of design is called *silverpoint*. The lines of a silverpoint drawing are made with a special pencil with a silver point. Silverpoint was a popular medium at the turn of the century, but this popularity faded as graphite pencils became more accessible.

Silverpoint can only be used to mark on certain surfaces. The only surfaces that strip tiny particles from a pencil point of silver are those with a clay or clay-like coating. Cream-colored, clay-coated paper called *cameo paper* or some stiffer surface (like a

Artists at work

■ FINE ARTIST
Drawing Income with Graphite

"I like to draw because it makes me feel good. It makes me aware and appreciative of certain facets of life. Do you think I could make a living at it, though?"

Most people who are interested in art soon channel their energies toward careers like commercial art or industrial design. Some fine art painters are diligent and talented enough to sell their works, but few make a living at drawing. Many fine artists have jobs in fields not related to art that provide them with steady incomes and the time to be creative.

If you specialize in a medium used by relatively few artists, graphite pencil for example, you might achieve some measure of success. Landscapes, portraits, still life arrangements, and abstract works are easily rendered in graphite. After determining the composition you want, you might sketch the basic shapes and their arrangement on either a sheet of high-quality drawing paper or the reverse side of a sheet of four-ply bristol board. Using a pencil with a moderately soft lead, this step might only take you thirty minutes.

Applying one technique, you might scribble in the sketch with cross-hatching strokes, determining the location of the dark and light areas. After three or four layers, the loose lines of the cross-hatching would disappear, and

your drawing would acquire a textured look. This is a detailed process because the darker areas might require from twelve to twenty-four layers of graphite. Working four to six hours a day, it might take you one to three weeks to complete a typical drawing.

Whatever medium you choose, self-discipline, flexibility, tenacity and dedication are essential requirements for a fine artist. If you do decide to make a living at your art, you will have to become part salesperson and business person also. It takes hard work and organization to attract an expanding audience of buyers and admirers.

Art schools can provide the training, experience and instruction essential to the development of fine artists. Few artists are self-taught. Some even obtain advanced degrees such as the Master of Fine Arts (MFA) in their specialty.

For now, you should take as many courses in painting, printmak-

ing, sculpture, design and drawing as you can. You should also take part in as many art activities as your schedule will allow. Set up a mini-studio in a corner of your room, have a sketchbook handy wherever you go and sketch constantly.

Free-lance designers, illustrators, mural and background painters employ similar techniques and require similar training. Many art teachers are often trained as fine artists and share the techniques they have learned with their students.

Many of the rewards received by a fine artist are not financial. As a fine artist, you can derive tremendous satisfaction from knowing that your work enriches the lives of others, and that your career might contribute to the development of contemporary society and the understanding of past cultures. ■

▲ The value range of silverpoint is somewhat limited. It has an interesting delicacy, however, and it takes on a patina as the silver tarnishes.

FIGURE 9.13   Private Collection. Courtesy of Nancy Lee and Charles Stewart.

wood panel or illustration board) that has been coated with gesso are the two surfaces usually used for silverpoint drawings. *Gesso* is a white, plaster-like surface used for drawing or painting.

You can see a silverpoint drawing done on a gessoed surface in Figure 9.13. The value changes in the drawing are subtle. Silverpoint produces a value range of only about 50 percent gray to white. This limitation requires the artist to be disciplined and precise. As a result, silverpoint drawings often are characterized by subtle gradations and delicacy.

In addition to value, another design quality affected by using silverpoint as a medium is line. Since the silver point tends to stay fairly sharp, the artist is limited in the kinds of line that can be used in silverpoint drawings.

Color is another element affected by using silver-point in a drawing. After exposure to air, silver tarnishes, or takes on a patina finish, somewhat like some metal sculpture. This means that its surface turns brown from oxidation. If you could see the drawing in Figure 9.13 in color, you would see that the entire surface has changed from gray to a kind of rich sepia (grayish brown). In this case, the element of color has changed because of the medium used.

CHAPTER 9 REVIEW

1. From whose point of view can design qualities be used to show how subjects really look?

2. Which qualities determine the success of a formal drawing; design qualities or literal qualities?

3. What is the difference between fine art and an illustration?

4. Do you think drawings for fine art can be used as illustrations? Why or why not? Do you think an illustration might possibly be considered fine art? Why or why not?

STUDIO 1

Formal Drawing of an Object or Animal

SUPPLIES

➥ **Pen and ink**

➥ **Drawing paper**

1. For your first formal drawing, make one similar to Figure 9.14. Use a familiar animal with a distinctive outline for your subject. Choose the element you want to emphasize (line, shape, form, value, texture, or space). Then decide which principles of art to use in emphasizing this element (balance, harmony, variety, gradation, movement, rhythm, proportion, or space).

2. The subject matter will express something to the viewer. The main purpose of the drawing, however, is to create a visual experience using the elements and principles of art. Do a series of thumbnail sketches to help you design your drawing.

3. Art student Judi Eudy decided to emphasize line in her drawing of a kangaroo in Figure 9.14. Knowing that the kinds of line are limited only by the imagination, she developed cross-contour lines made up of different patterns. These lines gave her drawing variety. Repetition—of the lines themselves, within each line, and of the directions of the lines—creates harmony and makes her drawing unified.

Computer Option

Choose a subject similar to the one shown in Figure 9.14. Using a freehand drawing tool, such as the Pen or Brush tool, sketch the contour of your subject. Do not be concerned if your sketch contains imperfections. Decide which element of art you would like to emphasize, and select a tool that will help you achieve your result. For example, the Paint Roller or Fill tool for form and value, the Line, Pencil, Rectangle, and/or Ellipse tools for line and shape. You can also use patterned fills for texture. Choose a principle of art to organize the work. When you have completed your illustration, consider deleting the outline or setting its color to white.

▲ **FIGURE 9.14   Student Judi Eudy's kangaroo can be classified as a pen line patterned drawing.**

Formal Drawing of a Model

SUPPLIES

⇢ Graphite or charcoal pencil

⇢ Layout or see-through paper

⇢ Additional drawing media of your choice

1. In this drawing you will again emphasize a certain element, but this time you will use the element to define the form of a person. Also, you will direct the viewer's attention to places you want to emphasize by using contrast. You can create contrast by a sudden change in the size or value of an element. Or you can interrupt the rhythmic repetition of an element by suddenly introducing another element.

2. Look at Ken Torres's ink line drawing in Figure 9.15. This portrait of a girl is probably a good likeness. However the most striking thing about the portrait is the artist's use of

▲ **FIGURE 9.15** Note how drawing student Ken Torres made use of dark lines to direct the viewer's attention to the most important parts of this portrait.

line. Notice how the thin, light lines contrast with the bold, dark lines of the girl's glasses. This draws attention to a carefully controlled point of emphasis at the eyes.

3. If you choose to emphasize space in your drawing, you could do this by drawing attention to the planes of the face located at different distances. Or you could repeat geometric shapes to define facial features. You could also choose to emphasize line, value, color, or texture. Remember that value and color are a product of light and sometimes shadow.

4. You will need to do several graphite or charcoal sketches to become familiar with the model's features. Make these sketches larger than thumbnail size. While you are designing your drawing, use overlays of layout or see-through paper. If you decide to emphasize shape, you can use the final overlay as a preliminary drawing and transfer it to the rendering surface.

Formal Wash Drawing

SUPPLIES

⇢ Graphite or charcoal pencil

⇢ Layout or see-through paper

⇢ Additional drawing media of your choice

1. Make a formal wash drawing using placement, repetition, and alignment to emphasize shape. By using several mixtures of the paint or ink and water, you can create several dark-to-light gradations to emphasize value. Use an outdoor scene or a still-life setup for subject matter.

2. Look at the wash drawing by Holly Stewart in Figure 9.16. It emphasizes all of the design elements of art and is definitely not imitational. Although it was based on figures and a street scene, most viewers notice this subject

S T U D I O 3   *Continued from page 181*

▲ **FIGURE 9.16** The people in student Holly Stewart's drawing were rendered with watercolor wash. How has the artist succeeded in creating an illusion of space in this work?

matter only after they have absorbed the visual impact of the drawing.

3. This visual impact results from manipulating space, which is suggested by the way shapes, lines, values, and pattern have been used. The many variations of these elements create interest. Placement and repetition were used to give the drawing an overall sense of unity.

4. Analyze this drawing by yourself, and then discuss your findings with the class. The following questions will get you started:

   - Why is the ellipse-shaped bottom of the barrel acceptable even though it is thinner than the ellipse at the top?

- Which shape dominates? What is it composed of? How does its placement strengthen its dominance?

- Where is line variety evidenced?

- How many parallel alignments can you find? Start with the edges of the picture. Consider the vertical and horizontal axes of individual shapes as well as lines and edges.

- Where can you find repeated shapes?

- Where are gradations and contrasts of value noted?

- How does the brick pattern contribute to the unity and interest of the composition?

Computer Option

Select a tool that can be used to create freehand lines, such as a Brush or Pencil tool. Set the line width of the tool to extra-thick, and set the color to a light gray (about 10 percent). Holding down the left mouse button, create several broad, sweeping lines of varying lengths. Increase the percentage of black slightly (to about 15 percent), and create several more lines that overlap the original ones slightly. Experiment with differing shades of gray and variations in line thickness to achieve interesting wash effects.

FIGURE 1
**What do you think this artist was more concerned with when creating this work—the literal
qualities or the design qualities? How does the *activity* of the worker help draw the viewer's
attention to the design qualities? What else has been done to emphasize their importance?
See page 167 for discussion.**

Jacob Lawrence. *Cabinet Maker.* 1957. Casein on paper. 77.4 x 57 cm (30½ x 22½"). Hirshhorn Museum and
Sculpture Garden, Smithsonian Institution, Washington, D.C. Gift of Joseph H. Hirshhorn.

FIGURE 2
As a student Annette Berlin drew this fantasy still life using an old department store mannequin, a catcher's mask, and other objects. See pages 173 and 189 for discussion.

Courtesy of the artist.

FIGURE 3
Student Nicole Brints used extreme enlargement in scale of small objects and textures to emphasize structure in this work. See page 174 for discussion.

Courtesy of the artist.

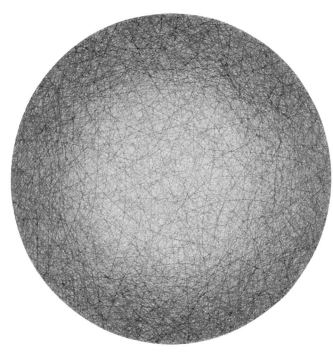

FIGURE 4
Paul Hanna's linear acrylic painting is called *Querencia No. 14*. It implies vast energy, but structurally it is carefully controlled. See page 177 for discussion.

Courtesy of the artist.

FIGURE 5
See page 177 for discussion.

Jim Howze. *No New Tricks.* 1993. Mixed media. 7.62 cm (3") diameter. Courtesy of the artist.

FIGURE 6
How has art student Shelly Settle changed the structure of the real-life images she used as sources for her drawing? See page 185 for discussion.

Courtesy of the artist.

FIGURE 7
See pages 186–187 for discussion.

Hugh Gibbons. *Arrangement at 12:17 p.m.* Oil on canvas. 114.3 x 182.9 cm (45 x 72"). Courtesy of
the artist.

FIGURE 8
One half of this painting is completely nonobjective, representing, perhaps, the confused feelings and emotions of the person whose face is seen at the right. Does the title of this picture help you interpret its meaning? See page 206 for discussion.

Jackson Pollock. *Portrait and a Dream.* 1953. Enamel on canvas. 1.5 x 3.4 m (4'10" x 11'2¼"). The Dallas Museum of Art, Dallas, Texas. Gift of Mr. and Mrs. Algur H. Meadows and the Meadows Foundation Incorporated.

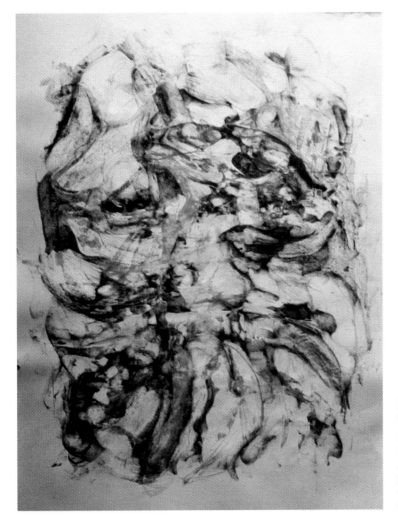

FIGURE 9
What emotions are expressed in this mixed media drawing by Linda Kennedy? Are these emotions related to a person or situation, or to the drawing process? See page 207 for discussion.

Courtesy of the artist.

FIGURE 10
Employing only a few brushstrokes and graphite, Manet was able to define the figure of a man dressed in the fashion of the time. Depending on the interpretation, the figure might evoke many different emotions. The artist did this piece as a study for his finished work, *The Absinthe Drinker*.

Edouard Manet. *The Man in the Tall Hat.* 1858–1859. Watercolor and graphite. 35.7 x 25.7 cm (14 x 10 1/16"). National Gallery of Art, Washington, D.C. Rosenwald Collection.

FIGURES 11, 12
As a high school student in 1985, Kathy Hicks King produced these wash drawings. Do you think she made many wash drawings like these during that time? Were these drawings done slowly or rapidly? How do you know?

Courtesy of the artist.

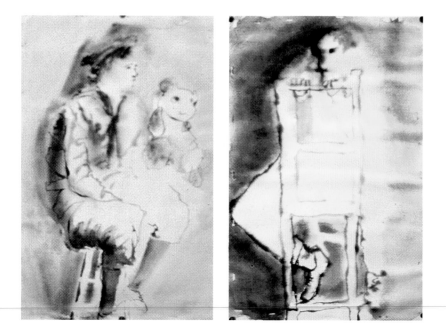

FIGURE 13
Kathy Hicks King painted this billboard, which won the National Obie Award for excellence in outdoor advertising. The sign was part of the *sesquicentennial* (150th anniversary) celebration for the state of Texas.

Kathy Hicks King. *Sesquicentennial.* Enamel on metal. 4.3 x 14.6 m (14' x 48'). Courtesy of the artist and Duplex Advertising Co., Temple, Texas.

FIGURE 14
This piece was commissioned by the Coca Cola Company. In spite of her busy schedule as an art teacher, Kathy Hicks King still finds time to produce commercial work, and exhibit fine art. The works of one of her students, Cody Bush, may be seen on pages 128 and 245.

Kathy Hicks King. Outdoor advertising billboard. Enamel on metal. 4.3 x 14.6 m (14' x 48'). Courtesy of the artist and Duplex Advertising Co., Temple, Texas.

FIGURE 15
This is a fine art piece executed recently by Ms. King. See page 208 for discussion.

Kathy Hicks King. *Fire Revealed.* 1993. Oil on canvas. 91.4 x 121.9 cm (36 x 48"). Courtesy of the artist.

FIGURE 16
Figures 16 through 20 are single figure washes that were executed by art students. They are done in less than twenty minutes each. Notice how free and expressive they are.

Ilana Reily. Courtesy of the artist.

FIGURE 17
See page 210 for discussion.

Marc Ferrino. Courtesy of the artist.

FIGURE 18
See page 210 for discussion.

Brian Hegvold. Courtesy of the artist.

FIGURE 19
See page 210 for discussion.

Apichart Chong. Courtesy of the artist.

FIGURE 20
See page 210 for discussion.

Miranda Howe. Courtesy of the artist.

FIGURE 21

As a student, Philip Ford produced this pastel drawing, *The Courtship*, based on childhood memories and the *commedia dell'arte* theater. What characteristics does this drawing share with the drawing of the old man in Figure 11.16 on page 217? See pages 208, 209, and 218 for a discussion of *commedia dell'arte* theater.

Courtesy of the artist.

FIGURE 22

Compare this mixed media work by Sara Waters called *Crossing . . .* with her drawing in Figure 11.9 on page 211. What are the similarities? What are the differences? See page 211 for discussion.

Courtesy of the artist.

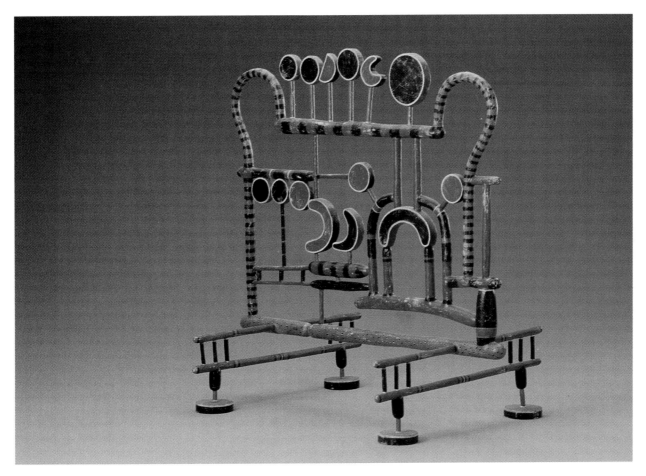

FIGURE 23
Cheatham's knowledge of human history, symbolism, and mythology give him
the creative ideas for much of the three-dimensional art he produces. See page
213 for discussion.

Frank Cheatham. *A Device for Determining the Magical Phases of the Moon.* Hardwood and acrylic.
Courtesy of the artist.

FIGURE 24
This work differs a great deal from that on page 89, but both were executed by the same artist. See page 89 for discussion.

Jane Cheatham. *July Window.* Courtesy of the artist.

FIGURE 25
This woodcut print by Paul Hanna is called *Owl and Heart Flower*. What makes the use of color so dramatic? See page 222 for discussion.

Courtesy of the artist.

FIGURE 26
This work was executed by art student Jamie Herring, who is a physically challenged individual. Through the use of a computer she is able to achieve artistic expression.

Jamie Herring. *Popcorn Abstraction.* 1988. Apple MacIntosh SE, ImageWriter II, (dot matrix printer with colored ribbon on paper) *SuperPaint* by Silicon Beach Software. 22.5 x 18.7 cm (8⅞ x 7⅜"). Private collection. Courtesy of the artist.

FIGURE 27
Colors are selected for each object, costume, and figure in a scene, and the computer adds color to each frame. It may take up to four hours to "colorize" one minute of black and white film. See page 272 for discussion.

Frame from *Sherlock Holmes and the Secret Weapon.* 1942. Courtesy of Hal Roach Studios, Inc. and Colorization, Inc.

FIGURE 28
The natural colors of these flowers have been changed by a software operation called pseudo-coloring. See page 272 for a discussion.

Courtesy of Gould Inc., Imaging and Graphics Division.

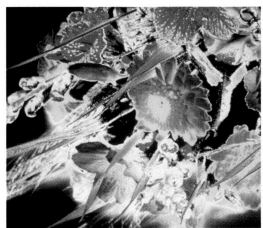

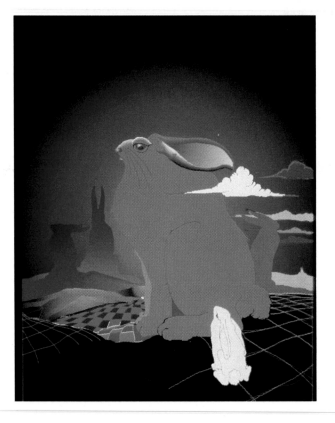

STUDIO 4

Drawing of Shapes Using Hatching

SUPPLIES

- ➼ Soft charcoal pencil
- ➼ Ruler (optional)
- ➼ See-through paper, vellum, or layout paper
- ➼ Pen and ink, or dry drawing medium of your choice
- ➼ Drawing paper

1. For this formal drawing, you will draw a collection of shapes starting with no less than three blind contour drawings on see-through paper, vellum, or layout paper. Select any kind of interesting objects as your subjects for these contour drawings. Use a soft charcoal pencil that makes a strong line.

2. Now lay the contour drawings on top of each other so that they overlap, creating many new shapes. Adjust the overlapping until you create shapes that form alignments that are interesting and hold the composition together.

3. When you have a unified composition that includes some size changes for variety, lay another sheet of see-through paper on top of the first three to make a composite reproduction of all the shapes. If the drawing becomes complex and obscures subject matter of your original drawings, don't worry about it.

4. At this point, you can decide whether you want to finish the drawing in a dry medium, in ink or by combining the dry medium with ink. If you use a dry medium, keep working on the same paper. If you want to work in ink, transfer the drawing to bristol board or a lightweight or medium-weight illustration board.

5. To provide visual interest, use two values of gray plus black and white. If you are using ink, apply washes of different values to do this. If you are using a dry medium make the values of gray by using lines.

6. Look again at Figure 9.9 on page 172 which combines dry medium with ink. Besides the areas of black and white, the areas of lighter gray in the drawing were made by a pattern of lines going in the same direction. You learned in Chapter 1 that this is called hatching. Remember that cross-hatching is overlaying these lines with a second pattern of lines going in the other direction. Cross-hatching was used to produce the darker grays in this drawing. The black areas were created with brush and ink.

7. Of course, you can control the values in your drawing by how thick and how close together you make the lines. You can also relate the direc-tion of the lines to the axis of any shape in the composition so you can enhance the unity of your drawing.

8. Before you start your pattern of hatching and cross-hatch-ing, practice to determine how to space the lines. If you wish, you can draw your lines with a ruler.

9. Perhaps you would like to eliminate outlines altogether and let value contrasts define the shapes. To do this, make the preliminary drawing in

Computer Option

To complete this activity, you will need a program capable of producing bitmapped images (this means with a bitmap-edit-ing Zoom tool). Begin by creat-ing or Opening from disk several contour drawings of simple objects. Cut and Paste the drawings so that they over-lap. Continue to work with them in this fashion, using the Undo command if necessary, until you have created an inter-esting and unified composition. Working carefully with the Brush or Line tool, fill some of the resulting shapes with pat-terns of thin lines going in the same direction. Use the Zoom tool (bitmap editor) to "touch up" any rough lines.

STUDIO 4   *Continued from page 183*

light graphite pencil, do the hatching in ink, and then erase the pencil lines.

10. Decide whether your drawing will be a bleed or a vignette. In a **bleed** *the shapes in the drawing reach the edges of the working area.* You might find it easier to create unity with a bleed because the straight, rectangular edges of the working area become part of the drawing and hold it together.

11. In a **vignette** (vin-YET), *the shapes often fade gradually into the empty working area around the edges of the drawing.* Other times they end abruptly, floating in their sea of negative space, never actually contacting the edge of the drawing.

This negative space can be used to emphasize the overall image of your drawing.

☞ TECHNIQUE TIP

Harmony and Variety

Whatever media you use, you have created a fairly complex design. It should be unified, however, by the careful placement of the horizontals and verticals in the rectangular working area or by the related directions in which you have placed the different shapes. You need not worry too much about variety at this point. Attaining an interesting amount of variation is rarely a problem. Achieving harmony is much more difficult.

Comparing the drawing process to making a stew might help you to understand this delicate relationship between variety and harmony. In cooking the stew, you want all the ingredients to blend together (be unified) into a good stew. Then you sprinkle in just enough spices (variety) to give the stew an interesting—but not too interesting—taste.

As an artist you want to do the same thing with your drawings. You want to devote most of your attention to the overall unity. Overall unity is achieved by adding just the right blend of harmony and variety.

STUDIO 5

Formal Drawing Using Shadow

SUPPLIES

➡ **Graphite pencil**
➡ **Charcoal pencil**
➡ **Pen and ink, or watercolor**
➡ **Drawing paper**

1. Select an object, place it before a light-colored, clean wall, put strong light on it, and make a formal drawing of the object and its shadows. If you can't find a light-colored, clean wall, use a paper

backdrop. If you wish, experiment with two light sources rather than one.

2. The drawing in Figure 9.17 is a visual idea that was created by taping a vine to the studio wall and flooding it from one side with artificial light. The dark but soft shadows are as important to the overall image as the object casting them. The cast shadows in this case are soft because the

light, which is almost as large as the vine, is also close to the vine. The closeness of the light gives the effect of two light sources, or of somewhat diffused (spread out) light.

3. The combination of defined shapes and soft cast shadows on the same surface melts into an interesting gestalt pattern. This image is more important than the vine itself. The pattern is what gives the

STUDIO 5   *Continued from page 184*

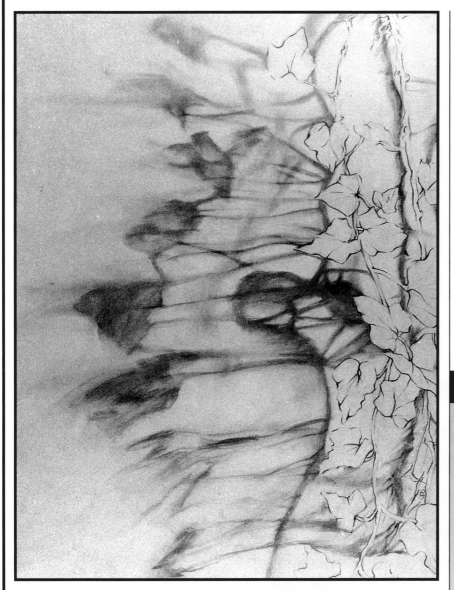

▲ **FIGURE 9.17**   Control of light and dark values gave this drawing by student Annette Berlin its strong formal character. How is variety demonstrated in this work?

Miner's work in Figure 11.6, page 210).

5. In this studio exercise, be certain to emphasize the design qualities, and minimize the literal qualities.

Computer Option

If your program includes a Motion Blur filter, try the following. Create or call up from disk a fairly lifelike drawing similar to the one illustrated in Figure 9.17. Copy it using the Duplicate or Copy/Paste command. Select the cloned image with the Scissors, Pick, or Lasso tool. Then open, the Filter menu (you will find it in the Edit menu) and specify Motion Blur. Set the direction of the blur to the left and the speed to 15 or 16, and apply the filter. Once the computer has redrawn the image, use the Zoom tool (bitmap editor) and Brush or Pen tool to restore sharp focus to the leftmost edges. Position the filtered image just to the left of the original.

drawing its effective design relationships. Of course, the fact that we can still recognize the vine adds literal qualities to this formal drawing.

4. Another example of a formal drawing with some literal qualities is Figure 6 in Color Section II. In this drawing by Shelly Settle, you can easily identify some of the real-life sources for the images you see in the drawing. Even so, she has made several structural changes pertaining to the elements and principles of art to create a stronger formal statement. (This drawing is also highly emotional. Compare it with Cherie

STUDIO 6

Formal Drawing of Fragmented Objects

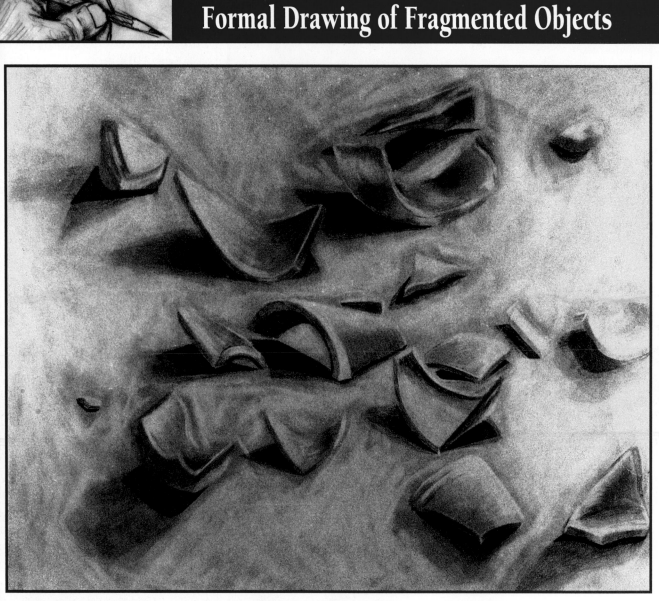

▲ **FIGURE 9.18**   This student drawing of a broken object is a product of careful composition derived from a seemingly unorganized source. How is the illusion of form realized?

SUPPLIES

⟶ **Drawing media of your choice**

⟶ **Drawing paper**

1. The drawing you see in Figure 9.18 is an effective formal drawing that came about as the result of a powerful expressive act on the part of an experienced painter and teacher named Hugh Gibbons.

2. Picture this, if you will: Students are sitting in a circle around a setup of pottery that they assume they are going to draw. The teacher enters, walks over to the setup, and says, "This is today's still-life setup, but before you start drawing, let me change it a little bit."

Then the teacher pulls out a hammer from under his coat and smashes all of the pottery! "Now draw it," he says.

3. Then he explains that the pieces are all individual shapes and forms that the students will have to observe carefully. The selective eye of each artist and the area of

STUDIO **6**   *Continued from page 186*

shattered pottery chosen by that artist will help determine the design qualities of the drawing. See Figure 7 in Color Section II for a formally well-structured, but expressive painting.

4. Now do your own formal drawing of something that has been fragmented. You can control the design by choosing the part of the setup you want to draw, enlarging objects for emphasis, and repeating shapes and patterns to create harmony.

Computer Option

Create or Open from disk a detailed illustration of an everyday object, such as a drinking glass, an animal, or a chair. Position the image in the center of the screen. Then, using a Pick, Scissors or Lasso tool, capture small, irregular portions of the image, and drag each to a different area on the screen. Attempt to arrange the pieces in a visually interesting way. If you wish, you can create the suggestion of form and cast shadows by using small patches of stippling or, if your program contains them, patterned fills.

STUDIO **7**

Enlargement of a Rubbing

SUPPLIES

- ❧ **Graphite pencil**
- ❧ **Drawing paper**
- ❧ **Drawing media of your choice**

1. Choose a rubbing from your sketchbook that you find especially appealing. Enlarge it four times its actual size for a finished drawing.

2. For a fairly accurate representation on a larger scale, draw a grid of ³⁄₁₆-inch (5 mm) squares on the small rubbing with a sharp pencil. Then, on the sheet for the finished rendering, duplicate this grid exactly using ³⁄₄-inch (20 mm) squares. This grid will be four times as large as the small grid and have exactly the same proportions.

3. Now copy the lines, values, and shapes from each of the small squares into the corresponding square on the large grid. Use any medium, but try to reproduce the value contrasts and gradations found in the small squares.

4. Put the drawing in a hinged mat. Even though the drawing is small, make the sides of the mat at least 2½ inches (6 cm) wide.

Computer Option

If you completed the Computer Option on page 173 which calls upon you to do a rubbing, open that file. If your program has rulers and guidelines, use those features to mark off a space approximately four times the size of your picture. Otherwise, simply "eyeball" the new dimensions. Use the Pick, Scissors, or Lasso tool to select your drawing. Drag the corner or corner handle of the image out to the space you have marked off or estimated.

| STUDIO 8 |

Formal Drawing of a Setup

SUPPLIES

◦ **Colored drawing media of your choice**

◦ **Drawing paper**

1. Draw your own setup using design relationships (combinations of elements and principles) to create a unified and interesting design. Use one large shape to occupy most of the space in the setup. Having this kind of anchor shape in the composition promotes unity. The smaller shapes around the anchor shape add variety and, if repeated, contribute to harmony. Harmony is further enhanced if the axis of the large shape is aligned with those of the smaller shapes.

2. Repeating some other art elements will contribute to the overall unity of your design. Most of the objects should be rendered in somewhat analogous colors, but also use a few objects in complementary or near complementary colors for contrasting accents.

▼ The setup for the etching in this illustration could have also been used for a drawing or a painting. Although the artist had the option of emphasizing any part of the setup, he chose to do his final rendering of this particular view. Is the art successful?

FIGURE 9.19   Giorgio Morandi. *Still Life with Coffee Pot.* 1934. Etching on paper. 29.8 x 39.0 cm (11¾ x 15⅜"). The Harvard University Art Museums, Cambridge, Massachusetts. Gift of Meta and Paul J. Sachs.

STUDIO 8   *Continued from page 188*

3. Decide whether to surround your composition with negative space, creating a vignette, or to crop in closely, as Berlin did in Figure 2 in Color Section II. For the vignette, apply some color and gradation in the negative area to keep that space related to the whole composition. For cropping, try a few thumbnail sketches first, and use cardboard cropping Ls to decide on your design.

4. Even though you will emphasize the design qualities in the setup, remember that the specific objects you choose to put in the setup will contribute to the character of your drawing and the viewer's psychological response to it. The selection, arrangement, and color of the objects and the cropping of your composition all depend on your selective vision.

STUDIO 9
Nonobjective Linear Drawing

SUPPLIES

→ **Dry color drawing medium or acrylic paint and drafter's ruling pen**

→ **Drawing paper**

1. Use a visual idea to create a formal drawing that expresses the action of the drawing process. For example, you could draw a square that has a complex pattern of criss-cross lines. You could use gradation from cool to warm colors and make a transition from the square outer shape of the drawing to a circular form on the inside of the square, still using criss-cross lines.

2. If you use a dry medium, be sure to keep your drawing instrument sharp. Acrylic paint should be thinned before you attempt to use it in a drafter's ruling pen, which makes consistent lines.

3. The working area of your drawing should bleed off the edge on all sides of the paper. You will want to wrap the finished drawing in acetate without matting it.

☞ TECHNIQUE TIP

Consistent Line

Paul Hanna achieved a consistent line in acrylic paint by using an automobile painter's pin-striping pen (Figure 4, Color Section II). This device distributes an even flow of paint onto a metal roller. The width of the roller determines the width of the decorative striping on the car or, in this case, the width of a line drawn on a canvas by an inventive painter.

Computer Option

Using the Rectangle tool, draw a perfect square. You can do this by holding down your program's "Constrain" key or keys (for example, Ctrl, Ctrl + Shift, Open Apple) while you draw. Switching to the Line, Brush, or Pencil tool, fill your square with a pattern of criss-crossing lines or, if your program features a Gradient Fill tool, a gradation from cool to warm colors. Build and add other geometric forms and shapes to create an interesting design statement.

3 Evaluation

■ APPLYING ART FACTS

On a separate sheet of paper, write the term or terms that best match each definition given below.

1. The aesthetic qualities used by formalists when analyzing and judging works of art.

2. A valuable tool that can be used to determine how the elements and principles of art are organized in a work of art.

3. Works of art that have not literal qualities or readily apparent subject matter.

4. The method employed to obtain a rubbing or frottage.

5. A popular medium at the turn of the century, it is used less frequently now that graphite pencils are readily available.

6. The term applied to the process of selecting a small area of a picture to use as an independent design.

7. A drawing technique in which one pattern of lines is overlayed with a second pattern going in another direction.

8. A drawing in which the shapes are placed so that they reach the outer edges of the working surface.

■ SHARPENING YOUR PERCEPTUAL SKILLS

CHAPTER 8

1. Use the design chart on page 158 to analyze Matisse's drawing of a Rumanian blouse on page 156. Compare the design relationships noted on your chart with those on charts completed by other students in your class.

2. Identify a work of art in Chapter 3 that you think a formalist would be inclined to judge favorably. In class point out the design qualities in the drawing that could be used to defend that favorable judgment.

3. Identify another work in Chapter 3 that you think a formalist would be inclined to judge unfavorably. In class explain why the work is unacceptable in terms of its design (visual) qualities. Conduct a class discussion in which attention is directed to identifying any other aesthetic qualities in this work. Can any of these aesthetic qualities be used to arrive at a favorable judgment?

CHAPTER 9

1. Select an art element identified on the design chart illustrated on page 158. Find a drawing in this book in which five or more principles have been applied to this art element.

2. Pick an object or person as the subject for a drawing. Make several realistic sketches of this subject, looking for an element and principle of art that you would like to emphasize. Make a final drawing emphasizing the chosen element and principle.

3. Complete three gesture drawings from a model, emphasizing value gradations on a large sheet of white paper. Work transparently in any medium so that your drawings are on top of each other. Select areas formed by the transparent overlapping and fill these in with black and two values of gray. Fill in the black areas first. Then render the two gray areas by hatching and cross-hatching. Leave some areas white. Maintain a two-inch margin around the entire drawing.

4. Use selective vision to identify an interesting or usual area or composition in a rural landscape or urban setting. Make a black and white photograph that captures your selected area or composition. Enlarge your photo to a minimum size of five by seven inches. Then complete a drawing that exaggerates the various objects and shapes in the photo. *Note:* Take several photos and select the photo to be enlarged from a contact sheet.

5. List the drawing tools and media you used in doing the studio exercises in Chapter 9. Which of these did you enjoy using the most? Which presented the most problems for you?

6. List the drawing techniques you learned and used in completing the studio exercises in Chapter 9.

■ MAKING CONNECTIONS

The following exercises are meant to illustrate the various ways art is tied to your education in other subjects.

1. **SOCIAL STUDIES (GEOGRAPHY).** Examine closely the drawing and painting of *Gas* by Edward Hopper (Figure 6.3, page 111; Figure 23, Color Section I). Where do you think the gas station might be located? In class discuss how the setting would differ if the station was located in another part of the country.

2. **MUSIC.** Use your *ears* when examining Vincent van Gogh's drawing of *Grove of Cypresses* (Figure 8.9, page 165). Can you think of a musical composition that captures the same sense of spiralling movement that van Gogh illustrates visually? If you play a musical instrument, can you compose a short score that echoes the rhythm in van Gogh's drawing? Perhaps other members of your class could create lyrics for your score.

■ THINKING CRITICALLY ABOUT ART

1. **DESCRIBE.** After examining Bacon's drawing of *The Painter* (Figure 9.1, page 166) for 15 to 20 seconds, close your book and write a detailed description of it from memory. Make sure that you include a listing of the elements of art as well as a precise description of the literal qualities. Read your description in class and listen while other students read theirs. Examine the drawing again. Were all the literal qualities and the elements of art accounted for in the descriptions provided?

2. **ANALYZE.** On a large bulletin board reproduce the design chart illustrated on page 158. Along with other members of your class find and cut out magazine illustrations that show the design relationships indicated by the intersections of the chart. For example, a photo of a performer on stage might show an emphasis of shape or form while another of a well-known sports personality might illustrate gradation of value. Place the magazine illustrations collected in the proper intersections of the design chart.

3. **COMPARE AND CONTRAST.** In class, compare Henri Matisse's drawing of *Head of a Girl with Braids* (Figure 8.8, page 164) with the *Portrait of a Lady* by Eugene Amaury-Duval, (Figure 1.13, page 13). How many students favor the Matisse? How many prefer the Amaury-Duval? Conduct a discussion in which the students in both groups provide their reasons for favoring one of these works over the other. What does this discussion reveal about the aesthetic preferences of class members?

Expressive Drawings

4

CHAPTER 10
Understanding and Judging Expressive Qualities

CHAPTER 11
Making Emotional Drawings

▲ **List the reasons this work might be considered successful as an expressive piece.**

James McNeill Whistler. *Weary.* 1863. Drypoint. 19.7 x 13 cm (7¾ x 5⅛"). National Gallery of Art, Wahington, D.C. Lessing J. Rosenwald Collection.

In Unit 4 you will focus on a third style of drawing—expressive drawing. In Chapter 10, "Understanding and Judging Expressive Qualities," you will make a final imaginary visit to the art gallery to consider how drawings can communicate feelings, moods, and ideas. As an emotionalist critic, you will interpret and judge drawings according to their expressive qualities.

After you have studied expressive qualities in drawings and discovered through art history how other artists have expressed emotion, you will learn techniques for personal expression in Chapter 11, "Making Emotional Drawings." Drawings with expressive qualities are often used to tell stories and to advertise products. By your choice of subject matter and the manner in which you draw it, using the formal elements, you can communicate a message to viewers in emotional drawings.

▲ Where do the stairs in this drawing lead? What appears to be on the stairs? What is found at the head of the stairs? What might lay beyond? How is dawn shown in this work? How does this drawing make you feel?

FIGURE 10.1 Harriet Feigenbaum. *Dawn.* 1973. Charcoal on paper. 259 x 130 cm (102 x 51½"). The National Museum of Women in the Arts, Washington, D.C. Gift of Wallace and Wilhelmina Holladay.

Understanding and Judging Expressive Qualities

Since you have already played the roles of an imitationalist and a formalist in previous chapters, we will ask you to become an emotionalist in this chapter. When you examine a drawing, you will focus attention on its expressive qualities. This is done in order to determine what feeling, mood, or idea it communicates. As an emotionalist, you will decide whether or not a drawing is successful in clearly communicating a message to viewers. Look at Figure 10.1 and read the caption. Answer and discuss the questions posed about the drawing with your classmates.

Since you are an emotionalist, you find that works of art with expressive qualities are especially appealing to you. When a friend tells you that a local gallery has scheduled an exhibition that includes emotional drawings, you arrange to attend.

objectives

After reading this chapter and doing the activities, you will be able to:

- Explain how an emotionalist judges drawings.

- Interpret the feelings, moods, and ideas expressed by artists in drawings.

- Judge drawings based on their expressive qualities and give reasons for your judgment.

Terms to Know

art appreciation
graphic designer's
verisimilitude

ou, the Emotionalist

The gallery is jammed with people, all voicing their opinions about the wide assortment of artworks on display. The room becomes silent when you enter; everyone is eager to see how you will react to the drawings. People edge closer as you pause before a black conte crayon drawing by the American artist Edward Hopper (Figure 6.3, page 111). They all watch as you study it closely.

Did You Know?

Hopper worked for twenty years designing book covers, illustrations, and advertisements for an advertising agency in New York City. He was forty-three years old when a gallery owner agreed to exhibit his watercolors. A few months after his first exhibition, which was highly successful, Hopper resigned from the agency. He spent the rest of his life drawing and painting.

Glancing up from the drawing, you notice that several of the onlookers are waiting for your reactions. What will you mention first? Will you review the clues you found as you tried to discover the meaning of the picture? If so, you might point out the narrow, deserted road; the line of dark trees bordering the far side of this road; the three gas pumps manned by a single small figure; and the tidy, compact service station with a sign that, like the tops of the gas pumps, provides no information at all.

You pause for a few moments, allowing your audience to think about these clues. Then you ask if anyone can explain what the work could mean, based on these clues. No one answers. Maybe they are afraid of making the "wrong" interpretation.

■ EDWARD HOPPER, PORTRAITIST

Edward Hopper can best be described as a portrait painter. His portraits, however, weren't of people; they were of places. Other portrait artists tried to capture the appearance and mood of people.

Hopper tried to capture the appearance and mood of places. He especially liked the man-made features that gave the modern landscape its unique character. His plain, carefully composed portraits of the modern city—monotonous, impersonal, and lonely—have rarely been equaled (Figure 10.2).

Hopper started working on his drawing *Gas* in 1940. Modern ways of transportation were rapidly changing America into a nation of commuters. People thought nothing of boarding buses, trains, and planes to travel great distances for business or pleasure.

Yet the favorite means of transportation was, by far, the automobile. More and more cars crowded into the highways. Superhighways had to be built to replace the narrow roads that had been adequate in the past. Soon people used highways instead of narrow country roads. The tiny service stations sprinkled alongside the old roads were doomed. These gas stations would meet the same fate as the hitching posts and watering troughs they had replaced earlier. Hopper observed this change and saw in it the subject for a painting.

Hopper's Methodology

The first thing Hopper had to do was find a gas station to paint. He wasn't satisfied, however, with painting just any service station. He was determined to find one that matched the image that had been slowly taking shape in his mind. After a long, fruitless search, he admitted that there was no such gas station.

SHARPENING YOUR SKILLS

What Does It Mean?

Study the drawing *Gas* and decide what it means to you. To do this, you must not only decide what feeling, mood, or idea it communicates, but you must also be prepared to indicate the clues in the drawing that led you to this decision.

▲ **How many people can you find in this picture? Why is this important to the mood or feeling that is communicated? Explain how the mood of this picture would change if people were shown walking in front of this line of stores.**

FIGURE 10.2   Edward Hopper. *Early Sunday Morning.* 1930. Oil on canvas, 88.9 x 152.4 cm (35 x 60"). Whitney Museum of American Art, New York, New York. Purchase, with funds from Gertrude Vanderbilt Whitney.

He then began a series of drawings combining features he had noted in several gas stations. In this way he was able to put his mental image into visual form, first as a drawing and finally as a painting.

Comparing the drawing and painting reveals that the design of the painting differs only slightly from that of the drawing. In the painting, the artificial light from the service station is stronger and the sign has been moved closer to the road. The road is shown curving out of sight in the darkness beyond the solitary building. The station in the painting seems to be in danger of being overrun by the high, flame-like orange grass surrounding it. The trees also seem more threatening, as though they were preparing to march across the deserted highway and surround the defenseless station.

The pose and appearance of the attendant have also changed. In the painting, he stands straighter and wears a vest and a tie. Why is he dressed in this manner? Is business at the gas station so slack that it is pointless for the attendant to change into work clothes?

It is impossible to say how many drawings Hopper may have made before beginning his painting of *Gas.* He often did thirty or more drawings in preparation for a painting. In this case, his patience and determination were rewarded with at least two memorable works of art. They show a place out of step with its time. The advancing twilight in both painting and drawing indicates more than the passing of another day. It marks the end of an era—an era symbolized by a lonely gas station on a narrow country road.

You explain that there could be several meanings for this drawing. You remind your audience that each one of them is influenced by his or her unique past experiences. These experiences may cause them to see and respond differently to the same clues in a drawing. You suggest two meanings for this drawing. The first can be understood easily and may not seem too exciting. The second meaning, however, is less obvious. The viewers will have to think about it carefully.

The Artwork Tells a Story

To introduce your first interpretation, you refer to the tops of the gas pumps, the sign, and the door and window of the tiny service station. All of these objects are illuminated by artificial lights. Light from the door and window can be seen on parts of the concrete drive, too. The dull sky, dark trees, and shadowed roadway suggest the approach of darkness.

It is dusk, and the lonely figure at the gas pumps is going through the routine of closing the service station for the night. The air is still. Only the occasional sounds made by the attendant disturb the stillness and remind us that the station isn't entirely deserted. You suggest that the approaching night, the absence of sound, and the single figure create a mood of loneliness.

You make another interpretation of the drawing that suggests a specific reason for the lonely mood. You ask your audience to look again at the road in the picture. Does it look like a busy highway? There are no signs of traffic at the moment. On the other hand, is there any reason to believe that there ever is much traffic on this road? Is this gas station there only to service the rare car that happens to drive down this remote country road? Why was it built in such an out-of-the-way location? Why is there only one person in evidence?

The people around you move closer, their curiosity aroused. You continue by explaining that conditions may have changed since the station was built. Maybe at one time this road was crowded, and business at the little service station was brisk. When automobiles were first manufactured, they could move only at a slow, deliberate pace. Since the passengers had more leisure time than people do today, they were content to enjoy a slow ride in the country. However cars—and people—have changed. Cars became more powerful, and more people owned them. People became more impatient and insisted on traveling from one place to another quickly.

These changes created a need for superhighways, which soon replaced the country roads. Left behind and almost forgotten were the service stations along those country roads. Like the one pictured in Hopper's drawing, they are reminders of a different time and a different, slower and more relaxed way of life.

It is always fascinating to learn how others have interpreted the same work of art. Unfortunately, there is no time for that now. Already someone is asking you to make a judgment about the Hopper drawing. Is it a good work of art? Decide for yourself if it is a successful drawing. Keep in mind, however, that you are an emotionalist. You base your decision on whether or not a drawing uses expressive qualities effectively. A work can be either imitationalist or abstract and still be judged on expressive qualities.

■ JUDGING HOPPER'S DRAWING

You might say that Hopper's drawing is an excellent work of art. It certainly succeeds in communicating an overpowering sense of loneliness. You might also state that it expresses an idea about the changes brought about by the passing of time and new ways of living. Anyway, you must make a decision—a decision which will indicate whether or not you appreciate Hopper's drawing. After all, **art appreciation** is an *act of making a judgment about a work of art and backing up that judgment with good reasons*. This means that you will have to defend your decision by pointing to the things you learned while studying the drawing. Already the crowd of people around you is becoming impatient to hear your decision. What will it be? (You can see Hopper's painting *Gas* in Figure 23 in Color Section I.)

■ INTERPRETING *GROSS CLINIC* BY THOMAS EAKINS

After deciding about the Hopper drawing, you move on to the other works on display. You pass by several before you stop at a large drawing by Thomas Eakins (Figure 6.5, page 113). Since you are an emotionalist, the work arouses your interest. You decide to look at it closely. As an emotionalist, study *Gross Clinic* and provide an interpretation of it.

■ JUDGING *SELF-PORTRAIT AT THE AGE OF TWENTY-TWO*

As you walk around the gallery, you are fascinated by what you can learn from drawings by studying their expressive qualities. Of course, expression isn't the main goal of every artwork. A drawing by the German artist Albrecht Dürer (Figure 8.6, page 161) is an excellent example of this fact. While interesting because of the artist's skill in making a lifelike self-portrait, it fails to communicate a mood, feeling, or idea. For this reason, as an emotionalist you give it a little more than a quick glance as you walk by.

SHARPENING YOUR SKILLS

Interpret Gross Clinic

As you try to decide what feeling, mood, or idea the drawing communicates, consider the following questions:

- What is happening here? What profession is being practiced?
- Do you usually picture people practicing this profession while they are dressed in street clothes? Are the street clothes in this picture modern or do you associate them with the past?
- Why has the distinguished-looking gentleman in the center (Figure 10.3) stopped working?
- This gentleman seems to be speaking. What could he be saying?
- Who are the people seated in the background? What are they doing?
- Why is the woman on the left hiding her eyes? (Figure 10.4)
- At what point in history could this scene have taken place?

Having answered these questions and others like them, you make first an interpretation and then a judgment. What emotions and ideas did the artist want to convey? Do you think this drawing is a successful work of art? What are the reasons for your decision?

◀ Compare and contrast the actions of these two figures. Do you think the dignified appearance of the man is emphasized by the cowering figure of the woman in the same picture?

FIGURE 10.3
Thomas Eakins. *Gross Clinic* (detail). 1875. India ink wash on cardboard. 60 x 48.6 cm (23⅝ x 19⅛"). The Metropolitan Museum of Art, New York, New York. Rogers Fund.

◀ **FIGURE 10.4**
Thomas Eakins. *Gross Clinic* (detail).

Artists at work

Delivering the Message with Style

"Last year I helped my mom pick out slides for the county fair photo contest and she won four awards. I'm really looking forward to working on the yearbook. What do you call people who do that for a living?"

Graphic designers are the *people who combine the written word with visual imagery to produce effective messages.* Some graphic designers act as senior art directors (also known as creative directors) and are the creative mainsprings of an advertising agency. They conceive ideas and develop strategies for advertising campaigns. They work with art directors, artists, marketing staff and clients to create effective programs for promoting many types of products and services. Today, some corporations employ their own art directors to design and maintain control over their products, packaging, and promotion.

Your success as an art director will depend largely on your creativity and your ability to work well with people. You will need a fertile mind to develop new themes that not only enhance the presentation of the content of your publication, but connect it to current events, attitudes, or trends.

As an art director, you must have good communication skills. You will need to convey your ideas to a wide array of other artists and indicate how their special skills will help develop the artistic theme of each issue. You must also have a strong desire for excellence, and the ability to analyze and criticize each completed issue, looking for ways to make next month's issue better.

Attaining a high supervisory position like that of art director requires expertise in several design areas and an extensive list of job accomplishments. You should attend a school that offers a strong program in graphic design (with an emphasis on publications, perhaps) and then concentrate on gaining successful graphic design experience.

Your idea about working on the yearbook is an excellent one. In high school, you might also consider working on the student newspaper and other publications. Keep helping with the photo club newsletter and look at similar publications to see how they develop their characteristic appearance.

Of course, you should take all the drawing, painting, graphic design, printmaking and art history classes that you can, but don't neglect English, literature, and history classes as these are essential to an understanding of writing and publishing.

Part-time work in a print shop, newspaper, or graphic design studio will also prove worthwhile, and any jobs that offer experience in printing and publishing are valuable.

Working as an art director for a corporation or advertising agency requires the same backgrounds and abilities, but these positions involve broader areas of interest and skill. A career involving typography, illustration, or photography might also appeal to you. You might also consider a teaching career in one of these areas.

Art directors combine the talents of many artists to create a publication that presents fresh and informative content with a consistent style and eye-catching look. They derive great satisfaction from meeting the challenge of producing work that entertains and informs the public. ■

■ IS *HEAD OF A GIRL WITH BRAIDS* A SUCCESS?

The loud whispering of excited voices attracts your attention. Looking about, you see people engaged in a lively debate in front of an ink drawing by the French artist Henri Matisse (Figure 8.8, page 164). Joining them, you are told that two earlier gallery visitors had expressed completely different opinions about this drawing.

This news doesn't surprise you since you played the part of the two gallery visitors in previous chapters. In Chapter 6 you were an imitationalist, and in Chapter 8 you were a formalist.

Suddenly you become aware that the people have stopped arguing. Everyone is looking at you. Apparently they are waiting to hear what you have to say about the Matisse drawing. You ask how the earlier visitors reacted to it. A volunteer from the group around you explains that the first visitor said it was unsuccessful because it lacked **verisimilitude**, *the appearance of being true or real.* The second critic, however, decided the drawing was successful because of its sensitive use of the elements of art, especially line.

As an emotionalist, do you agree with either of these two opinions? Of course not. Instead you choose to view the drawing from a completely different point of view. You ignore both the literal qualities and the design qualities. Instead, you focus on the expressive qualities evident in the Matisse drawing.

You note that the simply rendered face of the young girl in the picture shows only a trace of emotion. Her wide-open, dark eyes don't appear to be focused. Although her eyes are directed downward to her left, she doesn't seem to be looking at anything. Perhaps she is lost in her own thoughts or daydreams. If so, are her thoughts pleasant or unpleasant? It is difficult to answer that question with certainty. Unfortunately, the slightly curved line of the mouth fails to provide any more clues about her thoughts or feelings. Her mouth isn't completely relaxed, but we can't tell whether the girl has just finished speaking or is about to speak.

Using the expressive qualities to judge, you decide that this drawing is at least partly successful.

It does communicate a mood or feeling, although it is difficult to determine exactly what that mood or feeling is. The few clues available suggest a quiet, pensive moment. Something seems to have triggered the young girl's thoughts causing them to drift away from the here and now to a more fascinating inner world.

■ INTERPRETING AND JUDGING *OLD MAN FIGURING*

A drawing that is almost as simple in design as the Matisse drawing is on display nearby, and you walk over to it. This work by Paul Klee (Figure 10.5) should be easy to interpret. Like the Matisse work, it is an outline drawing, although it is overlaid with thin, irregularly spaced, horizontal lines. These lines act as a screen between the viewer and

▲ Explain why an imitationalist would probably consider this to be an unsuccessful drawing. What do you think a formalist would say about it? Did you immediately find it to be amusing?

FIGURE 10.5 Paul Klee. *Old Man Figuring.* 1929. Etching, printed in brown-black. 29.8 x 23.8 cm (11¾ x 9⅜"). The Museum of Modern Art, New York, New York. Purchase.

Make a Personal Judgment

You find another work in the gallery inviting because of its exciting use of expressive qualities (Figure 10.7). Study this drawing, and then make an interpretation (or interpretations) of it. Complete your study of the drawing by making a personal judgment about it. Remember that you are an emotionalist who relies on expressive qualities.

◀ What do you think the woman at the left might be looking at? Describe the expression on the face of the other woman. Do you think these women share a bond of affection? Why or why not?

FIGURE 10.7   Mary Cassatt. *In the Omnibus (recto).* c. 1891. Black chalk and graphite on wove paper. 37.8 x 27.3 cm (14⅞ x 10¾"). National Gallery of Art, Washington, D.C. Lessing J. Rosenwald Collection.

▲ **Why might this man be feeling depressed at the loss of a friend? Do you think you could have understood and appreciated this work if you had ignored its expressive qualities?**

FIGURE 10.6 Henri de Toulouse-Lautrec. *The Last Respects.* 1887. Ink and gouache. 65.4 x 49.2 cm (25¾ x 19⅜"). Dallas Museum of Art, Dallas, Texas. The Wendy and Emery Reves Collection.

■ JUDGING *THE LAST RESPECTS*

Before leaving the gallery, you study another work at some length. It is a large drawing by Henri de Toulouse-Lautrec entitled *The Last Respects* (Figure 10.6). You are attracted to it because it expresses a touching message in a quiet, respectful way. The bowed and bared head of a workman looking over his shoulder at a funeral procession communicates his sense of loss. The artist successfully avoided overdramatizing this scene by adding unnecessary details. The picture's restraint adds dignity to a simple scene of one human being offering a silent farewell to another. What is the relationship of the workman to the deceased? What could the workman be thinking? Could he be feeling ashamed because he has not joined the funeral procession? As an emotionalist, what judgment would you make about this drawing?

The emotional drawings you have seen in the gallery make you eager to create your own. Glancing at a clock on the gallery wall, you see that there is enough time to return to your studio to work. Of course your drawings will emphasize expressive qualities.

the portrait of an old man. The man is seen scratching his chin. His face expresses wide-eyed surprise. What causes that expression and what is the reason for the veil of horizontal lines?

Klee may have been trying to answer these questions when he titled his drawing *Old Man Figuring.* The gleeful expression on the man's face suggests that he has finally solved a problem or riddle. He smiles and his eyes open as he discovers the answer. He is separated from the viewer by a veil of ignorance, shown by the horizontal lines. He has figured out the problem, although the viewer is still puzzled by it. No one asks your opinion, but if someone did, you would say that the drawing is both clever and amusing. It is successful because it communicates humor in a sophisticated way.

CHAPTER 10 REVIEW

1. What does the emotionalist take into account when deciding upon a work's success or lack of success?

2. Explain what is meant by the expressive qualities.

3. How do the expressive qualities differ from the literal and formal qualities?

4. What would explain the fact that different people can arrive at different interpretations of the same artwork?

▲ Use your imagination to place yourself in the audience. The stage curtain is pulled aside, and Yvette Guilbert appears to take a curtain call. How did she appear? Did she give a loud and lively or quiet and restrained performance?

FIGURE 11.1 Henri de Toulouse-Lautrec. *Yvette Guilbert Taking a Curtain Call.* 1894. Watercolor, crayon. 41.6 x 22.9 cm (16⅜ x 9"). Museum of Art, Rhode Island School of Design, Providence, Rhode Island. Gift of Mrs. Murray S. Danforth.

CHAPTER 11

Making Emotional Drawings

Emotional drawings are those that make their most obvious impact through expressive qualities. As we explained in Chapter 5, however, very few drawings fit into only one style category. Few drawings are purely emotional, purely imitational, or purely formal.

In this chapter, you will learn that imitational images—literal qualities, or subject matter—are often required in emotional drawings to communicate the artist's feeling or idea (Figure 11.1). You will learn that the design qualities—the elements and principles of art—must be present in any drawing for it to function visually. You will also learn to use a mixture of media to create emotional drawings, use drawings to express humor, and create emotional illustrations.

Design Qualities in Emotional Drawings

An art movement concerned with the creation of a purely emotional visual art form made its appearance in New York in the 1940s and became an international phenomenon. Artists associated with this movement came to be known as Abstract Expressionists (see Chapter 3, page 64). The artworks produced by these Abstract Expressionists were characterized by an emphasis placed on spon-

SHARPENING YOUR SKILLS

Make an Action Drawing

SUPPLIES
- Compressed charcoal
- Red conte crayon, pastel chalk, colored pencil and technical pen or fine-line marker
- Bristol board

Try expressing some emotions by making an action drawing. Make some angry marks with a piece of compressed charcoal, red conte crayon, or pastel chalk. Next, make some fast marks with a colored pencil. These marks will be thinner and straighter than the angry marks and will probably go in only one direction. Choose a color that you think expresses speed.

For the next group of lines, use a technical pen or fine-line marker to make some slow lines—thin, black, spidery, leisurely lines that wander in and out and all around the drawing. Even though you are making an emotional drawing, it needs structure to communicate effectively. Make some of the slow lines overlap other lines to tie your drawing together and create unity.

▲ Though it isn't always evident in her finished pieces, Tina Fuentes derives many of her images from the human figure, as she did in *Moreno*.

FIGURE 11.2 Courtesy of the artist.

taneous personal expression rather than a concern for realistically rendered subject matter. Since subject matter was ignored, these works were entirely abstract or, more precisely, nonobjective.

They were expressive because the artists tried to communicate emotion by applying paint to canvases freely and spontaneously, often without concern for careful design. *The act of painting itself—and expressing the emotions the artists felt while painting—* was so important to these Abstract Expressionists that they referred to their work as **action painting**. You can see an example of Abstract Expressionism or action painting in Figure 8 of Color Section II.

Many expressionist artists today, however, realize the need for a more effective organization of visual structure, even in very expressive abstract work. Look at Tina Fuentes's drawing in Figure 11.2, for example. In this drawing Fuentes expressed emotion and energy, but she approached her drawing with control and created a unified image.

The mixed media drawing by Linda Kennedy (Figure 9 in Color Section II) has only one large abstract object filling the working area. The object—if it is an object—is extremely complex. Still, a rhythm is created by the brushstrokes combined with repetitions of color and value to help give the drawing an overall unity. This drawing is probably as close as a drawing can come to being purely emotional.

Both Kennedy and Fuentes experienced emotion in the almost athletic act of making the marks, and the marks remain as a record of their emotion. This kind of emotional drawing doesn't rely on subject matter to express its meaning. It uses structural or design qualities to express feelings about the process of drawing itself.

The charcoal drawing by Anita Mills (Figure 11.3) also uses design qualities to convey emotion. The effective design organizes subtle shapes, uses several horizontal and vertical alignments and succeeds in unifying the entire working area. The drawing also creates an interesting ambiguity between positive and negative space. The dark marks, however, are definitely expressive and suggest the strong emotion involved in their making. Many of these marks were made with an eraser, resulting in an unusual balance between creation and destruction of form.

Literal Qualities in Emotional Drawings

Even though you can make an emotional drawing without recognizable images, not all emotional drawings are abstract. Long before the Abstract Expressionists were expressing emotions about the act of painting, other artists were expressing emotion about subject matter. An outstanding example of an emotional drawing with subject matter is shown in Figure 2.14 on page 32. In this work, the artist attempted to communicate feelings about a subject by the way that subject was drawn. How successful was he? You can answer this question for yourself—by answering another question: Could you determine immediately what this figure was doing and feeling? If so, the artist succeeded.

Look at the drawing of an old woman's head by Geila Gueramian in Figure 11.4 on page 208. The artist expressed her message by the way she made the marks and by the extreme distortion of the facial anatomy. In Chapter 7, you saw the expressive distortion in Steve Haynes's portrait (Figure 7.33, page 139). Those distortions were moderate. The artist used them only to make the drawing more interesting. In Gueramian's drawing, however, exaggeration is largely what makes the drawing expressive. Along with the crinkly, spidery lines that cut into the face to form wrinkles and folds, and the harsh charcoal marks in the dark areas, the distortions suggest the

▲ Anita Mills took advantage of the flexibility of a dry medium and used it almost like paint in this drawing. Sometimes what is omitted or removed from a composition is as important as what remains.

FIGURE 11.3   Courtesy of the artist.

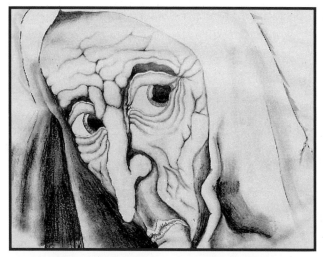

▲ FIGURE 11.4 **The expression and distortions are as important in this student work by Geila Gueramian as the kind of marks she used.**

resentment that can accompany old age. In Mike McAfee's drawing of a back fence overwhelmed by vines (Figure 11.5), the combination of pen line and graphite effectively expresses the tangled complexity and linear shadows of the scene—and nature's vengeance on an artificial barrier.

Emotion expressed in a realistic figure can often be seen in the body attitude or gesture of that figure (Figure 10, Color Section II). How could you use gesture to express fear, anger, or joy when drawing a figure? Can you identify any works of art illustrated in this book that do that?

In visual art as in other art forms—music, performance, and literature—there are *archetypes*. You respond to these archetypes on an emotional level

SHARPENING YOUR SKILLS

Drawing Single Figures in Wash

SUPPLIES
- India ink, pen, fiber-tipped pen, transparent watercolors
- Number 2 and number 5 round brushes
- Shallow dishes or watercolor palette
- Small sponge
- Medium-rough watercolor paper or block

Study the single figures in Kathy Hicks King's drawings, rendered when she was in high school (Figures 11 and 12 in Color Section II). In Figures 13, 14, and 15 you will find her later work; advertising billboards, and a fine art painting for exhibition purposes.

Pose a friend—in an interesting costume if possible—and make some similar wash drawings with pens and brushes. Don't make pencil sketches first. Spend about twenty minutes on each drawing, and make the figures about 14 inches (36 cm) high. Try to create drawings that are free and expressive (Color Section II, Figures 16–20).

Make two of these drawings each day for a week. Mat the best three of these drawings for display and for consideration to be included in your portfolio.

Computer Option

With the Pencil, Brush, or other freehand drawing tool, roughly sketch the contour lines of a human figure. (As an alternative, you may open from the disk a sketch which you previously completed.) Set the line width of the tool to extra-thick, and set the color to a bright pastel hue. Using broad mouse strokes, re-work the contour lines you drew. Again resetting the line width and altering the hue slightly, add additional lines and splashes of color. Continue to work in this fashion until you have produced a rich, shimmering wash effect.

◀ **FIGURE 11.5   Student Mike McAfee added expressive shadows with pencil to enhance the emotional appeal of his pen and ink back fence scene.**

because they are so recognizable. The young lovers, the villain, the buffoon, and the revered grandparent are archetypes.

Did You Know?

Commedia dell'arte is the name for a style of stage comedy that originated in Italy and was performed from the sixteenth to the eighteenth century. Like many of today's television situation comedies, it was based on a group of standard situations and a company of stock characters. The costumes and makeup they wore, the gestures they made, and their postures expressed the archetype role they played. Everyone loved these characters and expected certain attitudes and actions from them.

These characters included Columbine, the saucy sweetheart of Harlequin, who was a masked clown with colorful tights and a wooden sword. Other characters were the old man, Pantalone (or Pantaloon); Punchinello, the buffoon; and Scaramouche, the cowardly braggart. See Figure 21 in Color Section II for an example of artwork based on these archetypes.

Emotional Drawing with Mixed Media

Some approaches to expressing emotions are highly individual. Artists frequently invent their own ways to use both media and the art elements to express themselves.

Often the works of art they create are difficult to classify. They can be called paintings, sculpture, or photographs. Or they might be **collages** (*two-dimensional works of art created with items such as paper, cloth, photographs, and found objects*) or **assemblages** (*three-dimensional collages*) consisting of an assortment of objects attached to a surface. Since drawing is often involved in creating these works, we are including them in our discussion of emotional drawings.

Look at the work of Cherie Miner in Figure 11.6 on the following page. Although this work has no immediate recognizable images, it is full of emotion, which is expressed in the maplike quality of the shapes held together by the linear stitches. We suspect that the drawing contains symbolism based on

▲ The emotional qualities in Cherie Miner's work are evident not only in the use of collage and stitchery, but also in the symbolism of land forms and patchwork.

Figure 11.6 Courtesy of the artist.

the artist's personal background, but that meaning is hidden from us. Still, the work is interesting because of its expressive qualities, even if we don't know the origin of the symbols.

The work also makes use of interesting formal elements, although Miner hasn't stressed the principles of design in organizing those elements. The expressive qualities of the shapes and marks, however, are quite obvious. Making the marks was a fairly slow and calculated process, which means the emotion expressed is not about the action involved, but about the drawing's origins and formal elements. The drawing is abstract (it has no recognizable subject matter) and expressionist (it communicates emotion), but it isn't an Abstract Expressionist drawing. It doesn't express emotion about the act of drawing.

The bas-relief construction or assemblage by Fred Hudgeons (Figure 11.7) is another example of how drawing can be combined with other art forms to express a feeling or idea. **Bas relief** means *that some areas of the artwork project slightly from the surface.* The subject matter of this work isn't easy to recognize. It could be a section of some old building, deteriorating because of age and exposure to the weather. Perhaps it is the only section remaining of a once proud and sturdy structure.

Hudgeons uses drawing, painting, and other art forms to create a work that calls for a response from the viewers. Since some of the work's expressive qualities are created through the careful organization of design qualities, we could call this work an example of *structural expression.*

▶ Fred Hudgeons's massive work would seem out of place in a drawing text except that it depends on illusions that are created with drawing media.

Figure 11.7 Courtesy of the artist.

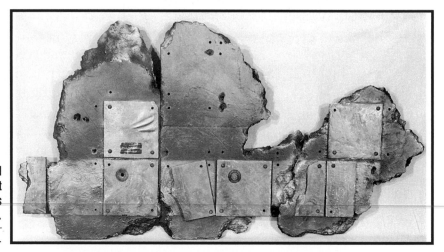

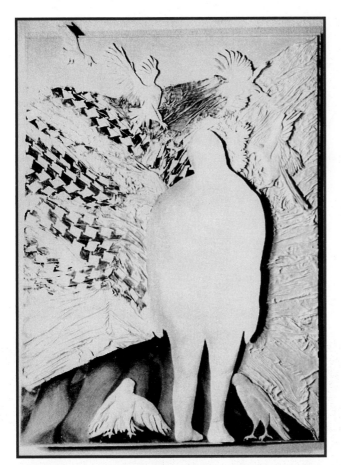

▲ Emotion and symbolism are evident in Nancy Merchant's complex mixed media drawing. What do the symbols mean to you? How would you interpret the meaning of this work?

FIGURE 11.8 Courtesy of the artist.

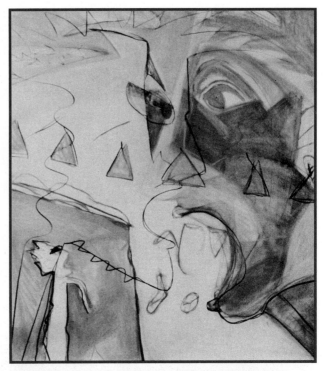

▲ Sara Waters's pastel and charcoal drawing is called *Having Words Again*. Do you think this is an appropriate title? Why?

FIGURE 11.9 Courtesy of the artist.

of Color Section II. The title of this imposing work is *Crossing*. Analyze it by observing the ways shape, line, and color are used. Can you interpret its meaning?

Humor and Symbolism

An emotional work of art need not express a serious idea to be successful. Many highly regarded works are humorous or playful. For example, look at the Verne Funk drawing in Figure 11.10 on page 212. This work could also be classified as a painting or a sculpture. The artist drew on a life-sized hollow clay column that had been fired like pottery in a kiln.

Funk used this work to poke fun at some dancers. The work is good-natured enough, however, not to offend the subjects of the joke. As you can see in Figure 11.11 on page 212, this work was exhibited along with several similar to it in a museum installation depicting a dance hall.

As an emotional work of art, Funk's dancers are successful, but they are more than simply entertain-

The work by Nancy Merchant (Figure 11.8) also uses the design qualities to elicit an emotional response from viewers. However, we can recognize human figures as well, so the artist has also used literal qualities.

Look at Figure 11.9. This charcoal and pastel drawing by Sara Waters is another example of using abstract images to express emotion. Examine this work closely. You probably noticed the large screaming face at the right—but did you also notice the tiny figure in the lower left corner? How do you think these two figures are related? What is the nature of that relationship? Waters has, with a few lines, shapes, and values created a work that causes viewers to re-examine their own, often strained, relationships with others.

Images are even more evident in the artist's large construction (which involves drawing) in Figure 22

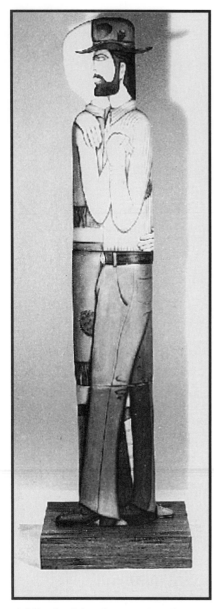

▲ Life-sized drawings on ceramic columns expresses Verne Funk's gently satirical sense of humor.

FIGURE 11.10 Courtesy of the artist.

▲ Verne Funk's works shown as a dance hall scene in a museum gallery. Do you think he is poking fun at anyone?

FIGURE 11.11 Courtesy of the artist.

▲ Suzanne Durland's humorous exaggerations and wandering line ask the viewer to respond to the playful emotions of childhood. Can you find other emotions expressed here also?

FIGURE 11.12 Courtesy of the artist.

▲ Don Durland's walking boots are an imposing image. How do they also express satire or humor?

FIGURE 11.13 Courtesy of the artist.

ing. In creating them, the artist also emphasized their design qualities by carefully selecting and fitting a variety of shapes, lines, and values comfortably on a slender column of clay.

Another artist whose work is notable for emotion and strong structure is Frank Cheatham, who has design work in the Museum of Modern Art and the Smithsonian Institution. He has designed the graphics for many items you might recognize such as the packaging for Testor's model-building supplies. Mr. Cheatham's recent work is predominantly

SHARPENING YOUR SKILLS

Mixed Media Construction Using Symbolism

SUPPLIES
- Materials of your choice, to assemble. (Examples: roll of wrapping paper, corrugated cardboard boxes painted with gesso.)
- Scissors or a mat knife to cut out pieces
- Felt-tipped markers to draw on the pieces
- Yarn, heavy string, or masking tape to hold pieces together

Work with other students to create a symbolic construction (assemblage). The construction will fill a three-dimensional space and should unite the wall and floor from any viewpoint. The size of your construction will be determined by the amount of space you can use.

Start by making rough sketches symbolizing some action, event, state of mind, or condition. The marks on the shapes you select or cut out should express how you feel about the subject. Make marks large enough to be easily seen. Photograph the construction before you take it down.

three-dimensional sculptural constructions in a mixture of various media such as wood, clay, leather, and metal. The creations are notable for the colorful drawings on the surfaces that have their source in the artist's deep understanding of human history, symbolism, mythology, and magic.

An example of these colorful images may be seen in Figure 23 in Color Section II.

The drawing of Suzanne Durland (Figure 11.12) also expresses some playful emotions. Although its design aspects are visually pleasing, the childlike innocence of this work holds the viewer's attention. Ms. Durland is half of a family team of artists. There is also humor in the art of Don Durland, her husband, but it is often expressed as gentle ridicule. You can see this quality in the almost ornate treatment of the subject in Figure 11.13. Durland's drawing, limited to a single elegant boot, effectively arouses the viewer's curiosity and stimulates the imagination. One cannot help speculating about the appearance and mannerisms of someone choosing to wear such a boot.

Creating Emotional Illustrations

An illustration, you will recall, is simply art that is used to help tell a story, give instructions, or make a product look attractive. The pictures in this book are illustrations. Thanks to the invention of printing, illustrations can be used to communicate with many people. In order to communicate, illustrations often need strong emotional qualities. A simple line drawing is the easiest kind of illustration to reproduce with modern printing methods.

A *line drawing, made up of solid blacks and whites* is referred to as **line art**. Future Akins's *Bedroom Heroes/ Cowboy's Fantasy* in Figure 11.14 on page 214 is an example of line art that dramatically uses the high contrast of white line on black.

Akins originally made a **linocut print**; that is, she cut her *design into a block of linoleum (a kind of floor covering), put ink on the surface, and pressed the paper onto the linoleum block to make the print.* By using this medium, she captured the white-on-black contrast and expressive line quality. This print was later reproduced

To an artist, a print is an artwork produced by applying ink to a surface on which the artist has created images and pressing paper against that surface.

Images are made by marking on, carving out of, or etching into a surface. The surface from which images are transferred to paper is referred to as the *printing plate*.

The surface may be:

- A linoleum block (for a *linocut*).

- A wood block (for a *woodcut*).

- A metal plate (for an *intaglio*).

- A stone or metal plate (for a *lithograph*).

- A silk screen (for a *serigraph*).

The surface can be used to make several prints of the same composition. Prints of the same composition are referred to as an *edition* and are usually individually signed, numbered, and titled by the artist.

Some art dealers advertise works as prints that are really only reproductions. Reproductions are created by photographing works of art through screens and color filters. The resulting film is used to make metal plates for a high-speed commercial press. These reproductions are lower in quality than prints and are less valuable because they aren't produced by the artist or made from plates on which the artist has created images.

▲ Future Akins chose linocut for this expressive, high contrast piece called *Bedroom Heroes/Cowboy's Fantasy*. It has been used as an art gallery poster. Can you use clues to interpret its meaning?

FIGURE 11.14   Courtesy of the artist and Lubbock Fine Arts Center.

by modern commercial means as an illustration for an art center calendar. Do you think the work succeeds in expressing an idea or emotion? What is that idea or emotion? What clues can you point to in the work that will support your interpretation?

Figure 11.15 on page 216 is another expressive illustration in line. It didn't start out as line art, however. It was done on a somewhat grainy paper with pen and then shaded with a black pencil. After this, it was reproduced on a photocopying machine. All of the gray values of the pencil shading were translated into black dots, which give the shading strokes a crude, almost stippled look. This approach expresses the tough and somewhat unpleasant personality of Mister Suitcase, a character in a story by the artist James Johnson.

■ FIGURES IN EMOTIONAL ILLUSTRATIONS

It is often the job of an illustration to convey emotions about people to viewers. The human subjects in a drawing may be real, as in a photograph advertisement of a product. Or they may be imaginary, as in a story illustration. In either case, the way the artist draws human subjects is important in communicating clearly the message of the illustration. Figure 2.2 (Chapter 2) is an expressive preliminary drawing for a *Saturday Evening Post* cover by Norman Rockwell. How did Rockwell express the sadness of parting in his drawing of the figures? Where do these people live? How do you know this? Which person is leaving, and where is he going?

The charcoal pencil illustration of the old mountain man (Figure 11.16, page 217) uses distortion of another kind to express emotion. This illustration

Artists at Work

Sharing Legends through Art

"Well, usually, I'm very shy, but I like to draw pictures and tell stories about them. Are there many artists who do that?"

*I*f your best way to connect with the world is to draw it, you might think about becoming a book illustrator. Actually, careers in book illustration provide opportunities for many talented artists. They interpret experience, preserve culture and pass it on to new generations.

Many illustrators began collecting and refining their drawings when they were your age. One launched his career at the age of eighteen. In his first book, he used bold, glowing colors and strong lines to express himself in the drawings for a story about a little boy.

You could produce a series of drawings and then create a story about them. You could also let someone else write a story for the drawings. You might also consider making drawings for stories that you have read. Some illustrators base their stories on folk tales and legends. The timeless, fundamental themes and universal appeal of these stories make them fertile ground for storytellers and illustrators.

To be successful as an illustrator, you must be able to draw and paint, above all else. Creating illustrations that parallel the written word also requires an understanding of the techniques of storytelling and a sensitivity to the nuances of language.

Schools that offer majors in illustration can help prepare you for many types of illustration work. While drawing and painting would make up much of your course of study, most art schools and many colleges offer classes in figure drawing, rapid sketching, printmaking and painting in all media that can expand your range of experience. A portfolio showing your skill and versatility is an asset when trying to land a job.

It is never too soon for an illustrator to start refining techniques and experimenting with styles. You should take all the drawing, painting and two-dimensional design classes available. You should also study history, English, literature, and narrative writing to help you become a more capable storyteller.

You should study illustrations in a variety of books, periodicals, brochures, album covers, and posters. Collect examples of different types of illustrations and file them according to artist, subject matter or style.

Your ability to draw and paint is also useful in all other fields of illustration: advertising, cartoon, fashion, product, storyboard and architectural rendering. Many successful art directors began their careers as illustrators. Some illustrators who have become masters of technique and media find another source of income by selling their paintings in galleries. The job of interpreting modern life in the light of ancient legends and myths can be rewarding and fulfilling, but all illustrators have the satisfaction of knowing that their unique visions represent an important cultural voice. ■

could have been done in ink or watercolor wash. Can you think of any reason why the artist chose to use pencil instead? Is the old fellow in the drawing a large man or a small one? (Look at the size of his hands in relation to his rifle.) Is he stalking a bear, seeing a ghost, or thinking about his lonely way of life? (Look at his clothing, the way he holds his head and shoulders, and the expression on his face.) What emotions does this old man stir in you? Do you fear him? Do you feel sorry for him or find him amusing? Why?

▲ The character of James Johnson's *Mr. Suitcase* is clearly expressed by the kind of line and reproduction method. Why would the artist choose to depict a suitcase in this way?

FIGURE 11.15 Courtesy of the artist.

SHARPENING YOUR SKILLS

Emotional Drawing of a Person

SUPPLIES
- Charcoal pencil
- Drawing paper, see-through vellum, or layout paper
- Drawing media of your choice

Draw a person's head and face using exaggeration to communicate emotion. You can work from either a model or a photograph.

First, use a charcoal pencil to make an imitational drawing. Note the shapes and planes of the face and how they fit together. Then overlay the drawing with a sheet of see-through vellum or layout paper. Reproduce the areas that will remain imitational in the finished drawing, and greatly exaggerate the areas you want to emphasize.

Using this overlay as a rough sketch, do a finished drawing in the media of your choice and exaggerate even more. Use the line variety to add interest to your drawing.

Computer Option

Select a tool that will create freehand lines, such as a Pen, Brush, or Pencil tool. Set the line width to fine, the color to deep gray (about 50 percent). With the mouse, draw the head and face of an imaginary individual; do not be concerned if some of the lines are rough. Now switch to your program's shape and/or Zoom tool (bitmap editor). Working on a section of your drawing at a time, exaggerate some of the lines and shapes, while refining (smoothing) others. Your finished portrait should have a strong emotional appeal.

▲ **FIGURE 11.16** What physical exaggerations do you see in this illustration of the old man? What do they tell you about him? Does the drawing's technique reinforce these ideas?

SHARPENING YOUR SKILLS

Color Emotional Drawing of a Person

SUPPLIES
- Charcoal pencil
- Drawing paper, see-through vellum or layout paper
- Color drawing media of your choice

Repeat the steps of the last activity until you are ready to do the finished rendering. Then decide how to use color to express emotion in the portrait.

An analogous color structure in hues and values of reds might express anger. Cool colors suggest tranquility. Purples and violets are often associated with the exotic or mysterious. Remember that a totally analogous color structure can be dull without some complementary accent and some value gradation. Pastel chalks are a good medium for this drawing since you can use brilliant colors and make expressive marks.

CHAPTER 11 REVIEW

1. What is meant by *expressive qualities*?
2. Name some visual symbols that most everyone recognizes.
3. Tell the difference between collages and assemblages.
4. Find a work of fine art in this book that exhibits humor. In a short paragraph write the title of the work, the name of the artist, the page where it appears, and tell what clues led you to your conclusion.

STUDIO 1

Eraser Drawing Using Stencils

SUPPLIES

- ↝ Layout or typing paper
- ↝ Rubber cement
- ↝ Medium-weight, medium-surface bristol board
- ↝ Charcoal or graphite
- ↝ Sandpad
- ↝ Felt pad, cotton, or tissue
- ↝ Kneadable eraser
- ↝ Charcoal pencil

1. In this drawing you will manipulate shapes to express an emotion. Start by cutting a variety of large and small simple shapes from layout or typing paper. Use rubber cement to glue these to a sheet of bristol board. Rubber cement will attach the shapes firmly, but after it dries you can peel off the shapes.

2. Now make some carbon dust from charcoal or graphite with your sandpad, and rub it onto the drawing with a felt pad, cotton, or tissue. Don't worry about applying the dust smoothly. An uneven application will give the drawing more character.

3. Carefully peel off the paper stencil shapes. Then draw into the gray ground with an eraser to connect some of the shapes and soften some of their edges. Complete your composition by alternating a charcoal pencil with the eraser, applying more carbon dust, or using more stencils for a transparent effect. Restenciling some areas will help relate the shapes to the surface and provide unity.

4. Do several of these drawings. Practice will improve them rapidly and noticeably. Choose the best ones to spray with fixative and mat.

STUDIO 2

Color Drawing of a Group of Figures

SUPPLIES

- ↝ Drawing media of your choice
- ↝ Drawing paper

1. Draw a group of figures like the one in Philip Ford's drawing (Figure 21 in Color Section II). This expressive pastel and conte drawing is based on *commedia dell'arte* characters from the Italian theater (see Did You Know? on page 211) as well as on some of Ford's childhood puppets.

2. For an idea for this drawing, consider occasions when people gather. A scene from a play or a crowd scene in history or literature would be good subject matter for this emotional drawing. Remember that you are making an expressive statement about the people and the event. Since you aren't drawing an illustration, you shouldn't try to tell a specific story.

3. Make a preliminary drawing to decide how to arrange the figures and objects to achieve unity. You can use large, non-detailed shapes for this rough drawing. For the finished drawing, concentrate on securing a unified arrangement of the shapes instead of a perspective drawing with accurate proportions.

4. Apply the marks in your drawing to express the emotion you want to convey. Use colors that you think suggest this emotion.

STUDIO 3

Drawing on Mixed Media Collage

SUPPLIES

- Graphite pencil
- See-through paper
- Various kinds of paper or fabric, found objects
- Colored pens or pencils
- Illustration board
- Glue or acrylic medium

1. For this activity you will create a mixed media collage and then use drawing to add line, value, and color.

2. First, find some items in your sketchbook that you like or about which you feel a strong emotion. Reproduce these items on overlays, refining or distorting their shapes to reflect the emotion you feel.

3. Transfer these shapes to different kinds of paper or fabric of your choice. Cut or tear them out. Enhance some of these shapes by attaching **found objects**—*natural or man-made objects found by chance*. For example, you could sew sequins to cloth or glue leaves to paper.

4. Draw on the shapes with colored pens or pencils to add line, value, and color. Then glue the shapes to the illustration board in a way that reinforces the emotion you are trying to express. Acrylic matte or glossy medium, the liquid used to mix acrylic paints, makes a good collage glue. White glue thinned with water can also be used. Finish the collage by drawing into it to unify areas of design.

Computer Option

If you routinely print out copies of your work, examine several computer drawings that you have completed in different styles and expressing strong emotion. On the printout for each, circle objects or figures that might be juxtaposed interestingly in an electronic collage. Then open the files in which these works are stored and, using the Pick, Scissors, or Lasso tool, select the objects. Use the Copy command to copy the objects, and save them in a new file. Experiment with positioning them in different ways on the screen. Add color, stippling, and patterned fills.

STUDIO 4

Drawing on a Three-Dimensional Object

SUPPLIES

- Cardboard box or tube
- White acrylic gesso
- Brush
- Sandpaper
- Magazine photographs
- Acrylic medium
- Drawing media of your choice

1. In this artwork you will poke fun at some well-known figure. You will need a long, narrow cardboard box, or a cardboard tube about one foot long. Paint the box or tube with two or three coats of white acrylic gesso, sanding between coats. When you are finished painting, the box or tube should have a uniformly white surface. For extra durability, paint the inside of the box also.

2. Find a magazine photograph of the face of the person you wish to use as your subject. Cut it out and glue it with acrylic medium to one end of the box or tube. Or you can transfer it in the manner described in the Technique Tip. Use any drawing media you like to finish the design. You can also add more photographs.

STUDIO 4 *Continued from page 219*

3. To protect your finished art, apply a coat of acrylic medium. Test the medium first, however, to make sure it won't dissolve any drawing media you have used.

4. You can see some examples of student drawings on three-dimensional objects in Figure 11.17. Even though you are using drawing to communicate playfulness, remember to control the design qualities to create a unified composition.

☞ TECHNIQUE TIP

Transferring Printed Photographs

To transfer a magazine or newspaper photograph to a white surface, soak the printed picture briefly in turpentine, lighter fluid, or some other solvent. Then lay the photograph facedown on the surface, and absorb the excess solvent with tissue. Rub the back of the photograph firmly with a smooth stylus or ballpoint pen.

After you remove the printed photograph, you will see its mirror image on the working surface. Turpentine transfers work best when you use freshly printed magazines or newspapers.

The *decoupage* method is another way to transfer magazine photographs. It takes more time than a turpentine transfer, but it produces a smooth and permanent transfer. Put about three coats of clear acrylic medium on the printed surface. When the surface is dry, soak and sponge most of the paper off the

Computer Option

If your program has the ability to show perspective (via a 3-D, Add Perspective, or Add Depth command), or apply envelopes to objects, try the following. Begin by examining the completed student artworks done with conventional media in Figure 11.17. Now locate a clip-art image of a famous person or type of individual; you may, of course, use such an image that you have created on disk. Copy or import the image into a new file. Use either a perspective command or apply an envelope to the image that will allow you to achieve one of the looks in Figure 11.17.

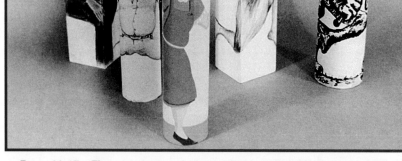

▲ **FIGURE 11.17** These student works began from an idea like the one used in Figure 11.9. They were done by (left to right) Susan Nall, Nancy Fagan, Brad Fuoss (two), and Rob Wilson.

back with water. Dry the image, and glue it to the surface with more acrylic medium.

✚ SAFETY NOTE

Using Solvents Safely

Turpentine, lighter fluid, and most other solvents are flammable. Be careful to keep them away from flame. Also, most of these materials emit toxic fumes, so work in a well-ventilated area.

Solvents can also harm your skin, so wear rubber gloves. Some solvents, such as turpentine, can blister your skin painfully if they soak through clothing.

STUDIO 5

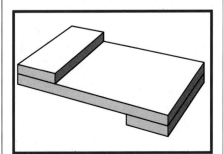

Linocut Greeting Card Illustration

SUPPLIES

- Drawing medium of your choice
- Linoleum block
- Gouge
- Tray or plate
- Brayer
- Water-soluble block printing ink (recommended)
- Wooden spoon
- Rice paper or other smooth, somewhat absorbent paper

1. A good way to use line art for an illustration is to print your own greeting cards. To do this, draw your design on a linoleum block, scoop out the negative areas, ink the block's surface, and use the block to make a print. First, make several correctly proportioned rough sketches of the image you have chosen for your illustration. You should realize that the image produced on the print will be in reverse, as if you are looking in a mirror.

✚ SAFETY NOTE

Cutting Blocks

When you use the gouge to scoop out the portions of the block that you don't want to be inked, always push the gouge away from you, using both hands. Never hold the block in your hand to cut it. Put it against the inside corner of an L-shaped block fastened firmly to a table or bench, or use a bench hook.

Since letters will also be reversed you should draw them in reverse on the block. We recommend that you omit lettering on your first linocut; you can leave space on your cards for a handwritten message or make a double-folded card and write on the inside.

2. When you have finished designing your illustration, draw it on a small linoleum block, 4 x 6 inches (10 x 15 cm) in size. You are now ready to cut out the design. Use a bench hook or fasten strips of wood to your workbench or table in the shape of an L, and place the block in

☞ TECHNIQUE TIP

Bench Hooks

Easily constructed wooden bench hooks are ideal for use during the cutting operations required in printmaking. Hooked over the edge of a desk or table, they hold linoleum or wood blocks in place and make cutting less hazardous.

FIGURE 11.18   Bench hook.

the corner of the L so that it won't slip when you push against it. Use a knife called a *gouge*, which is designed for cutting a wood or linoleum block. Cut away the parts of the block that you don't want to print in the design. *Note:* See the Safety Note "Cutting Blocks" for instructions on using the gouge.

3. The next step is to apply ink to the block. The rubber inking roller used for this process is called a brayer. The block printing ink you will use is a thick kind especially designed for block printing.

Computer Options

If your program includes Filter commands, examine the list (you will find it in the Edit menu) and see if a "woodcut" filter appears among the possibilities. Next choose a subject for your illustration that might appear on a greeting card of some sort. Using a freehand line tool (such as a Pen or Brush tool), do a rough drawing of your subject. Apply the woodcut Filter command. Use the Undo command to restore your drawing and reapply the Filter after experimenting with various settings. When you are pleased with the result, save your work.

STUDIO 5   *Continued from page 221*

4. Squeeze some ink from the tube onto a smooth, nonabsorbent surface, like an old tray or plate. Roll it smooth with the brayer. Then roll some ink onto the printing surface of your block, and lay the rice paper (or any other smooth, absorbent paper) over it. (Actually, rice paper isn't made from rice, but from fiber of the mulberry plant or an herb called rice paper tree.)

5. To print the design, rub the back of the paper with a wooden spoon or a similar smooth tool. You will have to practice to learn how heavily to ink the block and what tools to use for pressing the design onto the paper. *Note: A* **woodcut print** *is made the same way as a linocut print, except a block of soft wood is carved instead of the linoleum.*

6. After you have printed the design, clean the ink off all the tools with water.

✚ SAFETY NOTE

Cleaning Blocks and Brayers

You should always wipe any remaining ink from a block and brayer after you have finished printing. If you have used a water-based printing ink, you can use water for cleaning. If you have used oil-based ink, however, you should use a solvent such as turpentine. Remember that if you use a solvent, you should be careful not to inhale the fumes, get the solvent on your skin, or let it come in contact with your eyes.

STUDIO 6

Two-Color Woodcut Illustration

SUPPLIES

- Pastels
- Drawing paper
- Two or more wood blocks
- Gouge
- Tray or plate
- Brayer
- Water-soluble printing ink
- Wooden spoon
- Rice paper or other smooth, absorbent paper

1. Choose a story and illustrate it with a two-color woodcut print. You can see an example of this kind of print in Figure 25 in Color Section II. Make your print at least 11 x 14 inches (28 x 36 cm) in size. You can also see a good example of a woodcut print by Paul Hanna in Figure 11.19.

2. Use pastels for your rough sketches. Use only flat areas of color or colored lines since it is difficult to reproduce gradation on the wood block.

3. Basswood, the light wood of a linden tree, is one of the best kinds to use for a woodcut, but you can use any soft wood block. You can even use an old drawing board, but don't cut too deeply if the board is hollow.

4. Transfer the pastel sketch to the wood block, turn the sketch facedown on the block and rub the back side of the drawing with your hand. You can make corrections or add details by drawing directly on the block. Use the gouge to cut around the design on the block. Remember to clean off all remaining chalk before trying to ink the block because the chalk will stick to the inked brayer.

STUDIO 6   *Continued from page 222*

5. You will need one block for each color you want to use in the print. Often woodcuts are printed in black and one color, but if you have patience and enough blocks, you can print as many colors as you wish. Using more than one printing block requires a technique known as *registration*, or positioning the paper and the inked blocks so that the colors print in the correct places.

6. To obtain the correct color registration, prepare a printing block for each color. Transfer those parts of the drawing to be printed to the appropriate color block. Mark the outline of the block's corners on the drawing the first time you transfer it, and align the other blocks the same way when transferring the drawing to them.

7. To place the paper on the blocks in the same spot each time you print a color, tape the paper to the block for the first color, and mark the outline of the two sides and corner of the paper on the block. Measure where these lines forming the corner are located on the first block; then measure and draw them in the same place on all other blocks. You will have to tape the paper to the block on one edge so that it won't slip while you are rubbing with the wooden spoon.

8. On a woodcut, overlap the edges of the colored areas about ⅛ inch (3 mm) to avoid leaving a white space between colors. Print the more transparent colors and the colors with a lighter value first. The darker or more opaque colors will cover the edges of the others, making a clean division between colors.

▲ Paul Hanna's large woodcut, *Resistant Man*, has been featured in a number of exhibitions. How would you react if you encountered this figure on a deserted street late at night?

FIGURE 11.19   Courtesy of the artist.

9. Let the ink dry between each color printing. Water-based inks may dry in minutes, but you may need to wait an entire day for oil-based inks to dry.

4 Evaluation

■ APPLYING ART FACTS

On a separate sheet of paper, write the term or terms that best match each definition given below.

1. The aesthetic qualities emotionalists favor when making and defending judgments about works of art.

2. Two-dimensional works of art composed of papers, newsprint, photographs, and other items attached to a surface.

3. Artworks in which the expressive qualities are created through the careful organization of design qualities.

4. A line drawing composed of solid blacks and whites.

5. In the printing process, the term used to identify the surface from which images are transferred to paper.

6. A type of art in which some areas of the work project slightly from the surface.

7. A knife designed especially for cutting a wood or linoleum printing block.

8. The term used to identify a series of prints of the same composition.

■ SHARPENING YOUR PERCEPTUAL SKILLS

CHAPTER 10

1. Make a list of at least eight colors on the chalkboard. Discuss the various feelings or emotions associated with each of these colors. Identify and discuss the various color combinations that could be used to emphasize emotions.

2. Examine Harriet Feigenbaum's drawing of *Dawn* on page 194. If the artist had elected to use color in completing this work, which hues do you think she would have used to accent the feeling or emotion she hoped to communicate? Write these colors on a slip of paper and, along with other students in your class, turn these in. Compile a list of the colors identified by class members. Which were mentioned most often? Which colors were not mentioned?

3. Matisse's drawing of *Head of a Girl with Braids* (Figure 8.8, page 164) might appeal to a formalist, but would probably not be acceptable to an emotionalist. Assume for a moment that Matisse wanted to change this work to make it more expressive. How could he change it to accomplish this objective without altering the girl's impression? On a sheet of sketch paper, make a drawing in which you incorporate these changes to Matisse's drawing. Exhibit your work in class without indicating the emotion you were attempting to illustrate. Could anyone identify the emotion?

CHAPTER 11

1. Express the emotion of sadness in an abstract, nonobjective drawing. Try similar drawings in two or three different media. Which of these media seemed most suitable for expressing sadness? Repeat this exercise using different emotions as your "subject matter."

2. Complete a realistic drawing that expresses a personal emotion about the subject of drawing. Choose colors that help emphasize that emotion. Use pastels or a combination of pastels and colored pencils.

3. Decide on an emotion you want to express. Use found objects to create an assemblage that expresses that emotion. Do preliminary sketches in your sketchbook to develop ideas for your assemblage. You may want to draw on the parts of the assemblage to enhance the effect you hope to achieve.

4. Draw a group of five people engaged in some amusing or unusual activity. Use magazine or newspaper photograph transfers for the heads. Use the medium or media of your choice for the bodies. Work on illustration board and allow enough margin for a hinged mat.

5. Make a list of the drawing tools and media you used in completing the studio exercises in Chapter 11. Which of these did you enjoy using the most? Which presented the most problems for you?

6. List the drawing techniques you learned and used in completing the studio exercises in Chapter 11. Which of these techniques was used for the first time? Do you think you will use it again? Why or why not?

■ MAKING CONNECTIONS

1. **LANGUAGE ARTS.** Imagine that you are living in one of the second-story rooms illustrated in Edward Hopper's *Early Sunday Morning* (Figure 10.2, page 199). Write a description of the interior of the room and the view you would have from your window. Identify this window in class and read your description.

2. **HISTORY.** Visit your school or community library and research the surgical procedures practiced at the time Thomas Eakins created his drawing of *Gross Clinic* (Figure 6.5, page 113; details 10.3, 10.4, page 199). How have these procedures changed over the years? Present your findings to the class.

3. **ECONOMICS.** Edward Hopper's painting of *Early Sunday Morning* (Figure 10.2, page 197) was completed in 1930, just one year after the stock market collapse that heralded the Great Depression. Do research to identify the causes for this economic catastrophe. Present your findings in class and discuss how Hopper's painting reflects this period in our nation's history.

4. **MUSIC.** Conduct research to find out what kind of music was popular in the United States during the time of the Great Depression. What does this music and Hopper's painting tell you about the mood of the country during this period?

■ THINKING CRITICALLY ABOUT ART

1. **DESCRIBE.** On a sheet of sketchpaper, complete a detailed pencil drawing of the storefront that might be located next to the last shop seen on either end of Hopper's painting of *Early Sunday Morning* (Figure 10.2, page 197). Make certain that the drawing of this storefront measures exactly eight inches in height. Your drawing should remain faithful to the realistic style and the mood noted in Hopper's work. Exhibit your drawing along with those completed by other members of the class, mounted in a line on the bulletin board to replicate the line of storefronts noted in Hopper's work.

2. **ANALYZE.** As a class, carefully analyze the bulletin board display of shopfronts. Discuss ways of rearranging the different drawings to create a more unified composition.

3. **INTERPRET.** Discuss the mood communicated by the bulletin board display. Does it succeed in expressing a mood similar to that of the Hopper painting? How could a similar composition made up of storefronts be made to express an entirely different mood?

4. **JUDGMENT.** Did the class as a whole regard the composition as a success? What could have been done to make it more successful?

Special Topics in Drawing

CHAPTER 12
Linear Perspective

CHAPTER 13
Cartooning

CHAPTER 14
Computer Drawing

▲ The graceful linear style of King's work is due to her affection for drawings done by the Italian Renaissance artist, Sandro Botticelli. Are its literal design and its expressive qualities appealing?

Jessie M. King. *Book Illustration: Where I Made One—Turn Down an Empty Glass.* c. 1903–1905. Pen and black ink on vellum. 21.6 x 18.4 cm (8½ x 7½"). The Baltimore Museum of Art, Baltimore, Maryland. Purchase, Nelson and Juanita Greif Gutman Collection, by exchange.

Unit 5 provides information about and techniques for three special kinds of drawing: accurate perspective drawing, cartooning, and computer drawing.

Accurate perspective drawing requires special measuring tools. For the activities in Chapter 12, "Linear Perspective," you will expand on what you learned about freehand perspective drawing.

Creating effective cartoons requires a sense of humor and the writing skills to put humorous ideas into words. In Chapter 13, "Cartooning," you will read about the first steps toward becoming a cartoonist. You will also draw several types of cartoons.

In Chapter 14, "Computer Drawing," you will find information about using the computer as a drawing tool. You will soon discover that the computer offers new possibilities for the process of drawing.

▲ What impresses you most about this pencil drawing? Do you think the artist created a convincing illusion of deep space? What skills were needed to do this?

FIGURE 12.1 John Taylor Arms. *Coutances.* 1926. Graphite on paper. 25.4 x 14.6 cm (10 x 5¾"). McNay Art Institute, San Antonio, Texas. Gift of Alice N. Hanszen.

CHAPTER

Linear Perspective

Knowing how to make accurate perspective drawings in scale is essential in the fields of architecture and industrial design. This skill is also important in illustration and fine art. You can see examples of linear perspective used in drawings in Figures 12.1 through 12.4 on pages 228 to 231.

Architects' renderings, such as the one illustrated in Figure 12.2 on page 230 are made for several reasons. This kind of drawing helps the architect visualize a finished project from the two-dimensional plans he or she made earlier. The architect can show a drawing like this to the client to provide a better idea of how the project will look when it is completed. The drawing may also be used as an illustration to promote the sale of houses in a development. If used in this manner, it must be at least reasonably accurate in scale and arrangement of parts. Any serious distortion of the true size and shape would be unethical because the product would be misrepresented to potential buyers.

objectives

After reading this chapter and doing the activities, you will be able to:

- Draw the basic box for perspective drawings.

- Use a grid to locate points for perspective drawings.

- Make accurate one-point perspective drawings.

- Identify and use mechanical drawing tools.

Terms to Know

alidade
elevation
exploded view
foreshortening
plane table
true height line

▲ **FIGURE 12.2**   **This rendering by Dan Engen, a student of architecture, pays particular attention to reflections.**

Perspective Drawing Communicates

Steve Rich, an expert at linear perspective, made the expressive architect's sketch of a neighborhood scene in Figure 12.3. The drawing is somewhat free and undetailed, but it effectively communicates the character of a large area of housing.

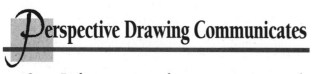

Did You Know?

Most scholars now believe that a Renaissance sculptor and architect named Filippo Brunelleschi (1377–1446) should be given credit for the development of linear perspective. It is thought that Brunelleschi used a mirror to discover perspective. The mirror revealed elements which could not be seen with the naked eye—for example, the squares of a tile floor or the beams of a ceiling appear in the mirror to converge in the distance. Indeed, the three-dimensional relationships are automatically transferred onto the mirror's two-dimensional surface just as they would be in a drawing using the laws of linear perspective.

The illustrator who did the rendering of the automobiles pictured in Figure 12.4 is obviously a master of freehand perspective. It is likely, however, that the artist made an accurate-to-scale linear perspective drawing of the cars before attempting this impressive rendering.

The technical illustration in Figure 12.5 is called an exploded view. In an **exploded view**, *the object is visually blown apart to show all of its components.* The artist had to draw the proportion and alignment of the parts accurately, showing where they fit. Technical illustrators must have knowledge of linear perspective even if they use prepared perspective grids or computers as aids.

World Class Buckle (Figure 12.6) is a fine art drawing done in charcoal pencil. It shows how perspective can be used for close-up drawings of objects. This drawing also used the idea of the exploded view, like the one in Figure 12.5. Do you think the exploded view is appropriate in this case?

No matter what kind of art you want to create, you need to know something about perspective drawing. There is no better way to improve your skill at accurate freehand drawing than to learn perspective drawing with the aid of measuring tools. Practicing linear perspective will even help you draw figures more believably.

In this chapter, we will present the basics of accurate perspective drawing. There are many good technical reference books on drafting and linear perspective that you can study to learn more

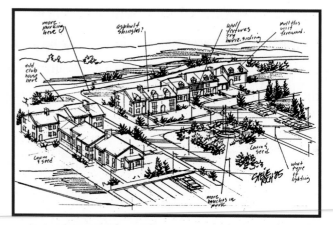

▲ **Steve Rich did this graphic overview of a development to illustrate a rapid perspective technique. Why do you think this technique would be useful to architects?**

FIGURE 12.3   Courtesy of the artist.

GTO 5.7 H·O RAM AIR, F-BODY SURBASE

◀ In the reproduction of this Mark Neeper rendering, the car done with an airbrush was shown in brilliant color. The car rendered with a dot pattern remained a black and white "ghost" image.

FIGURE 12.4   Courtesy of the artist.

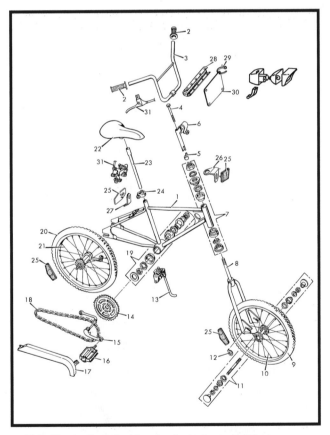

▲ This illustration of a bicycle shows how useful an exploded view can be in describing how something works.

FIGURE 12.5   Courtesy of The Murray Ohio Manufacturing Company.

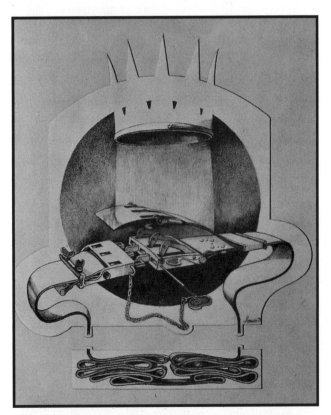

▲ **FIGURE 12.6**   *World Class Buckle* is a fine art drawing in charcoal pencil that makes use of the exploded view idea seen in the technical rendering in Figure 12.5.

details. The activities we suggest are a sample of the exercises you can find in many of these books. We will show you how to construct basic box shapes and put them in correct perspective. After you have constructed the boxes, you can draw objects inside them either freehand or by using perspective to accurately project images.

To do an accurate perspective drawing, you must have detailed and accurate measurements and sketches of anything you expect to include. An extra hour spent in research, sketching, and jotting down dimensions, or an extra hour spent in drawing or finding plans, can save you five hours on your finished art. You should return to the studio from your research with every bit of information you will need to do the entire drawing.

Did You Know?

The system of measurement used in perspective drawing actually doesn't affect the ways accurate perspectives are drawn. In fact, you could invent your own unit of measure as long as you used it consistently throughout the drawing—as you do when you use the human head as a unit of measure in figure drawings.

For example, if you are drawing a leather chair, you will need not just the dimensions of the chair's back, but also the distance between the buttons on its back, the buttons' diameter, the depth the buttons sink into the leather, and the exact angle at which the back of the chair tilts.

The Basic Box

The little ivory carving in Figure 12.7 was sawed out of a tusk over fifty years ago in Africa by a local craftsperson. We will use the elephant to show you how to draw a basic box. (We enlarged the carving, however, for our drawing. The elephant's actual height is about ¾ inch or 2 cm.)

An elephant, like all animals, is symmetrical. You learned in Chapter 1 that symmetrical means that something is the same on both sides of a central plane slicing through it. Many objects are symmetrical and an easy way to draw them is to construct the central plane in the basic box. In Figure 12.8, this central plane is defined by the thin, black line that runs around the center of the box. To draw the elephant, the "center slice"—or actually just an

---

SHARPENING YOUR SKILLS

A Basic Box for a Human Figure

This is a challenging but fun activity. Before beginning, review the handouts titled "Learn to Use a Proportional Window" (H-9) that your teacher distributed while you studied Chapter 7. Review all the steps in making an accurate proportional window for a model. Then try to apply them to doing a proportional basic box and grid for a person.

For this grid, of course, you can use the head as a unit of measure. Estimate proportions (measure) using your pencil. Remember to start with the floor grid for finding and marking how far back in the box and how far to the left or right various points are (the point of an elbow, the tip of the nose, etc.). Use the "center slice" grid to locate this height above the floor—then project this to a vertical line rising from the floor location just as you learned with the elephant. Two or three colored pencils will help you keep track of your marks.

---

extremely flat section—of the elephant was projected onto the central plane and expanded at all points to fill the box.

Figure 12.8 shows the basic box for the elephant carving. Notice the shaded portion on the ground that we drew first. Also note that the box is transparent, just as everything else in the drawing must be transparent.

In the bottom of a box, the lines going away from you into space would meet if they were extended to a shared vanishing point on the horizon. (See 1 in Figure 12.8.) Lines that aren't going away from you, such as Lines A-A and B-B, are parallel to the horizon. They don't converge anywhere. Lines C-C and D-D are also parallel to Lines A-A and B-B as well as to each other and remain that way.

After building the floor of the box on the ground our next task was to raise the corners to the proper height (Figure 12.8, Lines A-C and B-D). Then we connected the corners to form the top (Lines C-C, C-D, and D-D), and the transparent box was finished.

To find the central slice going through this box toward the vanishing point, we had to find the center of the bottom top, or one of the ends. To find the center of any square or rectangle in real space or in perspective, you draw an X from corner to corner. The center of the X is the center of the square or rectangle.

We drew the X on the ground to find the center of the floor of the box. A line drawn through this point to the vanishing point divides the floor into halves in perspective. Where this line crosses the ends of the floor, we raised verticals to cut the ends of the box in half. Where the verticals cross

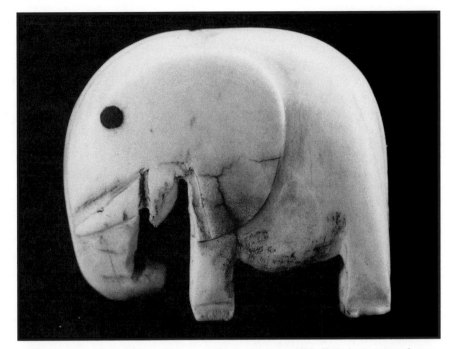

▲ **FIGURE 12.7**   An unknown African craftsperson carved this little ivory totem from a tusk over fifty years ago.

the top lines, we connected them with Line X-X to bisect the top of the box. (This line should also cross the vanishing point if it were extended. Seeing if it would reach the vanishing point is a good way to check the accuracy of the drawing.)

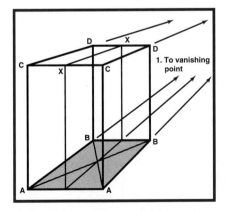

▲ **FIGURE 12.8**   This is a basic box drawn for the little ivory elephant.

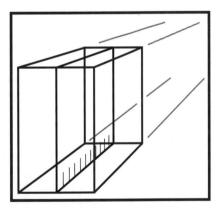

▲ **FIGURE 12.9**   The marks along the center line of the floor of the box indicate where we estimated the vertical lines of the grid should be drawn.

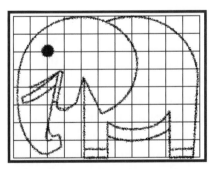

▲ **FIGURE 12.10**   Elevation or a flat view from one side of the elephant.

■ USING A GRID TO LOCATE POINTS

To draw a two-dimensional, paper-thin elephant on the center slice of the box, we had to locate points on that plane where various lines come together, or where various features of the elephant are located. Where did we locate these points first? On the ground.

Look at Figure 12.9 on page 233, where we located various points on the ground along the center line of the box (base of the center slice). Since we weren't working with a scale, or other tools of mechanical perspective, we located these points by estimation. We based our estimates on a grid, as in Figure 12.10 on page 233.

Figure 12.10 is a sketch of the side elevation of our little elephant. An **elevation** is *a scale drawing of the side, front or rear of a given object and shows no depth or perspective. It is drawn from a station point at a ninety-degree angle to the object and shows the entire image on a flat plane.* Over this elevation, we placed a grid of equal-sized squares. We marked the places where the vertical lines of this grid touch the ground on the base of the center slice in Figure 12.9. Notice that we allowed for foreshortening, the apparent shortening of forms so they appear to recede in space, by decreasing the distance between each of the verticals as they move back toward the vanishing point. **Foreshortening** means *shortening an object in a drawing to make it look as if it extends backward into space.* (A good way to do this is to start at the center, 5½ squares back, and work in both directions.)

Figure 12.11 shows the completed grid on the center section of the box. Since the vertical measurements for the grid squares on Line B-B are close to us against the picture plane, they remain equal in size. The squares can be marked on Line B-B at their actual or true height, so Line B-B is called a true height line. **True height line** refers to *any vertical line raised from the point where a reference line from a vanishing point touches the measuring line (ground line).* Actually, any vertical line at the front of a plane that goes back into space—if it is against the picture plane—can be a true height line for things in the receding plane.

Of course, the lines of the grid that go back toward the horizon from the true height line extend

to the vanishing point. The distance between them naturally gets smaller as they recede into space.

Look again at Figure 12.10. We said we were going to draw a flat elephant on the perspective plane in the box. The elephant in Figure 12.10 is flat, but it isn't in perspective. The grid in Figure 12.11 is in perspective, but it doesn't have an elephant on it.

We wanted to transfer the flat elephant to this grid. How? We started with just one point—the elephant's eye. In this case, the eye is two squares back from the front (picture plane/true height line) and six squares up from the ground. You can see the eye at that location in Figure 12.12.

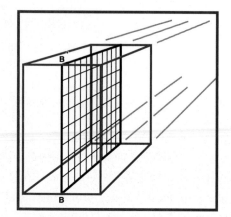

▲ **FIGURE 12.11   Completed grid on the center "slice" of the box.**

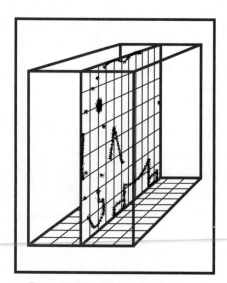

▲ **FIGURE 12.12   The eye and other points are located on the grid.**

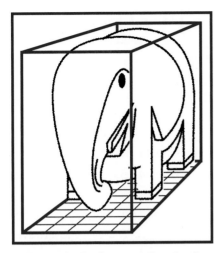

▲ **Figure 12.13   A perspective showing planes and volumes of the little ivory statue is the result of using a grid.**

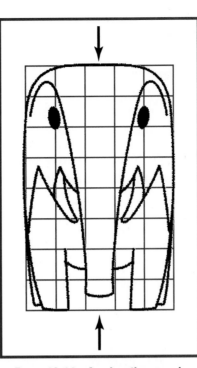

▲ **Figure 12.14   An elevation can show the front as well as the side. We could even draw one as a "slice" through the object; it would be called a section.**

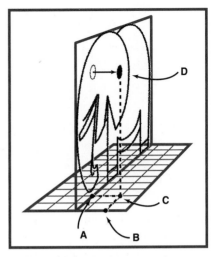

▲ **Figure 12.15   The eye must be located by marking three measurements: the distance from the front of the box, the distance from the center, and the height.**

Also, we put on the perspective grid the points where its tusks start and stop, the points where its feet are located, and other points where it touches the outside of the grid. We even located many of the points where the curved lines of its body cross lines on the grid. Knowing the location of these points made it easy to draw the elephant.

We have demonstrated an important skill. To locate a point in perspective accurately, you need to know only three measurements:

- The distance a point is back from the picture plane.
- The distance a point is from the side of the drawing.
- The distance a point is up from the ground.

If you know these three measurements, you can locate any point even if it is floating in the air.

If you can locate enough points on a plane, you can stretch them to the right and left into proper positions. Then you can connect the points and make the complete drawing of a form within the basic box, even if the form is irregular and curving.

Figure 12.13 shows our completed drawing of the elephant. Figures 12.14 and 12.15 show how we did it.

Figure 12.14 is another elevation of the ivory figure, but this time the elephant is viewed from the front instead of the side. After we constructed another grid in the same scale as the first one, we measured from the center to the eye on the right to see how far out from the center to place the eye. In Figure 12.15, Point A marks the distance on the ground from the eye to the front of the box (picture plane). Point B marks the distance 1½ squares from the eye to the right of the center plane.

We raised a vertical line from the intersection (Point C) and drew a horizontal line to the right from the eye in the central plane. The intersection of these lines (at Point D) was the expanded and real location of the elephant's eye. We could expand every point on the flat elephant that we wanted to in this way. Then we could see how to draw it as a volume instead of a flat plane. Note that the lower front line of the basic box—because it is against the picture plane—becomes a *measuring line* on which full measurements can be used, just as they can be used on the true height line.

*A*rtists at work

■ CIVIL ENGINEER
Drawings to Build On

"I want to build bridges and highways. Isn't math more important than drawing for someone like me?"

Civil engineering is the branch of engineering that deals mainly with land surveying, highway building, and construction of waterways and pipelines. Although expertise in math is important for making engineering calculations, many civil engineers report that as much as 60 percent of their work involves drawing.

In general, two types of drawings are needed to complete a civil engineering job. First, surveys and calculations are made in the field. As a surveyor, you would include in your report the measurements of the site and all natural and man-made features that will affect the new construction. Your ability to draw accurately would be essential.

Sometimes the information in the field might be too complicated to express in words. In that event, a plane table survey might be taken in which you would sketch the landscape. To do this, you would use a **plane table**, which is *a special drawing board mounted on a tripod (a three-legged stand)*. The plane table would be equipped with an **alidade** (AL-uh-dayd) that *indicates degrees and angles. This tool helps accurately plot maps.*

Increasingly, much of this work is done at computerized work stations utilizing CAD (Computer Aided Design) programs. These drawings must contain specific details since they will be used to guide construction.

In addition to skill in math, geometry, and drawing, you will need a grasp of design principles to help you design efficient infrastructure systems (fundamental facilities such as transportation and communication systems, roads, power stations and pipelines).

Many civil engineers graduate from college with a degree in civil engineering and become civil engineering trainees for large construction companies. Some come from architectural or drafting backgrounds, but all must have a solid foundation in drawing. Many civil engineering graduates choose to start working for a small firm that offers a variety of assignments and more opportunity for growth. Similarly, some choose to enter military service after graduation because the armed forces give

new engineers more opportunity to oversee large projects sooner than the private sector does.

Any part-time job in the construction field will give you valuable experience in construction techniques and technology. Especially worthwhile would be a position with a company that specializes in civil projects or the construction of large commercial buildings.

Opportunities for alternative careers can be found in all areas of structural engineering, architecture, and the construction industry. The heads of some large construction companies started as general contractors in the home building industry. Eventually, their firms became large enough to handle the special demands of large civil engineering projects.

The construction and maintenance of the nation's infrastructure is an important and demanding job. Civil engineers take pride in the fact that their work helps form the bedrock of civilization. ■

Adding Directional Lines

Return again to page 140 in Chapter 7 and review the part about sighting past your pencil to find some things that line up with each other (see Figures 7.36 and 7.37). Create another "spider web" of lines—with blue pencil maybe—and add some red "spider eggs" (dots) locating important points along these lines.

It's a real mess, isn't it? Well, maybe to everyone else, but you know what all those light spidery marks mean, and you can use them as a framework and a "code" to draw a great figure. Draw it with charcoal or ink right on top of your "spider web"!

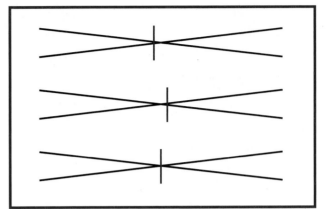

▲ FIGURE 12.16 In mechanical perspective, drawing accuracy is a "must." In which drawing does the vertical line pass through the true intersection?

■ ONE-POINT PERSPECTIVE

You have learned how to fit an object into a basic box in one-point perspective. Now you are ready to do a complete perspective—an interior or scene that you can transfer and render as a complete and accurate drawing in scale.

Remember that it is important to be accurate. Where do the two lines of the X cross in Figure 12.16? Not where the vertical line is in the top drawing, nor where it is in the middle drawing. Only the bottom drawing passes the vertical through the true intersection of the X.

Figure 12.17 on page 238 is a photograph of tools that are useful in making perspective drawings. They are placed on a drawing board with accurate edges and 90 degree corners. From left to right, they are:

Triangle (45 degree). Place the triangle firmly along the top edge of the T square to draw vertical lines. Depending on which side of the triangle you set on the T square, the triangle will allow you to make vertical lines or lines at 45 degree angles all across the paper.

Pair of dividers. Apply the measurements from the scale you choose to the drawing by using the dividers. The dividers will also allow you to hold a measurement and repeat it several times.

Compass. The compass is used to draw circles. Hold the points against the architect's scale to measure a proper radius (length from the center of a circle to its edge).

Architect's scale. The architect's scale looks like a triangular ruler). Use it to measure, not to draw straight lines.

Aluminum molding. Use four-foot long strips (which can be bought at lumber yards). Light aluminum molding can be used as a straight-edge for lines going to vanishing points. The best kind to buy forms an upside-down T when viewed from one end (Figure 12.18, page 238). Lines to vanishing points can be 6 inches (15 cm) long or longer on a large two-point perspective drawing. Stick a push-pin in the vanishing points to help you locate them with the end of the molding.

T square. The T square is used to draw horizontal lines. When using it hold the T square with its head hanging over the side of the drawing board on the opposite side from your drawing hand. If the head of the T square is flush against the edge of the board, it will slide up and down this edge so you can draw as many accurate horizontal lines as you like. Don't use the T square to draw vertical lines.

The remaining items in the photo include: Berol Verithin colored pencils, two drafting lead holders (you can use pencils), and an eraser.

Before you start the studio work for this chapter, memorize some abbreviations you will need for your first drawings. In these drawings, label points and lines in order to keep track of them. Abbreviations for the items you will need to label on your drawings are listed below. The most important ones are marked with an asterisk. The points and lines are:

- Horizon Line—HL*
- Picture Plane—PP
- Vanishing Point—VP*
- Right Vanishing Point—RVP
- Left Vanishing Point—LVP
- Center of Vision—CV*
- Measuring Line—ML
- Ground Line—GL*
- Measuring Point—MP*
- True Height Line—THL*
- Station Point—SP
- Distance Line—DIS
- Reference Line—REF
- Reference Point—RP

You will need some colored pencils so that you can color-code certain lines to avoid confusion. You might, for instance, use one color for the lines you use to set up the perspective, such as the frame of the picture plane, the horizon line, and the distance line. Another color can be used for structural lines, such as basic boxes, grids, and reference lines. The outlines of the form can be drawn with a fairly hard pencil at first, transparently. You can then go over the lines you would actually see with a darker pencil line. Be sure to keep all of your pencils sharp while you draw.

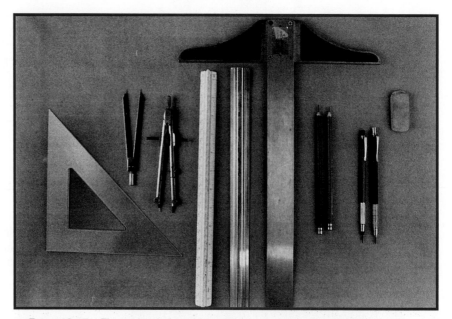

▲ FIGURE **12.17**   The tools on the table are the ones most often needed for mechanical perspective. (See the text for their names and functions.)

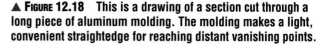

▲ FIGURE **12.18**   This is a drawing of a section cut through a long piece of aluminum molding. The molding makes a light, convenient straightedge for reaching distant vanishing points.

CHAPTER 12 REVIEW

1. What is a basic box and why is it necessary when drawing objects in perspective?
2. What purpose is served by using a grid in perspective drawing?
3. When making perspective drawings, what mechanical drawing tools would prove helpful?

STUDIO 1

Drawing a Basic Box in Perspective

SUPPLIES

↝ **Graphite pencil**

↝ **Ruler (optional)**

↝ **Eraser**

↝ **Drawing paper**

1. Follow the instructions below to draw a box like the one you have been studying. To begin, make the front end a simple vertical rectangle. The top and bottom should be parallel to each other, and the sides should be straight up and down. The sides should be parallel, also.

2. Next, pick a point somewhere above and to the right or left of the rectangle for a vanishing point. This vanishing point will be on an imaginary horizon line at eye level. Draw lines from each corner

---

☞ TECHNIQUE TIP

The Basics of Perspective Drawing

Before you study perspective further, review what you learned in Chapter 7, pages 122–130 and 144–151 about perspective drawing. Keep in mind that you should always:

- Put each object in your drawing in a basic box.

- Draw the shape of each basic box and object on the ground or floor first.

- Draw everything transparently.

---

of the rectangle to the vanishing point. (Use a ruler if you like.) These are the parallel lines of the four corners of the box moving away from you toward the horizon.

3. Now decide where to cut off the box at the back, and construct another rectangle just like the one in front. Of course, the back rectangle will be smaller because perspective has caused the sides, top and bottom to come closer together as they move toward the vanishing point.

4. To make the box easier to see in perspective, darken the lines that you could actually see if the box weren't transparent. (In Figure 12.8, page 233, these lines are A-A, A-C, C-C, A-B, C-D, B-D, and D-D. A cube or box has eight corners, each one formed by the meeting of three planes. From your eye level, you could see at least part of seven corners if the box were opaque.)

5. You are now ready to find the center of the floor of the box by drawing an X from corner to corner. Through the center of this X, draw another line that would extend to the vanishing point, starting at the front edge of the floor of the box and stopping at the rear edge. Raise verticals at the points where this line touches

---

the front and rear edges. These verticals will cross on the front and rear edges of the top panel, too. You can connect the points at which they cross to divide the panel in half. These lines will outline the center section through the length of the box.

6. Remember that anything in perspective is foreshortened. The length of the side panel of the box that you would actually see can be even shorter than the width of the front panel—unless the box is extremely long. Look again at the box we started to draw in Figure 12.8 on page 233. If you measure the visible length of the side panel and compare it with the width of the front panel, you will easily see foreshortening.

Computer Option

In order to complete this activity, your program must include a 3-D, Add Perspective, Add Depth, or other command that will show perspective. To begin, use the Rectangle tool to draw a simple box. Do not fill the object. Apply the perspective command. Experiment with changing the vanishing point and spatial depth.

STUDIO 2

Draw an Object in One-Point Perspective

SUPPLIES

- Graphite pencil
- Ruler
- Eraser
- Drawing paper

1. Draw some fairly simple object that is symmetrical but interesting in one-point perspective. You could use a vase or clay pot or an upholstered furniture piece. You could also enlarge something small, like an ink bottle or a padlock.

2. Measure the object you have selected carefully, and draw a pair of elevations of it on a grid of equal-sized squares. For a drawing that is to be about 9 x 12 inches (22.9 x 30.5 cm), use ½ inch (1.3 cm) squares. (This size is a little coarse for real accuracy, but a good size for practice.)

3. If you are enlarging an object, use accurate proportions. For example, to enlarge a padlock four times its real size you might decide that ½ inch on your grid should equal ⅛ inch on the padlock. This scale would make a 2-inch (5 cm) padlock 8 inches (20 cm) high in the drawing.

4. Next, draw a one-point, or parallel, perspective of the basic box for the object. To draw the basic box, you must duplicate your efforts in the previous activity. This time, however, you need to mea-

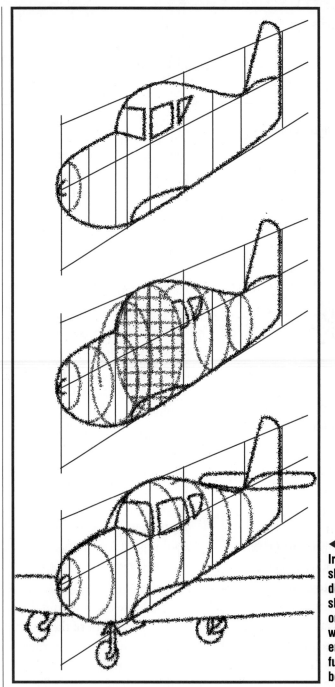

◀ FIGURE 12.19
Irregular, curving shapes are best handled by drawing the shapes of "slices" or sections first by working transparently. Could a carefully measured basic box be helpful here?

sure the box and center section to fit the proportions of the object you want to draw, at the size you want to draw it. Don't be disturbed by the fact that your vanishing point may be as much as 24 inches (60.9 cm) away from the drawing. This distance would be normal for a drawing of this size.

STUDIO 2 — *Continued from page 240*

5. Study Figures 12.9 through 12.15 on pages 273–279, and follow the same steps to make your drawing.

TECHNIQUE TIP

Drawing a Curved Object in a Basic Box

To draw the elephant, we expanded points from a center section outward, using a front elevation as a guide. You can use a different procedure to visualize a solid object with long, smooth curves, such as a boat hull, aircraft fuselage (Figure 12.19), automobile—or even a human figure—in a basic box. For such an object, use careful estimation or measurement, and draw the outlines of transverse (crosswise) sections at several points through the object instead of just the front.

Find the proper spot on the floor of the box, or on the central grid, and project each of these transverse sections into the box; then complete the outline.

STUDIO 3

Bring a Figure Drawing to Life

SUPPLIES

➥ **Drawing media of your choice**

➥ **Charcoal, conte crayon, or ink**

➥ **Vellum**

1. Looking at a drawing of a standing or seated figure that is stiff and lifeless is not visually exciting. If you have seen portraits of important people made by artists who could only copy photographs you'll know what we mean. Unfortunately, the way you've been working at this business of proportioning, the figure in a perspective box could produce the same stiff result. Copying the human figure in a proportional box or "cage" can produce a lifeless form. To add life to your drawing, try this:

2. Put a sheet of see-through paper, vellum or translucent layout paper over your drawing and tape it securely in place. This may prevent you from seeing your colored "spiderweb," but you should be able to see your image of the figure in a softer, somewhat dimmer way. You can now draw with charcoal or conte crayon—or even ink—right over your original drawing using these darker lines to make your drawing more lifelike.

3. How do you make existing drawing more lifelike? Well, for one thing, you make it more expressive. How do you do this? By avoiding the tendency to "play it safe" in favor of overstating or exaggerating the gesture. Draw on the see-through vellum directly on top of your constructed drawing using more expressive lines. Look for opportunities to correct the gesture and use exaggeration to make your figure appear more lively.

TECHNIQUE TIP

Vellum Is Durable

Worried about doing a finished drawing on a "flimsy" transparent vellum? Don't be. It's a lot easier than it looks. If you use a liquid medium you can even iron the back of the drawing to smooth out some of the wrinkles before matting. As a matter of fact, you can even buy 20 pound vellum of lasting quality that won't get brittle or yellow for many years.

▲ The woman at the table is staring in which direction? Is her gaze direct and open or is she trying to conceal it? What do you think is going through her mind? Did this drawing cause you to smile? Why?

FIGURE 13.1 George Grosz. *In the Restaurant*. 1910. Ink and graphite on paper. 27.6 x 22.5 cm (10⅞ x 8⅞"). McNay Art Institute, San Antonio, Texas. Gift in memory of John Palmer Leeper Sr.

CHAPTER 13

Cartooning

Cartoonists often say, "Cartooning is a serious business." In fact, it is a serious multimillion-dollar business. Cartooning can be compared to the fields of show business and professional sports. It is glamorous, those at the top of the field are highly paid, and only a very few who would like to be cartoonists can actually earn their living that way. Humor is often apparent in fine art pieces as well (Figure 13.1).

You may be among the very few who become professional cartoonists. Even if you don't, you can have fun with cartooning and contribute your own cartoons to everything from your school newspaper to your favorite candidate's election campaign. In this chapter, you will have an opportunity to draw three different kinds of cartoons. These are:

- The single-panel magazine gag cartoon.
- The editorial or political cartoon.
- The humorous comic strip.

objectives

After reading this chapter and doing the activities, you will be able to:

- Discuss the relative importance of the verbal and visual aspects of a cartoon.
- Name three types of cartoons.
- Develop a system for creating, organizing, and publishing gag cartoons.
- Make caricatures and draw a comic strip.

Terms to Know

balloon
caption
editorial cartoons
gag cartoon
roughs
saddlestitch
side stitch
syndicate

Cartoons Are Ancient

No one knows where or when cartooning actually started, but it is a very old form of drawing. The drawing in Figure 13.2 is a copy of one of the rock paintings at Tassili-n-ajjer ("Plateau of Rivers") in the North African desert. These paintings were made perhaps as long as six thousand years ago. Experts believe that this drawing was meant to be humorous. There is little doubt that one ancient Egyptian drawing is an unflattering caricature of the father of Tutankhamen, an Egyptian king.

Did You Know?

The name *cartoon* is sometimes given to drawings other than the kinds of cartoons with which you are familiar. Originally cartoons were full-scale preliminary drawings on paper for projects such as fresco painting on walls, stained glass, or tapestries. The detail of the drawing for Peter Roger's mural in Figure 13.3 is this kind of cartoon. (The word cartoon came from the Italian *cartone*, which referred to a cheap paper. Our word cartoon came from the same source.) The meaning of cartoon was expanded to include humorous satirical drawings submitted to English magazines in the mid-nineteenth century.

Today, we use the word cartoon to refer to animated film cartoons, comic strips, caricatures, and humorous drawings. The animated cartoons at the movies or on Saturday morning television are examples of cartoons produced by a team effort. These cartoons require the work of writers, senior creative drawing personnel, animators, and inkers.

Traditionally, a beginning animation cartoonist works as an animation cell inker. (You can see an animation cell in Figure 13.4.) Each tiny movement of an animated character must be drawn on a separate clear acetate cell and colored with inks that stick to the plastic. The cells are then photographed one at a time on frames of movie film. When the film is run rapidly through a projector or video machine and projected on a screen, motion is created. (Computer animation is discussed in Chapter 14.)

Cartoonists may belong to the same professional societies and subscribe to the same magazines as other artists. Cartoonists are really skilled story illustrators. Some of them draw characters for

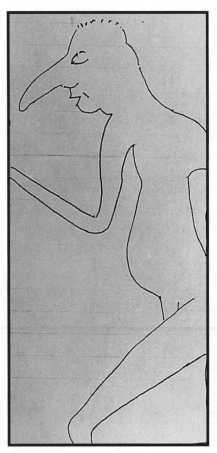

◀ **FIGURE 13.2** Perhaps one of the oldest cartoons in existence. It was painted on a rock in the North African desert.

▲ The word *cartoon* is used as the name of a preliminary drawing for a mural. This one was done by Peter Rogers in preparation for a mural (Figure 7.18, page 129).

FIGURE 13.3 Courtesy of the Museum of Texas Tech University, Lubbock, Texas.

comic books. They also illustrate continued adventure and human interest stories in newspapers, like Milton Caniff's *Steve Canyon* or Harold LeDoux's *Judge Parker* (Figure 13.5), which are followed by many faithful readers.

▲ This animation cell from a movie about the *Wizard of Oz* has the background on the bottom sheet and the figure to be animated on an acetate overlay.

FIGURE 13.4   © Rob Roy Productions, Seattle, Washington.

▼ Harold LeDoux, the cartoonist who illustrates the comic strip *Judge Parker*, is also a skilled painter.

FIGURE 13.5   © Field Enterprises/King Features.

Did You Know?

The *Judge Parker* strip (Figure 13.5) is a Sunday newspaper strip. Like most Sunday strips, the artist draws it in black and white. Color plates are made through a syndicate contract with another agency—usually the Greater Buffalo Press. The artist uses numbers keyed to a color chart that is published by the Greater Buffalo Press. These numbers tell the press what colors to print in which areas.

Even though they use the numbers, some artists also prefer to paint the strips with watercolor for their own reference. Among these artists is Hank Ketcham, whose *Dennis the Menace* has captured hearts all over the world.

▲ This cartoon witch obviously comes from an advertisement printed around Halloween.

Figure 13.6 Courtesy of *The University Daily*, Texas Tech University, Lubbock, Texas.

Cartoonists are primarily artists with a knowledge of composition, anatomy, and perspective. They illustrate strips but often don't write the stories. The *Judge Parker* strip, for example, is actually written by a man who prefers to remain in the background. He writes two other strips in addition to *Judge Parker*. The stories for *Judge Parker* are sent to LeDoux, who applies his considerable drawing skills illustrating them.

Comic strips, caricatures, and humorous drawings appear in magazines to illustrate articles, provide witty decorative filler material in various publications, and enhance advertisements on television or in newspapers. Figure 13.6 is one example of a cartoon used as an advertisement.

▲ The drawing above is amusing, but it could not be called a cartoon.

Figure 13.7 Jim Howze. *Pushfoot Halftrack Haybale Clown.* Courtesy of the artist.

The Cartoon Is a Verbal Art Form

If you are interested in becoming a cartoonist, the first thing you must understand is this: cartooning isn't primarily a visual art form. Yes, cartoons require drawing. Yes, good drawings and design can greatly increase the visual impact of cartoons. Cartooning, however, is not so much a visual art form as it is a verbal art form.

A cartoon begins as a verbal idea. A cartoon may not have a **caption** (*an accompanying comment or title*) or a **balloon** (*outlined dialogue or thoughts of a character in a comic strip panel*). Yet the cartoon still must express a situation or tell a brief story. A humorous drawing without a specific situation for provoking laughter doesn't fit our definition of a cartoon. For instance, the drawing in Figure 13.7 has a clown's nose tied to a bale of hay, but this is just a comic element in a carefully crafted drawing. Figure 13.8 is based on a humorous remark, but is not a cartoon. Look at Figure 5 in Color Section II. It too has some humor, but it is a fine art drawing employing pen and ink, then a photocopier, then more pen work, and a watercolor transparent wash applied on heavy vellum.

Since cartooning is a verbal art form, you must develop your imagination and polish your writing skills just as much as your drawing skills if you want to pursue a career as a cartoonist. If you prefer not to do your own writing, you will have to join forces with someone who can write. Most cartoonists, however, start out both writing and drawing their own ideas. Later, when they are established in the business, they might choose only to write or only to draw.

■ THE GAG CARTOON

Traditionally, many cartoonists begin their careers by drawing gag cartoons for magazines. A **gag cartoon** is *a cartoon that tells a humorous situation in one frame, sometimes with a caption, sometimes not.* Even though many major magazines went out of business when television became popular there are still national magazines for the general public and many specialized magazines that use cartoons.

▲ **This work is a tribute to a famous baseball personality. The artist also used a brush and computer images. Can you tell where?**

FIGURE 13.8   Jim Howze. *The Satchel Paige Memorial Calligraphicat.* Pen, brush and ink, and computer images. 48.3 x 40.6 cm (19 x 16"). Collection of O. V. Scott.

Gag cartoonists for magazines find themselves in a highly competitive field. Even so, cartooning for magazines is still a good place to start because it teaches discipline and practice. Also, these cartoons can be conveniently drawn at home and mailed to magazine publishers.

Gag cartoonists must be able to see the humorous possibilities in everyday situations. They must turn everyday situations around so that the humor emerges. After this, they must be able to convey an idea with an immediately understandable humorous drawing, usually along with a brief, well-edited caption (the sentence or phrase that makes the joke's point). Cartooning is really a show business kind of humor for the print media (magazines and newspapers). A good gag cartoonist could probably write for Jay Leno, David Letterman, or Arsenio Hall.

Besides drawing aptitude and writing skills, there are a few other characteristics required for success as a magazine cartoonist. First, you must have desire and perseverance. You must want the recognition and satisfaction that cartooning can provide badly enough to stay at it for years. Very few gag cartoonists were instant successes. Beginning cartoonists usually receive enough polite rejection slips from editors to paper the walls of their studios before someone finally buys one of their cartoons and publishes it.

Besides being persistent, you must be efficient. Gag cartoonists must produce a volume of work in an organized fashion. Artists need to send cartoons to several magazines on the average of once a month in batches of six to twelve drawings. That is a minimum of thirty good gags a month needed to approach just five magazines. To meet this requirement, a cartoonist would have to produce one good drawing a day—and an artist must usually draw several to produce one good cartoon.

A System for Successful Gag Cartooning

How can you get started as a gag cartoonist? How can you organize your work?

Keep a notebook. Form the habit of carrying a small notebook with you at all times. Many times a day you will see situations that could be very funny with a little twist of the imagination. If you try to remember the situations, you won't. Write them down. You could use a paper napkin if you have nothing else, but a professional would carry a notebook, or maybe even a small tape recorder.

Transfer notes to a card file. You won't need to write down very much of your idea to trigger your memory later. Suppose you are leaving for school, and you see a neighborhood dog chasing your cat. The cat climbs the sycamore tree in the backyard and smugly washes his whiskers to taunt the dog. The dog bounces around at the trunk of the tree, yapping in frustration until you finally send him home. In the process, some funny thoughts about dogs cross your mind. You take out your notebook and write, "Dog trees cat/dog's viewpoint." Then you go on to school.

That night at a regularly scheduled time you take out a card file of 3 x 5 index cards. You open your notebook to the five or six situations you have recorded during the day, and start editing. On one card you write:

SCENE: Cat in tree looking scared. Dog climbing tree with lineman's spurs or mountain climber's rope and spikes; dog nailing boards on tree.

CAPTION: None

This note records specifics for the idea. Later during your editing process you might add, "Dog dragging ladder toward tree with teeth," or "Dog floating in air attached by long hose to helium tank."

Find the appropriate market. Now that you have a well-developed idea, you must choose the best place to market it. The dog and cat gag is probably not suitable for a pet owners' magazine, which might not wish to emphasize conflict between pets. The idea obviously wouldn't fit an automotive or yachting magazine. Since it looks like a good gag for a wide range of the reading public, you decide that it is a general gag. You put a file number in the upper part of the card that indicates this category. After this number, you put a period or a dash and put another set of digits to indicate the number of the gag; for example, "1.247." This idea is the 247th in the group of general gags, 1.

If you write down when and where you send a drawing, you can also avoid resubmitting an idea too soon to a magazine that has already rejected it once. Also record in your file when a cartoon has been sold, and to whom.

To help you sell cartoons more quickly, here are some tips:

■ List subjects (like hobbies or professions) that you know something about.

■ Find as many publications—magazines and newspapers—as you can that publish cartoons on the subject.

■ Send cartoons about the subject from the viewpoint of an insider who would immediately recognize technical or biographical references. (Make sure the gags aren't harshly critical of the hobby or profession.)

■ Know the magazine's and editor's needs.

Many specialized magazines welcome submissions by people who know and sympathize with their particular audience. If your father or mother is a doctor or autoworker, if you build models or hunt, or if you work part time in a familiar occupation, you probably have sources of good gags for magazines concerned with these fields.

Perhaps earlier you were told by the cartoon editor of a certain general publication that he or she doesn't use animal cartoons. Remind yourself by a note on the card not to send this cartoon to that editor. You will save yourself a sure rejection. (Remember, though, that the magazine will probably be in existence for a long time, but the editor may move to a different magazine.) Now you can file your gag and go on to the next card. You can develop a large idea file by this process in a short time.

Keep a rough file. Meanwhile, you must be drawing these ideas, so start a file of roughs, too. **Roughs** are *sketches that indicate the general idea for finished cartoons. They show the size, position, and relationship of images in each cartoon.* Do your roughs on sheets of high quality typing paper.

Make inked drawings look professional. Revise your drawings in ink on the same kind of paper. Although some more expensively produced magazines may send drawings back for revision or more finished work, most magazines will photograph those inked roughs for reproduction. Therefore, make your inked drawings as finished and professional as you can. Neatly type the caption below the drawing or print it in black ink. Figure 13.9 is an example of finished cartoons with captions.

Identify each item. On the back of the inked roughs, up in a corner, put your name and address. You can use a rubber stamp to save time. Also write the file number that corresponds to the idea on the 3 x 5 file card. File all of your inked roughs that aren't being mailed to an editor. File the first pencil roughs with the inked drawings. If a finished drawing gets lost in the mail, you will still have the original on file.

Keep a record of your submittals. Always note in the file when and where each drawing was sent. If you do this, you can avoid sending the same idea to two different magazines at once. A few editors don't mind this, but assume that an editor wants to be the only one considering your idea unless he or she tells you otherwise.

" Cap'n, the Tide's coming in."

◄ **Here are two cartoons based on a visual pun by Paul Hanna. You can see that Hanna experimented with two different techniques. The top cartoon is pencil and photocopy, while the bottom cartoon is stippled.**

FIGURE 13.9   Courtesy of the artist.

"CAP'N, THE TIDE'S COMING IN."

THE EDITORIAL CARTOON

Cartoons that humorously express opinions on politics or social issues are called **editorial cartoons**. Many editorial cartoons use political figures for subject matter. Bill DeOre of *The Dallas Morning News* drew the cartoon in Figure 13.10 that effectively portrays American presidents as insects. In some countries an editorial cartoon like this would endanger the cartoonist's life. In the United States, however, editorial cartoonists can criticize government officials.

Some people call these cartoons *political cartoons*, but the drawings often use other subjects besides politics. Figure 13.11 is a nonpolitical editorial cartoon by the witty and talented Etta Hulme (pronounced like Home). Figure 13.12 is another nonpolitical editorial cartoon. It was drawn by Dirk West, who is a sports cartoonist for the *Lubbock Avalanche-Journal*. West is quite popular with readers who follow Southwest Conference college athletics.

▲ An editorial cartoonist like Bill DeOre must be quick in both wit and drawing. He must analyze important issues in the day's news and meet very short deadlines.

FIGURE 13.10   Courtesy of the artist and *The Dallas Morning News*.

SHARPENING YOUR SKILLS

Practice Caricature Sketching

SUPPLIES
- Pencil
- Sketchbook

Study well-known figures around town. List the most prominent features noted for five of these people (for example, long nose, full lower lip, or large Adam's apple). You will find that older people are usually easier to caricature than teenagers, and pretty girls and children are particularly difficult. With a sketchbook and a pencil, sketch all of your five subjects every day for a week to practice exaggerating their prominent features. Share your sketches with other students without revealing the names of your subjects. Can they identify them?

Computer Option

If you have done any lifelike electronic portraits of popular celebrities or other famous individuals, open one from disk. Study the work, and decide which of the person's facial features might best be exaggerated. Select your program's Shape tool and/or Zoom tool (bitmap editor). Zoom in on a section of the feature you plan to distort. Working carefully, move, shorten, or lengthen the lines and/or objects which make up that section. Zoom out and then in again on another section, repeating the process. Continue working in this fashion until you have completed your caricature.

◀ **Etta Hulme has a keen eye for the absurd side of our society. There are few women in the field of cartooning right now, but they are among the best cartoonists in the field.**

FIGURE 13.11 Courtesy of the artist and *The Fort Worth Star-Telegram.*

◀ **Dirk West uses a Pentel Sign Pen for much of his editorial cartooning.**

FIGURE 13.12 Courtesy of the artist and *The Lubbock Avalanche-Journal.*

On page 252 you will find a career profile of an editorial cartoonist and a description of the job. The job requires good reading and writing skills and demands speed and stamina. Editorial cartoonists have to come up with an idea each day. This idea must usually be based on a news event that occurred that same day—and it has to be funny.

It is also essential that an editorial cartoonist be an expert at the art of caricature. In Chapter 7 you learned that a caricature is a humorous drawing of a person who is easily recognizable because of the exaggeration of the person's features.

To develop your talent as a caricaturist, study the work of famous historical caricaturists (like Honoré

Artists at Work

Opinions into Images

"I'm always doodling and drawing caricatures, but my favorite thing is teasing my friends with my cartoons. Everyone thinks they're funny. Could I get paid to do that?"

Political cartoonists have been skewering politicians and poking fun at public figures for generations. They use drawing as a form of communication to entertain, criticize, or convince. Editorial cartoonists respond to current issues and events, developing insights into political situations, delineating the character of people, and finding humor in problems and their possible solutions. Good editorial cartoonists have fertile imaginations and can communicate a point of view.

As a syndicated editorial cartoonist for a newspaper, you would be expected to generate new ideas daily. Every morning you would begin by reading newspapers and magazines. Worldwide situations, political events, local happenings, sports, the weather or other subjects can provide the spark for an idea. Ideas and opinions are the lifeblood of every cartoon. When some issue attracts your attention, you will need to decide on your position. This is an essential step since an editorial cartoonist must try to communicate a specific point of view. The next step is to create an interesting and humorous visual image of your idea.

Many tools are available to the cartoonist. You might exaggerate a problem or person in one cartoon. Another time you might use irony or reversal by having the characters in the drawing say the opposite of what you think.

Cartooning is an extremely competitive field. There are approximately 250 full-time positions for editorial cartoonists in the United States. It takes hard work and dedication to produce effective work and market it successfully.

No specific degrees, diplomas, or backgrounds are essential for selling cartoons to publishers. Fresh ideas, an interesting style and insightful stances are your best calling card when looking for employment. Good school art experience can help you find alternative career opportunities and make important personal contacts.

You should continue to draw constantly. This is a good time to develop a cartoon style of your own. Study the styles of other cartoonists in newspapers, magazines, and greeting cards.

Comic strip and gag cartoonists must also generate ideas and express them visually, but it takes interesting ideas, intriguing characters, and unique style to interest a syndicate in your comic strip. A **syndicate** is *a business concern that sells many different materials for publication in newspapers or periodicals simultaneously*. There is a broader market for cartooning, however. The advertising industry regularly makes use of cartoons for newspapers, magazines, and television to sell products and concepts. The illustrations in children's books, manuals, and how-to-do-it instructions all use techniques similar to those required in cartooning. Animators and greeting card designers also require similar skills.

Whether selling products or swaying public opinion, cartoonists take satisfaction in generating ideas and images that inform as well as entertain. ■

◀ Dick Locher, who did the caricature of Walter Mondale in this political cartoon from the late 1970s, is one of the busiest cartoonists around. Look at Figure 13.13 to see why.

FIGURE 13.13 © Tribune Media Services, reprinted by permission.

▲ In addition to his editorial cartoons, Dick Locher and his helpers must do 365 *Dick Tracy* strips a year.

FIGURE 13.14 © Tribune Media Services, reprinted by permission.

Daumier, Figures 2.14 on page 32 and 2.15 on page 35) and contemporary artists. Try doing some caricatures of well-known people from photographs. Carry your sketchbook at all times, and practice drawing caricatures of people you see. As you practice, your ability to emphasize or exaggerate tell-tale features about a person will improve.

You may not become another Dick Locher (see one of his editorial cartoons in Figure 13.13). Who knows, though? You might also choose Locher's other career. He is now the principal artist for the

comic strip originally drawn by Chester Gould about the ageless crime fighter, *Dick Tracy* (Figure 13.14).

One word of caution about drawing caricatures: it isn't fair to make fun of anyone's physical disability. (This rule might be waived for an older person who is extremely famous or for a popular actor. The confidence of these people would probably not be shaken, and they would probably thrive on the attention. It would still be in bad taste, however, to make the disability a point of criticism.)

▲ *Bloom County* by Berke Breathed was a strip that was popular with young adults. Breathed did a comic strip in college called *Academia Waltz*. Do you get the joke in the cartoon above? If not, the photograph below might provide some clues.

FIGURE 13.15 © 1987, Washington Post Writers Group, reprinted with permission.

▲ FIGURE 13.16 Millions of dollars yearly are spent on products that originate with cartoons. They helped make Charles Schulz, creator of *Peanuts,* one of the highest paid entertainers in the United States.

■ THE HUMOROUS COMIC STRIP

Many people consider comic strip artists to be the kings and queens of cartooning. Artists like Cathy Guisewite, creator of *Cathy*; Dick Browne

and Morte Walker, who draw *Hagar the Horrible, Beetle Bailey,* and *Hi and Lois*; and Jeff MacNelly, who does *Shoe* and is also an accomplished political cartoonist, are admired by many young imitators.

The earnings of the top comic strip cartoonists rival those of sports heroes and television personalities. These artists often earn more from "spin-off" licensed products, however, than from drawing the comic strips. The products are manufactured under a license from the newspaper syndicates that distribute the comic strip.

For example, Charles Schulz shares the profits from the sale of *Peanuts'* dolls, stationery, and mugs with United Features Syndicate. Opus dolls, based on Berke Breathed's *Bloom County*, are becoming popular. Even Mr. Peanut dolls are on the market; they are a spin-off not from a strip but from the corporate trademark of Planters' Peanuts. See Figure 13.15 for *Bloom County* and Figure 13.16 for examples of licensed products.

Remember, though, that most cartoonists must work hard for a long time to get their strip accepted by a syndicate. Literally hundreds of comic strips are submitted to cartoon editors of major syndicates each month. Although editors receive thousands of submissions a year, each editor can probably afford to buy only two or three new strips each year. The owners of the syndicates invest

▲ These preliminary drawings by Bud Blake were done for his *Tiger* strip. Blake is much admired for his excellent drawing and fluid, expressive line.

FIGURE 13.17   © King Features.

thousands of dollars in launching each new comic strip. This investment results from the cost of advertising the strips to newspaper editors and paying salespeople to contact all the newspapers.

For the most part, the newspaper editors who buy strips say they can't afford additional space for comics, so buying a new strip often means eliminating an old one. This kind of substitution is sure to make some faithful readers of the old strip angry. Therefore, syndicate editors, who buy the strip from the cartoonist, and newspaper editors, who buy it from the syndicate, have to be sure that a new strip will appeal to many different kinds of

Comic Strip	Number of Words
Hi and Lois	29
Marvin	24
Steve Canyon (story strip)	52
Dick Tracy (story strip)	35
Barney Google and *Snuffy Smith*	32
Garfield	39
Hagar the Horrible	19
Archie	26
Blondie	30

▲ **FIGURE 13.18**   Number of words used in professional comic strips from one edition.

people. Also, busy readers should be able to grasp the gag quickly. Most importantly, the new strip has to be funnier than most of the other comics already in the newspapers.

The comic strip cartoonist must have the same skills as the single-panel gag cartoonist. The comic strip artist, however, can use three or four panels to develop the gag situation. This space allows the artist to prepare his or her audience as a television comedian does. In Figure 13.17, Bud Blake has given you an insider's peek at some of the rough sketches done on tissue for his comic strip *Tiger*. Many comic strip artists use sketches like these to plan their strips.

Most contemporary successes in the comic strip field rely on a gag-a-day format for their humor. This pace requires a huge gag writing output. Comic strip artists (as well as single-panel gag cartoonists) often use the services of professional gag writers. If you start a successful comic strip, don't worry—gag writers won't be hard to find. In fact, they will come looking for you. However, selecting some that can cooperate in producing your kind of humor may be difficult. Writers and artists who work together as a team from the beginning of their careers are fortunate.

Before you attempt a comic strip for your school newspaper or for syndication, count the words that are used in each of several comic strips. Use strips from the national syndicates for daily (not Sunday) newspaper publication. The word totals for strips in

▲ **Chris Conley expressed the feeling of the average student facing a library photocopying machine on a bad day. The artist was a mass communications major in college.**

FIGURE 13.19   Courtesy of the artist and *The University Daily*, Texas Tech University, Lubbock, Texas.

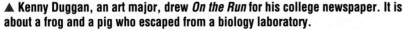

▲ **Kenny Duggan, an art major, drew *On the Run* for his college newspaper. It is about a frog and a pig who escaped from a biology laboratory.**

FIGURE 13.20   Courtesy of the artist and *The University Daily*, Texas Tech University, Lubbock, Texas.

a newspaper we looked at are indicated in the chart (Figure 13.18, page 255).

We found an average of less than thirty words per strip for the ten strips. Remember that these are the strips that editors have found people will read. You must edit until your gags are economical in word use and are immediately understandable by most people (or at least by most people in your selected audience).

Besides counting the words in each strip, count the number of panels in the strips. What is the average number? What is the maximum? Did you

find any with five panels? Probably not, because there isn't room. Many papers reduce their strips to around 6½ x 2 inches, (16.5 x 5 cm) or in printers' measure, 39 picas long and 12 picas high.

You will probably want to make cartoons twice this size, but keep the drawings in correct proportion.

Some successful comic strip artists start cartooning while they are still in school. Berke Breathed, for instance, drew *Academia Waltz* at the University of Texas long before *Bloom County* was created. For some comic strips by student artists, look at Figures

▲ **Student Langston Brown's cartoons often appeared in the *Lubbock Westerner*, his high school newspaper. With his ironing board surfer, he demonstrates the zany imagination required to succeed.**

FIGURE 13.21 Courtesy of the artist.

13.19–13.22. The editor who accepts these strips for the Texas Tech *University Daily* tries to encourage campus cartoonists, but she also buys *Bloom County, The Far Side*, and political cartoons by Ben Sargent and Jeff MacNelly from syndicates. Langston Brown, of the Lubbock High *Westerners*, was a talented high school cartoonist. His work appears in Figures 13.21 and 13.22.

CHAPTER 13 REVIEW

1. Why is it accurate to describe cartooning as a verbal as well as a visual art form?
2. What are the steps involved in developing a system for gag cartooning?
3. Why is a sketchbook an important aid for someone hoping to develop his or her skills as a caricaturist?
4. What interests should you cultivate in order to become a successful editorial cartoonist?

▲ **FIGURE 13.22** **A comic strip by student Langston Brown.**

STUDIO 1

Set Up Your Gag Cartoon System

SUPPLIES

- → Notebook
- → File cards (3 x 5")
- → Card file
- → Pencil
- → Typing paper
- → Drawing file
- → Pen and ink

1. Set up your own gag cartooning system. Keep a notebook and idea file as described earlier. Make entries in the notebook and transfer ideas to file cards every day for a week. Then start doing pencil roughs of your best ideas, and file these drawings.

2. Discuss your ideas with your friends and, if possible, with a journalism or English teacher. You will find differences of opinion about which ideas are funny. If nobody thinks an idea is funny, it probably isn't. However if someone looks at an idea, smiles, or chuckles, and says, "Hey, that's really funny," you should be encouraged.

3. You have to make the final decision about which ideas are best. Develop the roughs for these ideas into a more finished form. Then start looking for places to have them published.

4. At first, you might have to give your cartoons away instead of selling them. You can get valuable training, however, by cartooning for the school newspaper, community bulletin boards, school election and program posters, club announcements, and newsletters. Sometimes a parent-teacher group needs a cartoon on a printed hand-out, or the back page of a program for a school play might use a little humor. If your humor would be appreciated by a general audience, ask the editor of a shopper (a small newspaper composed of advertisements and local news) for a little space.

5. Don't worry too much about developing a cartooning style. If you keep on drawing, your style will develop. You can study the styles of famous gag cartoonists and their influence will be good for you as long as you don't try to directly copy their styles. Your own personality will assert itself eventually if you continue to revise and improve on the styles you see published.

STUDIO 2

Do a School Newspaper Comic Strip

SUPPLIES

- → Pencil
- → Drawing paper
- → Black ink
- → Pens and brushes
- → Light bristol board

1. For this cartooning project, prepare about eight weeks of a comic strip for the school newspaper.

2. Write an outline first if you are creating a continued story strip; then break it down into strips and panels. If your strip fits the gag-a-day format, write descriptions of the characters in the strip and how they are supposed to react.

3. Remember to do proportional roughs. Revise the drawings and transfer them to light bristol board. Use no more than thirty words, and letter them legibly in the panels first. Then complete the drawings with black ink.

STUDIO 3

Form a Comic Book Publishing Group

1. An especially enjoyable project is to organize your art class into a comic book publishing group. Producing a comic book will require three teams of students: a story team, a drawing team, and a production team. Working effectively will require coordination and cooperation from all team members.

2. The story team should consist of one to four people, who will elect one member to be the leader of the team. The team leader will rule on differences of opinion and who will serve as a contact with other teams. The team should be composed of writers who are doing well in English classes. After some exchange of ideas, the most imaginative student should put down the story in outline form while others fill in details and write dialogue.

3. The art team should have at least five people. The best drafter should do the figure drawing. This person should draw somewhat roughly with pencil on a layout pad, showing the action of the figures, the picture panels, and the

speech balloons. Three team members will be inkers who put layout paper or see-through vellum over the rough drawings and reproduce them in ink. As they go over the roughs they will refine the drawings, still maintaining the character of the art in the roughs.

4. One or two members of the team will do the dialogue and the lettering. The first characteristic of lettering should be easy readability. All capital lettering usually works best; and remember, your audience won't read it if there is too much text. The lettering and dialogue team need to coordinate when to give the samples of their lettering to the drawing team so plenty of space can be left in the balloons.

5. It is the job of the production team to print copies of each page and the cover. This team is also responsible for collating and assembling the book. First, they will put together a dummy book in cooperation with the drawing and writing team leaders. From this dummy they will be able to tell how many pages are

needed and the order in which they must be assembled. For instance, it is likely that page one will be printed on one side of the first sheet of paper and the last page will print on the back side if they are to be stapled together in the saddlestitch manner (see the Technique Tip below).

6. The production team needs to be aware of the limitations of the photocopier they will be using. For example, what are the size limitations for paper; how much detail does the copier reproduce; can it do duplex copies?

TECHNIQUE TIP

Saddlestitch or side stitch?

Saddlestitching means *fastening all the pages together through the center fold*, or the *gutter*, with two or three vertically-aligned staples. An alternative to saddle stitching is **side stitching** or *stapling through the outside edge on one side of the stacked pages*. This method is necessary if you do not have a stapler with a long enough arm to span a full page (about 8½ inches or 21.6 cm).

▲ Using the computer as a tool, the artist employed the elements and principles of art to create this nonobjective work. Study the art above and Figure 26, Color Section II; then name the elements and the principles you see employed.

FIGURE 14.1 Jamie Herring. *Popcorn Abstraction.* 1988. Apple MacIntosh SE, ImageWriter II, (dot matrix printer with colored ribbon on paper) *SuperPaint* by Silicon Beach Software. 22.5 x 18.7 cm (8⅞ x 7⅜"). Private collection. Courtesy of the artist.

CHAPTER 14

Computer Drawing

You have learned a strategy for looking at drawings with a discerning eye. Perhaps now you understand why you respond to different drawings in different ways. You have engaged in experiences producing drawings that communicate unique ideas or that solve unusual design problems. You also have discovered many of the ways that artists throughout history have portrayed reactions to their world through their drawings.

You might ask yourself, "What other ways of drawing are there that might reflect the time in which I live?"

Today, artists are using a new drawing tool—the computer—to portray the world of the twentieth century around them, to solve problems in design, to create formal artworks, and to express their feelings and emotions by electronically employing the elements and principles of art (Figure 14.1). They are finding that the computer is a valuable tool for both studio and commercial art. Animators for television and movies use the computer to speed up the time-consuming process of making changes on frames of film.

objectives

After reading this chapter and doing the activities, you will be able to:

- List tools for creating images with computers.

- Explain how a computer can be used to make two-dimensional images.

- Name types of programs for drawing three-dimensional images on a computer.

Terms to Know

application program
computer graphics
computer program
pixel

Benefits of Computer Drawing

Imagine that you are about to make a drawing. You are able to choose from many different drawing tools—for example, charcoal, conte crayon, colored pencil, or pen and ink.

Today you could also use a computer to make a drawing. Drawing with a computer is much like drawing with any other medium. As you probably know, computer equipment, (the keyboard, the central processing unit, and the monitor for example) is called *hardware*. It provides you with many tools for drawing. *Artworks created with a computer* are known as **computer graphics.**

After you have chosen your drawing tool, you must decide on the technique to use to create the visual effect you want. You might use contour drawing, gesture drawing, gradation, linear perspective, or atmospheric perspective. Can you use all of these techniques on a computer? Yes, you can. You can create a visual image with a computer using many familiar drawing techniques. Instructions, called *software*, tell the computer what to do to create images.

A computer is a machine that allows people to store, manipulate, and rearrange information. This information can take the form of numbers, letters, or images. As an artist, you are concerned with how you can use a computer to create images.

Instead of making marks on paper with a drawing instrument, computer artists draw with light on a computer screen. They create images in real time and real motion. That is, artists can draw images, move them about, and change them instantly while the images are displayed on the screen. Artists can also freeze an image they select from an entire group of images.

After an image has been completed, it can be stored by the computer for future use. An image can also be printed on paper or some type of film (slide, video, or photographic). This printed image is referred to as *hard copy.*

■ HARDWARE FOR COMPUTER DRAWING

The basic parts of computer hardware are the central processing unit, the keyboard, and the monitor (Figure 14.2). The central processing unit is the "brain" of the computer. It is the part inside the computer that processes information and performs the commands that artists give it. The keyboard is like a typewriter keyboard. Artists use this keyboard to send commands and information to the computer.

The computer's viewing screen is like a television screen, and it is called a *monitor*. Artists create and manipulate the images displayed on this screen. Most monitors display images only in one color, but many artists purchase color monitor screens for their computers.

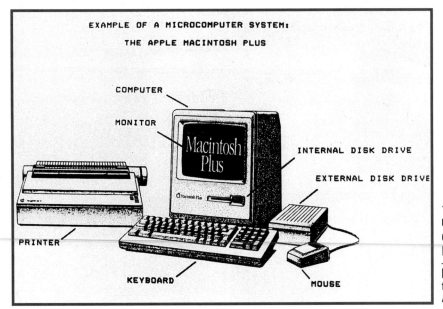

EXAMPLE OF A MICROCOMPUTER SYSTEM:
THE APPLE MACINTOSH PLUS

COMPUTER
MONITOR
Macintosh Plus
INTERNAL DISK DRIVE
EXTERNAL DISK DRIVE
PRINTER
KEYBOARD
MOUSE

◄ **A simple microcomputer system can be used to create drawings. Identify the piece of equipment that can be used to draw lines that appear on the monitor.**

FIGURE 14.2 Macintosh is a trademark licensed to Apple Computer, Inc. Line art courtesy of Apple Computer, Inc.

Did You Know?

The word *computer* comes from the Latin word *computare* which means "to count." The word *graphics* comes from the Greek word *graphikos* which means "to write." As you have learned, a computer "counts" or processes all information in the form of a binary computer code consisting of two digits, "1" and "0." Like the Morse code that uses "dots" and "dashes" strung together in different combinations to stand for alphabet numbers and letters, the computer uses "0's" and "1's" strung together in different combinations to stand for alphabet letters and numbers. Even images are processed in the computer as numbers. Through the use of computer hardware, peripheral devices and computer software, when an artist "draws" an image using a computer, the image is "digitized" or translated (Figure 14.5) to the computer as an array of numbered point locations on a *Cartesian* coordinate system. Therefore, when you "draw" with a computer, you actually are creating or "writing" images to appear on the computer monitor screen as points or pixels of light—through the computer's process of "counting" numbers!

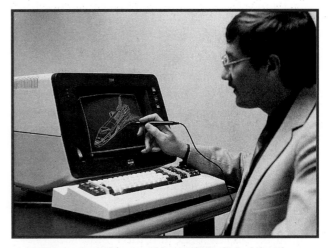

▲ **Light pens have been used to create technical drawings for computer-aided design (CAD).**

FIGURE 14.3 Courtesy of David McGaughey, programmer analyst, Advanced Technology Learning Center, Texas Tech University. Image of Columbia is from the program AutoCAD from Autodesk, Inc.

▲ **Movements of a mouse are translated into lines to create an image. Notice the contour drawings of the shoe on the monitor.**

FIGURE 14.4 Courtesy of Denise Hanna.

The monitor screen is mapped out electronically like a piece of graph paper. *Each square on the electronic graph of the screen* is called a picture element, or **pixel**. Artists move a *cursor* to make an image on the screen, pixel by pixel. The cursor is a point of bright light on the monitor screen that marks a position.

Input-Output Devices

Different tools can be attached to the computer for use by artists. These are called *peripheral* or *input-output devices*. Input devices allow artists to give commands or information to the computer to create images. One of these, the light pen, is an electronic pen connected to the computer. Artists use it to "draw" directly onto the computer's monitor screen (Figure 14.3). The graphics tablet is like an artist's sketchpad. Artists draw images on this flat piece of equipment with a type of electronic pencil called a *stylus*. The resulting image appears on the computer's display screen.

A "mouse," another input device, is a bulky drawing tool shaped like a box on wheels, small enough to fit in the palm of a hand. Artists can roll the mouse on a tabletop as though drawing on the table's surface.

Inside the mouse is electronic circuitry that translates movements into pixel locations to make lines on the monitor screen. Artists can also use the mouse to manipulate images by rolling it in certain directions and pushing control buttons (Figure 14.4).

An optical scanner is another tool for creating images. It can electronically scan (look at) a piece of copy or an image and convert information into a form that can be "read" and stored by the computer. Similarly, a digitizer scans images or photographs. It digitizes, or converts, colors or values into electronic bits of information. Artists can call up this digitized image and change it (Figure 14.6).

Output devices print an image onto other media so artists can have a copy of it. For example, artists might want to use a printer. A computer printer is like a small printing press. Information that the computer has read, manipulated, displayed on its monitor, or stored can be printed on paper. Some printers can also print on other kinds of surfaces, such as plastic. Most printers reproduce only black and white images but images can be reproduced in color with more expensive color printers.

Artists can also have an image transferred to paper by using a digital plotter. A digital plotter draws the image on the monitor screen on paper. Two or more armatures, each holding a pen, move vertically, horizontally, and diagonally to plot a contour line image that was created on the screen. A digital plotter gives architects and interior designers a quick method to make blueprint and layout drawings.

Some equipment can be used for both input and output. Artists use these devices first to enter information into the computer and then to retrieve information from the computer. Using optical scanners and digitizers along with other equipment, photographic and filmed material can be entered directly into a computer system. Artists can view and change these images on the computer monitor. Then the computer can replace the images on film.

For example, with a television video camera, a film frame grabber, and a digitizer connected to the computer, artists can freeze images from video film and transfer them to the computer. Images selected from frames of film can be changed. With specialized equipment attached to the computer, the final images can be transferred back to video film. This type of process is being used today to computer "colorize" copies of black and white movie film (see Figure 27 in Color Section II).

■ SOFTWARE FOR COMPUTER DRAWING

Computer software designed for artists is used to create a variety of two-dimensional or three-dimensional images and to create the illusion of motion. How does this software work?

Computers must process information as a series of *on* and *off* electronic switches. Instructions (software) for a computer must be written in a special format so the computer can read the instructions and process them electronically. *Software that tells a computer how to perform commands* is called a **computer program.**

The program instructions are usually recorded on a magnetic medium, such as a disk or tape. This disk or tape is placed in the computer's disk drive or tape player, which spins the disk or tape while the computer is being used. The computer reads the instructions by translating the presence (*on*) or absence (*off*) of magnetic spots on the disk or tape.

Artists activate the computer program by inserting the disk or tape into the computer and typing a command telling the computer to read the instructions. These instructions tell the computer how to carry out the commands it receives.

Some artists can write instructions themselves for the specific jobs they want the computer to perform. If this is the case, they can begin the drawing process by typing instructions on the keyboard.

Most artists, however, use application programs for specific drawing techniques. An **application program** is *software in which instructions to the computer have already been written by a computer programmer (a*

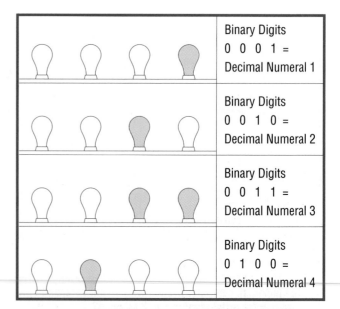

	Binary Digits 0 0 0 1 = Decimal Numeral 1
	Binary Digits 0 0 1 0 = Decimal Numeral 2
	Binary Digits 0 0 1 1 = Decimal Numeral 3
	Binary Digits 0 1 0 0 = Decimal Numeral 4

▲ **FIGURE 14.5 Because digital computers have only two possible states (off and on) and operate much like a light switch, they work on the binary system.**

▲ This advertisement shows the process of entering a photographic image into an Apple Macintosh computer system with a Thunderscan digitizer. At what point in the process can the artist manipulate the design?

FIGURE 14.6 Used with permission. © 1986, 1987, Thunderware, Inc. All rights reserved.

◀ The illusion of deep space in this image was created by the use of linear perspective.

FIGURE 14.7   David Herrold. *Nautical Interior.* 1984. Courtesy of the artist.

person who writes computer programs for others). Artists use an application program to draw new images or change images already stored. The computer's electronic memory, part of the central processing unit, stores these new or changed images temporarily while the computer is being used. When artists finish a work session, the images can be stored permanently. They are transferred onto magnetic floppy or hard disks, video or laser disks, or videotape. When artists want to use the images again, the storage disk or tape is inserted into the computer.

Many application programs have been written specifically for artists. These programs save artists time because the artists don't have to write the instructions themselves. Let's look at some application programs used by artists to create:

- Two-dimensional images.
- Three-dimensional images.
- Animation.

Two-Dimensional Programs

Artists interested in creating graphic designs can use a two-dimensional computer program. The image they create on the computer monitor consists of a set of pixels. Artists use various *draw* or *paint* commands to create a line or a colored area of pixels or bit maps.

Artists can manipulate sizes and types of lines, colors, shapes, forms, simulated textures, and even electronic brushstrokes. For example, artists can create line drawings similar to contour drawings. Or artists can draw shapes and fill them with different values or colors (Figure 14.7). The computer can instantly change a value or color scheme for any image displayed on the computer monitor. With a graphics tablet and the right kind of software, artists can use the computer for gesture drawing. Artists can create images that show motion or action (Figure 14.8).

The computer can also be useful to artists who draw from photographs. With some two-dimensional computer programs, artists can use picture processing. Artists digitize an image or photograph to enter it into the computer for display on the monitor screen. Then the image on the screen can be changed.

◄ **Artists can use a graphics tablet and stylus to draw lines with freedom and spontaneity.**

FIGURE 14.8 Tom Christopher. *Running Horse.* 1984. Courtesy of the artist.

With some types of two-dimensional image software, artists can create the illusion of three-dimensional space. Programs limited to black and white require artists to use black and white values to create this illusion. With color programs, artists can use color gradation to give their images a three-dimensional appearance. Some programs also allow artists to use value gradation to create atmospheric perspective. With other programs, artists can easily experiment with gradation and atmospheric and linear perspective to create images that look three-dimensional.

Three-Dimensional Programs

Software is available to create models for three-dimensional objects and their environments, thus producing convincing illusions of objects in space. Some programs tell the computer to "remember" the dimensions of an object drawn on a screen. Then artists can rotate the object, determine its

SHARPENING YOUR SKILLS

Contour Computer Drawing

To become familiar with the drawing tools you are using with your computer, make simple contour line drawings of objects like shoes, a hand, or the contents of your wallet or purse. Practice looking only at the subject you are drawing without watching the lines as they appear on the computer monitor. If you are using a mouse, it may be difficult to draw accurate diagonal lines and circular shapes. Next, draw a contour line portrait.

Artists at Work

■ AEROSPACE ENGINEER
Designing with Computers

"I'm into computers and outer space. How is learning to draw going to help me?"

The use of computer graphics has revolutionized many areas of graphic design. Computer aided design (CAD) programs are used by engineers and industrial designers to draw and analyze a wide variety of products, including some destined for use in space.

Imagine yourself as a project engineer working for a company that has contracted to define and model the space station assembly sequence for NASA (National Aeronautics and Space Administration). Your office might be at the Langley Research Center in Hampton, Virginia. It would be packed with state-of-the-art computerized work stations, graphics terminals, and laser printers.

On a typical day you might work at a computer terminal assembling the space of the current design. Part of your job might be to update the model of the space station as new information is provided. A change in the design of one part affects the entire space station. These changes can be monitored by using the computers to create a sequence of graphic designs that simulate actual processes. Pictures obtained from these models can help engineers understand the physical properties of the spacecraft and analyze the structure for control requirements, orbit lifetimes, and steady-state microgravity volumes.

In addition to a solid background in math and science, you will need a strong desire and ability to work with computers and a firm foundation in graphic design. Patience, curiosity and insight into both design and computer programming are important attributes for an aerospace engineer.

A degree in mechanical, aeronautical, or aerospace engineering is essential for someone who wants to become an aerospace engineer. In addition, you will need to take as many courses as possible in computer science and programming. You should select a school that has computer graphics classes as part of its graphic design curriculum. Some aerospace firms hire engineering students for summer work as part of co-op programs with colleges.

Part-time work in any drafting office or architectural firm that uses computers will help you get started. Take all the drafting and mechanical drawing classes you can, as well as design, drawing, and sculpture.

Opportunities for alternative careers can be found in all areas of computer programming, design and use. Industrial designers use computers to design everything from electric shavers and hair dryers to automobiles and high speed rail systems.

If you do choose to become an engineer in the space program, not only will you have the appreciation of the engineers who use the drawings you have created on the computer, but you will have the satisfaction of knowing that your work contributes to the important mission of learning more about space and the distant reaches of the universe. ■

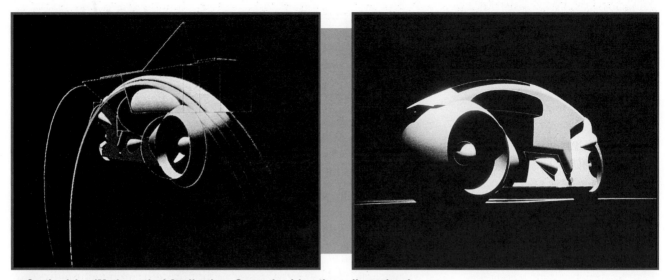

▲ **Synthavision (Mathematical Applications Group, Inc.) is a three-dimensional modeling software based on the principles of combinational geometry. The diagram at left shows how simple forms made from geometric shapes can be joined more smoothly to create the finished form.**

FIGURE 14.9   *Tron* image of a light cycle © 1982, The Walt Disney Company.

proportions, and duplicate it. The computer also can remember where the object was positioned. Other objects can be placed in front of the object or behind it.

There are other, more complex three-dimensional programs, but they are hard to write, and their use requires a great deal of technical knowledge. The computer must be given a set of instructions that tell it how to display a three-dimensional image from any angle. These three-dimensional images are amazingly accurate and realistic. Some of the more sophisticated software techniques used to convey this visual accuracy are described below.

Polygonal Modeling. In polygonal modeling, a model of a three-dimensional form is created out of lines using a technique similar to linear perspective. The final contours of the form are expressed as a mesh of polygon-shaped facets or surfaces. The computer assigns surface characteristics to each facet of the polygonal mesh and blends the boundaries between the facets. The final view of the object has the appearance of a smooth, finished solid form (Figure 14.9).

Texture Mapping. A photograph of an actual textured object, such as a piece of wood or a sponge, can be scanned by the computer and then stored in its memory. With a texture mapping program, the computer can be directed to wrap that texture around a form that has been modeled and stored in the computer's memory. In this way different textured surfaces can be applied to the same form.

Solids Modeling. In combinational geometry, models of three-dimensional forms, such as boxes, spheres, and cones, are programmed into the computer's memory. The computer is instructed to add and subtract forms to create images (Figure 14.9).

Ray Tracing. Ray tracing describes objects according to paths of light rays moving around those objects and reflected from one object to another. Ray tracing reproduces highly complex lighting effects, such as reflected illumination, mirror reflections, refraction (bending of light), and shadows (Figure 14.10, page 270).

Fractal-Surface Imagery. Fractal-surface imagery is used to model uneven ground. A form is created from a mesh made of triangular shapes. The computer calculates changes in distances between the triangles of the mesh. This calculation randomly fractures (divides) the triangles into a large number of irregular facets. This process is repeated until the individual triangles are so small that their edges can no longer be distinguished.

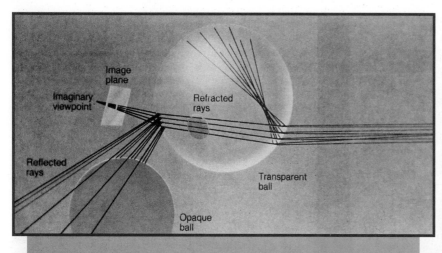

◀ The diagram (at left) shows how an image is determined by calculating the light ray paths reflecting off or absorbed by the surface of an object. Find the shape of each sphere reflected in the surface of its neighboring sphere (below).

FIGURE 14.10 Michael Collery and Shaun Ho. *Algorithmic Dream.* Christmas, 1983. Diagram by Mark E. Alsop, 1984, based on material provided by Pat Hanrahan and Paul Heckbart, New York Institute of Technology. Image courtesy of Cranston Csuri Productions, Inc.

Particle System Software. This software can re-create the appearance of clouds or fire. Each particle or piece created by the computer is randomly spaced and circulated. As the particle moves, the computer alters its color, degree of transparency, and size. Particle systems can also be used to create the illusion of haze or distance, which produces an effect like atmospheric perspective.

Animation Programs

The third type of computer graphics application program is animation. Animation programs use the computer's capability for displaying real motion in real time. The computer can create an object and then move, or animate, that object. Artists can tell the computer to move the object in a certain direction through a certain space. Each view displayed on the monitor screen can be recorded on film, frame by frame.

To move a modeled object and display that movement on the monitor, a set of commands to specify motion must be given to the computer. The computer also must be given instructions for the projected path of the object through space, along with calculations to define any motion of the object itself while it is being projected along that path.

Every sequence of movement through time and space can be frozen through stop-action timing. The sequence of images is flashed on the computer screen at the rate of twenty-four frames a second. These images are recorded on film to create the illusion of motion (Figure 14.11).

The computer can also be programmed for a process known as *in-betweening*. Animators give the computer one frame of action and a frame of action that would occur a number of steps later. The computer then fills in the in-between steps. The computer does this by calculating the predicted action in the missing frames. Once the programming for these calculations is established, in-betweening saves animators hours of work (Figure 14.12).

Today computer artists and scientists working in the area of animation are trying to create a special kind of computer animation called *motion blur*. This effect is like the illusion of vibrating movement. Artists suggest this effect in a picture when

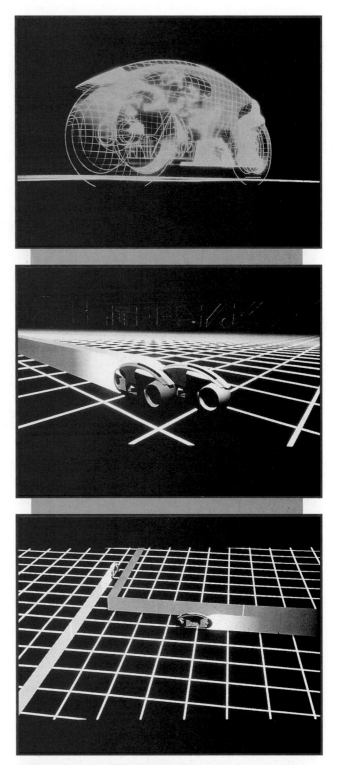

▲ These images show different film frames from the race of the light cycles in the Walt Disney film *Tron*. The light cycles first are energized (lattice grid), then speed across a videogame grid.

FIGURE 14.11   © 1982, The Walt Disney Company.

▲ **In-betweening software can be used in animation. How much time do you think this function can save an artist at the drawing table?**

FIGURE 14.12 Mike Newman. *Metamorphosis* (interpolation between two groups of unlike shapes). 1981. Produced at a Dicomed D38 design station using D1-48 film recorder. Courtesy of Dicomed Corporation.

they repeat the shapes of an object and vary its tone and color. When an object is subjected to motion blur on a computer, it appears on a frame of film as if surrounded by ghostly blurs of its repeated shape. Motion blur is created through the principles of ray tracing.

The Computer and the Creative Process

As you have seen, the computer can be used in many ways to make drawings. The computer is also useful to artists as a design tool. It gives them new ways of seeing and new solutions to design problems.

The computer can act as an additional eye for artists. In this respect, it is like a camera, enhancing our view of the world. The computer can sensitize us to certain features of this world, including color and space.

With a camera, artists can alter color through the use of different colored lens filters or types of film. A computer also allows artists to experiment with the effects that different color choices have on a visual image (see Figures 28 and 29 in Color Section II).

Artists can use a camera to capture different angles of a subject or to zoom in for a closer view. In the same way, a computer can display several views of an object or scene. It can also zoom in for a closer look. The computer can change an object's position or relationship to other objects appearing on the monitor. Besides showing a variety of exterior views of an object, the computer can display a cutaway view of an object's interior.

The computer can also help artists increase their creative output. It helps artists find more solutions to artistic problems, and it enhances the quality and originality of those solutions.

The computer can quickly create many solutions to the same artistic problem. For instance, assume that an artist wants to use a particular design and color combination for a drawing. However, the artist can't decide whether to include a background or which color combinations would be most effective. The artist could use a computer to create quickly and easily several different versions of the design. Then he or she could choose the best version and make that drawing on paper. The artist wouldn't need to redraw the same image several times to decide on the best design (Figure 14.13).

Artists can also experiment with design in more specific ways using the computer. They can use software to:

- Select and manipulate art elements and principles.

- Enlarge or reduce images.

- Add animation.

- Enter other images to be combined with those they have created by scanning or digitizing.

- Distort images to create unusual effects.

- Reproduce images by printing them on different kinds of surfaces.

Using computers encourages artists to take more risks during the creative process. When experimenting with an image on the computer screen, artists can erase it, change it, or save it for later use in a fraction of the time they could do these things without the computer. Artists can store images and make more changes at any time. Because the computer offers so many opportunities to change images, it increases artists' chances for finding highly original solutions to visual problems. Since artists can manipulate images in unusual ways with a computer, they can visualize solutions that would be impossible otherwise.

▲ **Dr. Kim Smith creates computer graphics for television news broadcasts. Note the graphics tablet and stylus that he uses to draw images.**

FIGURE 14.13   Courtesy of KBLK Channel 13, CBS affiliate, Lubbock, Texas.

It is certain that more and more artists will recognize the computer's great potential. They will use it to create works of art unlike any produced in the past—unique drawings that reflect the unique environment in which they are created.

CHAPTER 14 REVIEW

1. List art-related fields in which the computer is now employed as a tool.

2. What does the term *hardware* mean? What does *software* mean?

3. Name two peripheral or input-output devices.

4. List the three application programs explained in this chapter.

UNIT 5 Evaluation

■ APPLYING ART FACTS

On a separate sheet of paper, write the term that best matches each definition given below.

1. The term used for a technical illustration in which an object is visually blown apart to show all its components.
2. Shortening an object in a drawing to make it look as if it extends backward into space.
3. A vertical line located against the picture plane, at the front of a plane that goes back into space.
4. The tools needed to draw horizontal and vertical lines.
5. Lines that originate on the ground plane in a drawing and go to a vanishing point.
6. Cartoons that humorously express opinions on politics or social issues.
7. Drawings created with a computer.
8. Instructions that tell the computer what to do to create images.
9. A completed computer image that is printed on paper or some type of film.
10. Software that tells a computer how to perform commands.

■ SHARPENING YOUR PERCEPTUAL SKILLS

CHAPTER 12

1. Find a work of art illustrated in Chapter 3 that uses linear perspective incorrectly. Point out what is wrong with the perspective in this work. Explain the reasons why the artist was unable to provide an accurately rendered perspective drawing.

2. Select an object or a piece of furniture to draw. Measure it and decide on a scale at which you wish to draw it. Using this scale, draw a plan and an elevation for a basic box that would just fit around the object. Using a separate color, draw a grid of small, equal-sized squares.

3. Draw a one-point perspective of a basic box. Determine the distance two times the height of the box. Place the vanishing point at this distance above the ground line and about the same distance to one side.

4. Compile a list of the mechanical drawing tools you used in doing the studio exercises in Chapter 12. Which did you find to be especially useful?

CHAPTER 13

1. Is cartooning primarily a verbal or a visual art form? Explain your answer.

2. List three types of cartoons. Bring to class examples of each to be used in a bulletin board display.

3. Carry a notebook for a week. Record situations that could be cartoon possibilities. At the end of the week, pick the three best ideas and make rough pencil drawings of each one. Write your captions. Then do finished drawings in ink. Set up a filing system for your cartoons.

CHAPTER 14

1. Make a list of all the tools mentioned in Chapter 14 that are used to make computer drawings.

2. Write a brief report in which you explain how a computer can be used to make two-dimensional drawings. This report should be written expressly for readers who lack knowledge and experience with computers.

3. Divide the class into two sections, pro and con, and debate the following statement: The computer is a mechanical tool that has little to offer the creative artist.

■ MAKING CONNECTIONS

1. **LANGUAGE ARTS.** Prepare a brief story line that would lend itself to a humorous comic strip. Identify the main character in this story and describe him or her in detail. This description should include a detailed account of the character's appearance and personality.

2. **FINE ARTS.** Read the character description prepared in Number 1 above to the class. Ask classmates to create drawings illustrating the character using exaggeration and distortion to emphasize the physical and personality traits. Finished drawings should be put on display and the class asked to determine which ones seem especially effective in capturing the appearance and personality of the character you described.

3. **SOCIAL STUDIES.** Work with two or three other students to develop a political campaign for an honest big-city mayor fighting an uphill battle for reelection. Decide on what campaign promises should be made and discuss how these can be effectively presented to the voting public in a hard-hitting political cartoon. Working as a team, design and complete the cartoon with ink. Place the cartoon on display in the classroom and ask other students to offer their opinions about your candidate.

4. **HISTORY.** Visit your school or community library and gather as much information as you can about Thomas Nast, a political cartoonist of the past century. Bring to class examples of Nast's cartoons. Explain why Nast is an important figure in our country's history.

■ THINKING CRITICALLY ABOUT ART

1. **DESCRIBE.** Write a detailed description of three characters found in comic strips today. Read your descriptions in class. Were other students able to identify the characters?

2. **ANALYZE.** Examine the comic strips in your local newspaper. Which one seems to be drawn especially well? Does the artist of this strip make consistent use of certain elements of art? Explain.

3. **COMPARE AND CONTRAST.** Study several computer images in this and other books. Do you notice any differences in the ways that the elements and principles of art have been used compared to the ways artists use these same elements and principles to design non-computer art?

4. **INTERPRET.** Examine Langston Brown's cartoon (Figure 13.21, page 257). Write a humorous caption for this cartoon.

5. **JUDGE.** Assume that you are a publisher faced with the task of selecting a new comic strip for your newspaper. Look at examples of comic strips in various newspapers and select one that you feel would be a good choice for your publication. Cut out this strip, bring it to class, and place it on display. Explain why you chose this particular strip from among the many that were available.

Artists and Their Works

Amaury-Duval, Eugene, French, 1808–1885, painter
Portrait of a Lady (Portrait de Femme), 13; Fig. 1.13

Arms, John Taylor, American, 1887–1953
Coutances, 230; Fig. 12.1

Atkins, Future, American, contemporary
Bedroom Heroes/Cowboy's Fantasy, 214; Fig. 11.14

Bacon, Peggy, American, 1895–
The Painter, 166; Fig. 9.1

Bellows, George Wesley, American, 1882–1925, painter, printmaker
Studies of Jean, 63; Fig. 3.28

Blake, Bud, American, contemporary, cartoonist
Tiger strip, 255; Fig. 13.17

Breathed, Berke, American, contemporary, cartoonist
Bloom County strip, 254; Fig. 13.15

Canaletto, Italian, 1697–1768, painter
Ascension Day Festival at Venice, 54; Fig. 3.20

Carracci, Annibale, Italian, 1560–1609, painter
A Domestic Scene, 52; Fig. 3.17

Cassatt, Mary, American, 1845–1926, painter
In the Omnibus, 203; Fig. 10.7
Girl Arranging Her Hair, CS I-2; Fig. 3

Catlett, Elizabeth, American, 1915–, sculptor, painter, printmaker
Sharecropper, 2; Fig. 1.1

Cézanne, Paul, French, 1839–1906, painter
Bathers Under a Bridge, 23; Fig. 2.3

Cheatham, Frank,
A Device for Determining the Magical Phases of the Moon, CS II-11; Fig. 23

Cheatham, Jane,
July Window, CS II-12; Fig. 24

Christopher, Tom, American, contemporary
Running Horse, 267; Fig. 14.8

Collery, Michael, American, contemporary
Algorithmic Dream, 270; Fig. 14.10

Daumier, Honoré, French, 1808–1879, painter
Fright, 32; Fig. 2.14
Two Lawyers, 35; Fig. 2.15

Degas, Edgar, French, 1834–1917, painter
Study for a Portrait of Edouard Manet, 56; Fig. 3.22
The Theatre Box, 66; Fig. 4.1; CS I-7; Fig. 13
The Violinist, 82; Fig. 5.2

Delacroix, Eugène, French, 1798–1863, painter
An Arab on Horseback Attacked by a Lion, 55; Fig. 3.21

Dixon, Ken, American, contemporary
Origin of the Evening Star, CS I-12; Fig. 18
Passing Through, 92; Fig. 5.18
Reading the Signs–Blue Skies Again, CS I-12; Fig. 19

Dowlen, James, American, contemporary
Big Bun, CS II-16; Fig. 29

Dürer, Albrecht, German, 1471–1528, painter, printmaker
Lamentation, 162; Fig. 8.7
Self-Portrait at the Age of Twenty-Two, 161; Fig. 8.6

Eakins, Thomas, American, 1844–1916, painter
Gross Clinic, 113; Fig. 6.5
Perspective Studies for John Biglin in a Single Scull, 115; Fig. 6.6

El Greco, Spanish, 1541–1614, painter
Saint Jerome, 51; Fig. 3.16

Exekias, Greek, 550–525 B.C., potter, painter
Vase with Ajax and Achilles Playing Morra (dice), 42; Fig. 3.6

Feigenbaum, Harriet, American, 1939–, painter, draughtsman
Dawn, 194; Fig. 10.1

Ford, Phillip, American, contemporary
The Courtship, CS II-10; Fig. 21

Fragonard, Jean-Honoré, French, 1732–1806, painter
Grandfather's Reprimand, 117; Fig. 6.7

Garcia, Antonio Lopez, Spanish, 1936–, painter, sculptor, draughtsman
Remainders from a Meal, 69; Fig. 4.3

Gauguin, Paul, French, 1848–1903, painter
Nave Nave Fenua, 60; Fig. 3.25

Gibbons, Hugh, American, contemporary
Arrangement at 12:17, CS II-4; Fig. 7

Giotto di Bondone, Italian, c. 1266–1337, painter
Madonna and Child, 45; Fig. 3.10

Gorky, Arshile, American, 1905–1948, painter
Portrait of the Artist's Wife, "Mougouch", 8; Fig. 1.7

Goya, Francisco, Spanish, 1746–1828, painter
Disasters of War, 23; Fig. 2.4

Greuze, Jean-Baptiste, French, 1725–1805, painter
A Tired Woman with Two Children, 68; Fig. 4.2

Grosz, George, American, 1893–1959, painter
In the Restaurant, 242; Fig. 13.1

Guardi, Francesco, Italian, 1712–1793, painter
The Stairway of the Giants, Ducal Palace, 154–155

Hanna, Paul, American, contemporary, painter, engraver, cartoonist
cartoons, 249, 250; Fig. 13.9
Owl and Heart Flower, CS II-13; Fig. 25
Querencia No. 14, CS II-3; Fig. 4
Resistant Man, 223; Fig. 11.19

Herring, Jamie, American, contemporary
Popcorn Abstraction, 260; Fig. 14.1; CS II-14; Fig. 26

Herrold, David, American, contemporary
Nautical Interior, 266; Fig. 14.7

Hokusai, Katsushika, Japanese, 1760–1849, printmaker
Boy with a Flute, 14; Fig. 1.14

Hopper, Edward, American, 1882–1967, painter
Early Sunday Morning, 197; Fig. 10.2
Gas, CS I-14; Fig. 23
Jumping on a Train, 13; Fig. 1.12
Study for Gas, 111; Figs. 6.3; 6.4

Ho, Shaun, American, contemporary
Algorithmic Dream, 271; Fig. 14.10

Howze, Jim, American, contemporary
No New Tricks, CSII-3; Fig. 5
Pushfoot Halftrack Haybale Clown, 246; Fig. 13.7
The Satchel Paige Memorial Calligraphicat, 247; Fig. 13.8

Ingres, Jean-Auguste-Dominique, French, 1780–1867, painter
Portrait of Count de Nieuwerkerke, 24; Fig. 2.5

Johnson, James, American, contemporary
Mr. Suitcase, 216; Fig. 11.15

Kandinsky, Wassily, Russian, 1866–1944, painter
Improvisation 28, CS I-6; Fig. 12

Kelly, Ellsworth, American, 1923–, painter
Briar, 11; Fig. 1.10

King, Kathy Hicks, American, contemporary
Fire Revealed, CS II-8; Fig. 15
Outdoor Advertising Billboard, CS II-8; Fig. 14
Sesquicentennial, CS II-7; Fig. 13

King, Jessie M., Scottish, 1876–1948
Book Illustration: Where I Made One—Turn Down an Empty Glass, 228–229

Klee, Paul, Swiss, 1879–1940, painter
The Mocker Mocked, 7; Fig. 1.3
Old Man Figuring, 201; Fig. 10.5

Glossary

This section contains important words and phrases used in *Creating and Understanding Drawings*. You may wish to refer to this list of terms as you read the chapters and complete the activities.

aberrant scale   Type of proportion achieved by making an object or figure in a drawing appear abnormally small or large.

abstract   Artwork, based on recognizable objects, presented in a highly stylized manner that stresses the elements and principles of art.

Abstract Expressionism   Art movement in which artists working in New York in the 1930s and 1940s expressly employed media and design qualities to create works with little emphasis on recognizable subject matter.

acrylic paint   Most commonly used name for synthetic pigments and media.

action painting   Term used by Abstract Expressionists to describe the act of painting itself—and expressing the emotions the artists felt while painting.

actual texture   Kind of texture that the viewer of an artwork can touch.

aerial perspective   Decreasing the value and value contrasts for objects that appear farther back in a composition. This technique is used to create the illusion of space.

aesthetics   Ideas about what makes a work of art beautiful or satisfying.

alidade   Tool that indicates degrees and angles. This tool helps to accurately plot maps.

analysis   Art-criticism operation in which the principles of art are used to learn how the work is organized or composed.

application program   Software (instructions) that tells a computer to perform specific tasks.

appreciation   Act of making a judgment about a work of art and backing up that judgment with good reasons.

architect's scale   Tool that looks like a triangular ruler and is used to measure, not to draw straight lines.

archetype   A perfect example of a type or a group.

Armory Show   Huge exhibition of European and American art, originally called the International Exhibition of Modern Art, which opened in New York City on February 17, 1913. It introduced the American public to the most advanced movements in European art and motivated many American artists to start the experiments that began the modern era in American art.

art criticism   Process of examining, understanding, and judging a work of art. It involves four steps: description, analysis, interpretation, and judgment.

art historian   Person who judges artists and their works by deciding how much they have influenced art history.

art history   Information about the artist who created a work of art and when, where, how, and why it was made.

artisan   A skilled craftsperson.

Ashcan School   Term laughingly applied to a group of early twentieth-century American artists that resisted traditional European styles and subject matter, choosing instead to draw and paint the American scene—the streets, alleys, cafés, and theaters.

assemblage   Three-dimensional work of art made by attaching many pieces to a surface.

asymmetrical (informal) balance   Balance created in a work of art by giving unlike objects in the composition equal visual weight.

atmospheric perspective   Decreasing the intensity of hues for objects that appear farther back in a composition. This technique is used to create the illusion of space and to suggest the effects of light, air, and distance.

background   Area of a picture that appears farthest from the viewer.

balance   Principle of art that arranges elements in a work of art to create a sense of stability.

balloon   Outlined dialogue or thought of a character in a comic strip panel.

Baroque   Style of artistic expression prevalent in the seventeenth century which created a pattern of contrasting areas of light and shadow that gave a look of dynamic, continuous movement.

bas-relief   Work of art in which some areas stand out from the surface.

binocular vision   Seeing from two angles with both eyes at the same time and combining the two images into one so that a three-dimensional image is created.

bit maps   Squares on the electronic graph of a computer screen. An artist fills these squares on the screen to create an image.

bleed   Drawing in which the shapes reach the edges of the working area.

blind contour drawing   Drawing method which concentrates on the contours of the object being drawn and in which the artist does not look at the paper. It is an exercise in a valuable but limited way of seeing things. It is perhaps the only kind of drawing that doesn't use the gestalt principle of drawing the overall image first.

cameo paper   Cream-colored, clay-coated paper usually used for silverpoint drawing.

camera-ready   Art that is photographed to make a printing plate.

caption   Comment or title accompanying a cartoon.

caricature Drawing of a person that exaggerates the person's features to be humorous or to suggest an idea about the subject.

cartoon Term that refers to animated cartoons, comic strips, caricatures, and humorous drawings; it can also refer to full-scale preliminary drawings for fresco or mural work.

cast shadows Shadows cast by shapes onto other surfaces.

center of vision In one-point perspective, the vanishing point. In two-point perspective, the place opposite the eye of the observer.

charcoal A black or very dark-colored, brittle substance that consists mainly of carbon.

charcoal pencils Compressed charcoal in pencil form.

collage Two-dimensional work of art made by attaching many pieces to a surface.

color Element of art derived from reflected light. The sensation of color is aroused in the brain by response of the eyes to different wavelengths of light. A color has hue (color name), intensity (strength), and value (lightness or darkness).

colored chalk Dry, powdery sticks of pigments.

colored pencils Waxy pencils with strong, durable colors.

compass Tool that is used to draw circles.

compressed charcoal Made by binding together tiny particles of ground charcoal.

computer graphics Drawings created with a computer.

computer program Software (instructions) that tells a computer to perform commands.

cone of vision Imaginary cone with a circular base on the picture plane in which the artist views an object to be drawn in two-point perspective.

conte crayon Brand name for the best-known brand of drawing crayons.

contour drawing Drawing the edges, or contours, of figures or objects. Contour drawing records details of shape and structure.

crayons Among the oldest of all art media. Available in both pencils and square sticks, in varying degrees of hardness. Crayons provide a wide range of colors, and they can be applied to many different surfaces. Because of the adhesive strength of the binder, crayon marks are almost permanent and difficult to erase.

cropping Decreasing the area of a picture to use in an independent design.

cross contour Line that describes the volume of a form, rather than the outline.

cross-hatching Sets of overlapping parallel lines used to create value.

Cubism Inspired by Cezanne's paintings, an art movement that produced works composed of cubes of color arranged to create the illusion of solid form.

cursor Point of bright light on a computer screen that marks a position.

Dadaism Art style influenced by a period of pessimism and unrest after World War I. Artists associated with this movement felt that European culture no longer had a purpose or meaning, and that art objects should no longer be beautiful or meaningful, but ordinary and meaningless.

description First art-criticism operation, which involves asking and answering questions designed to help you discover everything in a drawing.

design qualities Uses of the elements and principles of art to create a unified, interesting artwork. These qualities are emphasized by the theory of Formalism.

design relationships The way art elements and principles are combined.

distance line Line on which the station point is located, dropped vertically from the center of vision. It measures the distance of the viewer from the picture plane.

dividers Tool used to apply measurements from the architect's scale to a drawing. Dividers are also used to hold a measurement and repeat it several times.

dry media Media used in drawing that include pencil, crayon, chalk, and charcoal.

edition Prints of the same composition. They are usually individually signed, numbered, and titled by the artist.

editorial cartoons Cartoons that humorously express opinions on politics or social issues.

elements of art Basic components artists use to create works of visual art. The elements of art are line, shape, form, value, texture, space, and color.

elevation Drawing that shows the entire image on a vertical plane, with no depth or perspective.

Emotionalism Theory of art that is used to judge a work of art by its expressive qualities (how well it communicates a feeling, mood, or idea to the viewer).

emphasis Principle of art that combines elements in a work of art to point out their differences.

engraving Work of art which is made by cutting into a surface, inking the surface, and pressing paper against it to make a print.

exaggeration Enlargement of figures or objects or their parts in a work of art to communicate an idea or feeling.

exploded view Technical illustration in which the object is visually blown apart to show all of its components.

Expressionism   Art movement that stressed the artist's need to communicate to viewers his or her emotional response to a subject.

expressive qualities   Feelings, moods, or ideas communicated to a viewer through a work of art. These qualities are emphasized by the theory of Emotionalism.

Fauvism   Art movement that used a heavy, bold application of brightly colored paint to express emotion.

figure   Human form in a work of art. Also any positive shape.

fine-line marker   Fiber-tipped pen.

finished art   Art in which the idea is expressed to the artist's satisfaction.

foreground   Area of a picture that appears closest to the viewer.

foreshortening   Shortening an object in a drawing to make it look as if it extends backward into space. This method reproduces proportions a viewer sees.

form   Element of art that is three-dimensional and encloses space. Like a shape, a form has length and width, but it also has depth.

formal drawing   Drawing that reveals little concern for literal qualities or realistically rendered subject matter, a lack of concern that often results in artworks that are abstract or nonobjective.

Formalism   Theory of art that is used to judge a work of art by its visual qualities (by its organization of the elements of art through the principles of art).

formalist   Considers only the design qualities—the elements and principles of art—to analyze and judge drawings.

form shadows   Shadows on the side of forms away from the light source.

found objects   Natural or man-made objects found by chance and used in a work of art.

freehand drawing   Drawing done without measuring tools or tracing.

frottage   The image that results from putting a piece of fairly smooth, flexible paper over an object with a raised image or textured surface and rubbing pencil lead or graphite stick over it; a rubbing.

gag cartoons   Cartoons that show a humorous situation in one frame, sometimes with a caption, sometimes not.

gesso   White, plaster-like surface used for drawing or painting.

gestalt   German word that means pattern or form.

gesture drawing   Drawing gestures or movements of the body. Gesture drawing quickly records an entire image.

Gothic International style   An elegant, flowing style of painting that was practiced throughout western Europe during the late fourteenth and early fifteenth centuries.

gouache   Any opaque water-based white paint that is mixed with watercolors to produce an opaque effect.

gradation   Principle of art that combines elements in a work of art by using a series of gradual changes.

graphic designer   Person who combines the written word with visual imagery to produce effective messages.

ground   Negative shape or shapes.

hard copy   Computer image printed on paper or film.

hardware   Physical parts that make up a computer system.

harmony   Principle of art that combines elements in a work of art to stress similarities of separate but related parts.

heroic figure   Ancient Greek artists' representation of a human figure. It is eight heads tall, a bit taller than life-sized (7½ heads tall).

highlights   Areas on a surface that reflect the most light. In a drawing, these areas are shown by light values to create the illusion of depth.

horizon line (eye level line)   Line at which earth and sky seem to meet.

horizontals   Drawings that are wider than they are long.

illustration   Drawing used to tell a story, give instructions, or make a product look attractive.

Imitationalism   Theory of art that is used to judge a work of art by its literal qualities (by how well it imitates the real world).

Impressionism   Art style that reproduces what the eye sees at a specific moment in time—not what the mind knows is there.

india ink   Black drawing ink that is available in two types: waterproof and soluble.

input-output devices   Tools such as a stylus or a mouse that can be attached to the computer for use by artists. These devices allow artists to give commands or information to the computer to create images.

intaglio   Print made from ink trapped in the grooves in an engraved metal plate.

interpretation   Art-criticism operation which involves using the "clues" gathered during investigation of a drawing to reach a decision about its meaning (or meanings).

judgment   Art-criticism operation which involves thoughtful and informed response to a drawing.

Ka   Ancient Egyptian word meaning the spirit.

landscape   Work of art that uses natural scenery as subject matter.

layout chalk   Chalk in small, hard, square sticks.

line   Element of art that is a continuous mark made on a surface by a pointed instrument.

line art   Illustration made up of solid blacks and whites for commercial printing purposes.

linear perspective   Technique for creating the illusion of depth for three-dimensional objects on a two-dimensional plane. Parallel lines meet on distant vanishing points on the horizon.

linocut print   Print made from an inked linoleum block.

literal qualities   Realistic representation of subject matter in a work of art. These qualities are emphasized by the theory of Imitationalism.

lithograph   Print made from an inked stone or metal plate. A drawing is made on the plate with a greasy crayon or ink (tusche).

Mannerism   Emotionally-charged art style that evolved in the sixteenth century from a mixture of Italian Renaissance influences and the drawings and paintings of northern Europe.

matknife   Box knife or utility knife, also used for cutting mats.

matting   Surrounding an artwork with a cardboard border. Drawings for an exhibition or an artist's portfolio are often matted, as are framed drawings.

measuring line (ground line)   Horizontal line defining the bottom of the picture plane (indicating where the picture plane meets the ground).

measuring point   Any point on the horizon used to project a depth measurement into a perspective drawing.

mechanical drawing   Drawing done with the help of measuring tools.

media   Materials used by an artist to create a work of art. (Singular is *medium*.)

mixed media   Artwork in which several media are combined to obtain desired effects.

model   Person who poses for a work of art.

monitor   Computer's viewing screen.

movement   Principle of art that combines elements in a work of art to create the illusion of action.

murals   Works of art painted and drawn directly on walls.

negative shape (ground)   Empty space surrounding a shape or form.

Neoclassicism   Reaction to earlier Baroque and Rococo art styles in which artists returned to the classical art of ancient Greece and Rome and the Renaissance masters for their inspiration.

nonobjective art   Style that has unrecognizable shapes and forms. These works contain no apparent reference to reality.

one-point (parallel) perspective   Perspective in which all receding lines meet at a single vanishing point that corresponds to the center of vision.

opaque   Quality of a material that doesn't let any light pass through.

outline contour   Line that shows the overall shape around the outer edge of a form.

overlapping   Placing one object in an artwork in front of another, partially concealing the object behind. This technique is used to suggest depth.

parallel perspective   Simplest kind of perspective in which the lines formed by the sides of the road, walk, or track seem to come together at a vanishing point on the horizon.

pastels   Chalks that, depending on the kind and amount of binder, can be powdery, waxy, or oily. They can be applied to high-quality surfaces, usually special pastel papers, by hand or with rubbing techniques. Both round and square sticks are available in sets that can include up to almost fifty hues.

pencil   Drawing and writing tool that consists of a slender, cylindrical casing around a marking substance.

peripheral devices   Tools that can be attached to the computer for use by artists. These devices allow artists to give commands or information to the computer to create images; also called input-output devices.

pharaohs   Rulers of ancient Egypt.

picas   Printing unit of measure in which six picas comprise an inch.

picture element—pixel   Square on the electronic graph of a computer screen. An artist fills pixels on the screen to create an image.

picture plane   Surface of a drawing or plane on which images are projected.

plagiarism   Unlawful and unethical copying of another artist's idea to present the idea as original.

plan   Drawing showing lines of an object from directly above on a flat plane without perspective.

plane table   Special drawing board mounted on a tripod.

Pointillism   Art style, also known as Neo-Impressionism, that was developed in the last quarter of the nineteenth century by Georges Seurat. Seurat applied tiny, uniform dots of pure color to his canvases.

points   Printing unit of measure. There are twelve points in each pica, and six picas in an inch.

political cartoons   Cartoons that humorously express opinions on politics but often use other subjects as well.

Pop Art   School of art that focused attention on the unimportant products of contemporary culture.

portfolio   Collection of samples of an artist's work.

portrait   Picture or image that is an attempt to achieve a likeness or representation of a particular person.

positive shape (figure)   Shape or form in two- or three-dimensional art.

powdered charcoal   Has the same material makeup as compressed charcoal. It can be used for shading and other special effects realized by rubbing and erasing the powder sprinkled on the drawing surface.

presentation   How a finished artwork is prepared to be shown to someone else.

principles of art   Ways artists organize the elements of art in works of visual art. The principles of art are balance, emphasis, harmony, variety, gradation, movement, rhythm, proportion, and space.

printing plate   The surface from which images are transferred to paper.

proportion   Principle of art that combines elements in a work of art to create size relationships of elements to the whole artwork and to each other.

prototype   A model.

Realism   Art style that rejected both ideal or classical subjects and romantic subject matter in favor of contemporary life rendered in a lifelike way.

Realists   Artists that rejected subject matter that glorified the past or romanticized the present. They painted everyday events the way these subjects really looked.

reference line   Line extending from a point on the picture plane and receding along the ground to a vanishing point.

reference point   Point on the measuring line (ground line) where a reference line begins.

rendering   Use of media to create a finished artwork.

rhythm   Principle of art that repeats elements in a work of art to create a visual tempo.

Rococo   Art style popular at the beginning of the eighteenth century that used a free, graceful movement; a playful application of line; and rich colors.

Romantic style   Art style that emphasized the expression of feelings and emotions in drawings and paintings completed in a spontaneous manner.

rough   Practice drawing done in preparation for a finished drawing.

rubbing   Method of reproducing textures by rubbing a drawing instrument on paper placed over a textured surface; also called *frottage*.

saddle stitching   Fastening all the pages together through the center fold, or the gutter, with two or three vertically aligned staples.

scratchboard   Illustration board that has been coated with a chalk-like substance that can then be coated with ink. The image is then scratched into the surface.

serigraph   Print made through a silk screen using stencils.

setup   Group of objects arranged as a subject for drawing.

shape   Element of art that is an enclosed area determined by line, value, texture, space, or any combination of these elements. A shape has two dimensions, length and width.

side stitch   Stapling through the outside edge of a booklet on one side of the stacked pages.

silverpoint   Drawing made with a special pencil that has a silver point.

simulated (visual) texture   Kind of texture suggested or implied in an artwork.

sketch   Drawing done quickly in preparation for a finished work of art.

sketchbook   Pad of drawing paper used by artists to record ideas and information for works of art and to practice drawings.

sketching   Type of drawing in which artists try out ideas before making works of art.

software   Instructions that tell the computer how to manipulate information.

space   Element of art that is the distance around, between, above, below, and within an object. Also a principle of art that creates the illusion of three dimensions in a work.

station point   Point of view from which a drawing and measurements for a drawing are made.

still life   Nonmoving objects that are subject matter for a work of art.

stippling   Technique of using patterns of dots to create values and value gradation.

structural expression   When a work's expressive qualities are created through the careful organization of design qualities.

studio   Room where artists work.

stylus   Metal pen-shaped instrument.

Surrealism   Art movement that tried to express the world of dreams and the workings of the mind with pencil and brush. It became a significant force in Europe throughout the 1920s and 1930s, and spread to the United States during World War II.

symmetrical (formal) balance   Balance created in a work of art by duplicating elements on either side of a line dividing the composition in half.

syndicate   Business concern that sells materials for publication of newspapers or periodicals simultaneously.

tactile   Appealing to the sense of touch.

tempera paint   Water-soluble gouache paint that can be secured in liquid form or as a powder to be mixed with water.

texture   Element of art that appeals to the sense of touch.

thumbnail sketch   Small sketches drawing quickly to record ideas and information for finished drawings.

tondo   Archaic term used to describe a painting that is round instead of square or rectangular.

translucent   Quality of a material that allows some light to pass through.

triangle   Tool which is placed along the top edge of a T square to draw vertical lines or lines at 45 degree angles.

true height line   Vertical line raised from the point where a reference line from a vanishing point touches the measuring line (ground line). This line can be used for actual measurements for any objects or lines along the reference line.

T square   Tool used to draw horizontal lines.

two-point (angular) perspective   Perspective in which different sets of receding lines meet at different vanishing points.

unity   Total visual effect achieved by carefully blending the elements and principles of art in a composition.

value   Element of art that refers to light and dark areas. Value depends on how much light a surface reflects. Value is also one of the three properties of color.

value gradation   Gradual change from dark to light areas used to create the illusion of three dimensions on a two-dimensional surface.

vanishing point   Point on the horizon or eye-level line at which receding parallel lines meet in a perspective drawing.

variety   Principle of art that combines contrasting elements in a work of art to create visual interest.

verisimilitude   Appearance of being true or real.

vertical axis   Imaginary line dividing an object, figure, or composition in half vertically.

verticals   Drawings that are taller than they are wide.

vignette   Drawing in which the shapes float in the empty working area without touching the edges of the drawing.

vine charcoal   Charcoal in its most natural state. It is made by heating vines until only the charred, black sticks of carbon remain. These thin carbon sticks are soft, lightweight, and extremely brittle.

visual texture   Suggested or implied texture.

visual vocabulary   Elements and principles of art.

wash   Term used to describe the medium made by thinning ink or paint with water.

wash drawing   Drawing made with a brush and mixtures of ink or paint thinned with water.

watercolor block   Pad of watercolor paper for sketching.

watercolor paints   Consist of extremely fine, transparent pigments in a medium of water or gum and are available in tubes or sectioned pans. They result in a transparent effect that distinguishes this medium from other, more opaque paints.

wet media   Include ink, acrylic, watercolors, and tempera paints.

woodcut print   Print made from an inked wood block.

Bibliography

Cheatham, Frank R., Jane H. Cheatham, and Sheryl A. Haler. *Design Concepts and Applications.* 2nd ed. Englewood Cliffs, NJ: Prentice-Hall, 1987. A thorough introduction to the visual language that is especially informative for the beginning student.

Deken, Joseph. *Computer Images: State of the Art.* NY: Stewart Tabori & Chang, 1983. A gallery of color computer images created for the fields of science and art. Available in paperback.

Feldman, Edmund Burke. *The Artist.* Englewood Cliffs, NJ: Prentice-Hall, 1982. Discusses many different kinds of creative artists and their reasons for making art.

Feldman, Edmund Burke. *Varieties of Visual Experience.* 4th ed. Englewood Cliffs, NJ: Prentice-Hall, 1992. An excellent introduction to the major art styles and several theories of art. Also provides a fine explanation of the steps involved in art criticism.

Gatto, Joseph A., Albert W. Porter, and Jack Selleck. *Exploring Visual Design.* 2nd ed. Worcester, MA: Davis Publications, Inc., 1987. Introduces the elements and principles of design in a way that beginning students find easy to comprehend.

Gombrich, Ernst H. *The Story of Art.* 15th ed. Englewood Cliffs, NJ: Prentice-Hall, 1989. A fine introduction to the entire history of art written in a manner that is especially well suited to newcomers to the subject.

Janson, H.W. and Anthony F. Janson. *A Basic History of Art.* 4th ed. Englewood Cliffs, NJ: Prentice-Hall, 1991. A comprehensive survey of the major periods of art history presented in a straightforward style.

Malraux, Andre. *The Voices of Silence.* Trans. Stuart Gilbert. Princeton, NJ: Princeton University Press, 1978. An absorbing presentation of art history which ignores the typical classifications in favor of a new and exciting set of categories.

Mayer, Ralph. *The Artist's Handbook of Materials and Techniques.* 5th ed., rev. and expanded. NY: Viking-Penguin, 1991. Includes specific, practical information and advice on the materials and techniques most commonly used by artists.

Mittler, Gene A. *Art in Focus.* 3rd ed. Mission Hills, CA: Glencoe, 1994. Involves students in a sequence of aesthetics, criticism, and history experiences applied to artworks from prehistoric times to the present. Also contains studio activities.

Peck, Stephen Rogers. *Atlas of Human Anatomy for the Artist.* NY: Oxford University Press, 1951. Structures of the body are analyzed and studied in detail.

Prueitt, Melvin L. *Art and the Computer.* NY: McGraw-Hill, 1984. Discussion by a pioneering computer artist of a large selection of computer-generated art. Available in paperback.

Ragans, Rosalind. *ArtTalk.* Mission Hills, CA: Glencoe, 1995. An approach to art history, criticism, aesthetics, and studio experiences applied to visual arts and crafts.

Simmons, Seymour, and Marc Winer. *Drawing: The Creative Process.* Englewood Cliffs, NJ: Prentice-Hall, 1977. A concise, easy-to-read overview of the basic materials and tools used by artists to create and preserve drawings.

Stolnitz, Jerome. *Aesthetics and Philosophy of Art Criticism: A Critical Introduction.* Boston: Houghton Mifflin, 1960. A readable introduction to the theories of art and an approach to the evaluation of art.

Taylor, Joshua C. *Learning to Look: A Handbook for the Visual Arts.* 2nd ed. Chicago: University of Chicago Press, 1981. Begins with a study of specific works of art and extends to a consideration of broad visual arts principles and techniques.

Index

Photo Credits